BRITISH BATTLE TANKS

AMERICAN-MADE WORLD WAR II TANKS

DAVID FLETCHER
AND STEVEN J. ZALOGA

OSPREY PUBLISHING
Bloomsbury Publishing Plc
PO Box 883, Oxford, OX1 9PL, UK
1385 Broadway, 5th Floor, New York, NY 10018, USA
E-mail: info@ospreypublishing.com
www.ospreypublishing.com

OSPREY is a trademark of Osprey Publishing Ltd

First published in Great Britain in 2018

Some of the material in this book has been previously published as: New Vanguard 3: *Sherman Medium Tank 1942–45* by Steven J. Zaloga; New Vanguard 33: *M3 & M5 Stuart Light Tank 1940–45* by Steven J. Zaloga; New Vanguard 113: *M3 Lee/Grant Medium Tank 1941–45* by Steven J. Zaloga; New Vanguard 123: *Swimming Shermans* by David Fletcher; New Vanguard 139: *Sherman Crab Flail Tank* by David Fletcher; New Vanguard 141: *Sherman Firefly* by David Fletcher; New Vanguard 159: *Staghound Armored Car 1942–62* by Steven J. Zaloga.

Artwork by Jim Laurier, Hugh Johnson, Peter Sarson and Tony Bryan, © Osprey Publishing Ltd

Unless otherwise stated all photos in this book are © The Tank Museum

A catalogue record for this book is available from the British Library.

ISBN: HB 9781472820068; eBook 9781472821522; ePDF 9781472821522; XML 9781472821539

18 19 20 21 22 10 9 8 7 6 5 4 3 2 1

Index by Alison Worthington
Originated by PDQ Digital Media Solutions, Bungay, UK
Printed in China at C&C Offset Ltd.

Front cover: © Tank Museum
Back cover: © Tank Museum

Osprey Publishing supports the Woodland Trust, the UK's leading woodland conservation charity. Between 2014 and 2018 our donations are being spent on their Centenary Woods project in the UK.

To find out more about our authors and books visit **www.ospreypublishing.com**. Here you will find extracts, author interviews, details of forthcoming events and the option to sign up for our newsletter.

CONTENTS

INTRODUCTION

Generally speaking American-built tanks were regarded with suspicion by British tank crews. They were seen as crude, lacking the sophistication of their British counterparts, particularly in respect of transmission. They were certainly a lot simpler than British tanks. Some of the criticism was justified, although some was not, and much was probably based upon the 'not made here' syndrome that British soldiers applied to all foreign machines. American tanks' internal fighting arrangements, whose deficiencies were probably due to a lack of any real experience of having to fight tanks in action, were not at all popular. Insufficient range, due to a limited petrol capacity, was another valid cause for complaint. Major General Vyvyan Pope, the one-armed Director of Armoured Fighting Vehicles, was so against the British use of American tanks that he even proposed setting up production lines in India, so that Britain could go on building its own tanks away from any risk of invasion.

The British, like the French, thought that American factories should be producing British-style tanks to order, but American opinion, as voiced by the President, was against the very idea. The general belief was that Great Britain, like the Continental countries, would succumb to Nazi invasion before long and that America might then be left with a type of tank on their hands for which they had no use. The Americans' idea was that they would increase production of American-designed tanks instead, and in the event that they were not sold abroad, they would at least be suitable for the US Army in due course. However, this approach was not particularly popular and to begin with the British were slow to take advantage of it. Once they did start to appreciate the rugged simplicity of American designs and started to impose some ideas and the results of combat experience on American tank designers, they accepted the new tanks with equal enthusiasm, although those regiments that continued to operate British tanks remained biased until the end of the war and after. Most extreme of all was Lieutenant General Sir Giffard Le Q Martel, whose opinion, in effect, was that the Americans had been good enough to lend us a few of their tanks to tide us over while we were building the next generation of our own tanks, and that we continued to use some Sherman tanks until the end of the war. This is a rather gross interpretation of what really happened, since in north-west Europe, not to mention Italy and even Burma, the Sherman predominated with British, Commonwealth and other Allied forces right through to the end.

If we overlook the two Christie machines that arrived in Britain in 1936 and 1938, the first one of which served as a model for all the British Christie Cruisers built up to 1945, then the first American tanks to arrive in Britain were the 36 M2A4 light tanks that were delivered in 1941. That they were not terribly well received goes without saying, for the general British view of tanks built in the USA, or indeed anywhere other than in Britain, was one of amused tolerance. As the inventors of the tank, and the first to use them in combat, most British people, within the military and without, believed that British tanks were the best and that all foreign machines were inferior. Major General Douglas Pratt inspected a wooden mock-up of the new M3 medium tank in October 1940 and reported to London that it was 'as high as the Tower of Babel', while the government's resistance towards acquiring American tanks was still very strong.

Looked at from a historical distance this attitude seems hard to justify, for a combination of financial stringency, military short-sightedness and indeed industrial indifference had saddled Britain with some truly dreadful tanks that the test of combat would soon expose. It would take almost the entire war to sort out Britain's domestically built tanks.

In the meantime, although it was then not immediately obvious, the British Army would have to rely on tanks, and indeed other machines, designed and built in the United States – there was really no alternative. Yet the British, then in the main a somewhat insular nation, had been brought up to consider that only things Made in Britain were any good, and that foreign products left a lot to be desired. This applied to things made in America as much as anywhere else.

In any case the matter was almost becoming academic. Britain was rapidly running out of its gold and dollar reserves and Britain's orders were being cancelled due to a lack of wherewithal to pay for them. A disastrous situation was looming, and was only solved when President Roosevelt, commencing his third term in office, proposed the Lend-Lease Act, which came into law in March 1941. Now Britain could have more or less all the American equipment it wanted, without having to worry about payment. The Americans had improved tanks on the way, and Lend-Lease meant that they could be obtained in adequate numbers and take some of the pressure off British manufacturers.

The Sherman was a case in point. By the time of the Normandy invasion it equipped more British tank regiments than any other type, so much so that British crews began to think of it as a British tank. The British Army fought in its Shermans until the end of the war. Not that this meant that all American tanks were prime examples of the progressive tank designer's art. Take the M26 Pershing for instance. Although America's most modern tank at the end of the war, and a distinct improvement on the Sherman, it was still not that good. A few were hurried over to Europe for the final weeks of the war against Germany, but a US Army officer, Captain Elmer Gray, in response to a question from American tank crews who asked if the M26 was a match for the German Panther and King Tiger, said 'Hell no, but it's the best tank we have yet developed'. In fact the 90mm gun on the M26 was inferior in penetrating power to the old British 17-pounder (76.2mm) except at longer range and even then not by very much.

Lieutenant General Martel, whose opinions should always be taken with a pinch of salt, pointed to a fundamental difference between the British and American approaches to tank design. He said that the British began at the top with a gun, turret and fighting compartment and expected the automotive designers to design a suitable chassis to fit, whereas the Americans worked upwards, starting with a highly reliable automotive chassis and then fitting a hull and turret to suit. This isn't entirely true,

for most tanks whether British or American were designed as a complete entity, but it contains an element of truth about the two countries' priorities.

This theory probably accounts for a remark made by a retired British officer to the author some years ago. This man had joined 7th Armoured Division just after the end of the war. This division had been equipped entirely with British tanks, Cromwells, for the North-West Europe campaign, with some American Stuarts in reconnaissance units. He told me that he had heard that American tanks were only modified tractors and not a patch on their British counterparts – a typical example of regimental bias of the time, which may have been derived from what Martel had written. American tanks weren't perfect, but then neither were the majority of Britain's. They were however reliable, and available in substantial numbers. This book attempts to show them, warts and all and how they served with British units during World War II.

LIGHT TANK M2A4

The escalation of warlike activity in Europe, particularly the combatants' experience with tanks during the Spanish Civil War and in the early years of World War II, had some influence in the United States. Military pundits who specialized in armoured vehicles, such as Gladeon Barnes and John Christmas, were advocating more effective weapons and thicker armour, while others were pushing for greater production, arguing that having experimented with light tanks for years, and producing each type in relatively small batches, it was time to settle on a modern design and build the tank in larger numbers.

Thus the M2A4, although by no means the first American tank with a single turret, or indeed armed with a 37mm gun, was better armoured than its predecessors and mounted a respectable anti-tank weapon for its day, the 37mm gun M3. American Car & Foundry built 365 and the Baldwin Locomotive Works a further ten about a year later. Such were British reservations about American tanks that only a sample batch of 36 (four of which went to Egypt) was ordered in June 1941.

The M2A4 was powered by a seven-cylinder Continental W-670-9A air-cooled radial engine which, having been designed as an aero-engine, was looked at askance by British tank experts. However, it developed 250hp which gave the tank a top speed of 34mph, and proved in time to be eminently reliable while it lasted. What is more, the driver had a five-speed synchromesh gearbox alongside him that was easy to change and drove front-mounted sprockets, as on British light tanks. The suspension was the tried-and-tested vertical volute spring bogie system originally patented by Harry Knox, which seems to have given a comfortable enough ride. If there was a justified criticism of the tank it was its fuel capacity – just 54 US gallons giving a road range of 70 miles. This compared unfavourably with the 109 Imperial gallons of the Crusader, which gave a range of over 100 miles on its internal tanks, with a further 30 gallons in the auxiliary fuel tank. And of course the M2A4 did not have an auxiliary fuel tank. The tank had 1in of armour on all vertical surfaces.

The crew positions came in for some understandable criticism. The driver and hull machine-gunner both had seats although the folding plates in front of them were seen as vulnerable and an infernal nuisance when either crewman wanted to dismount; the driver had an additional armoured flap that could be folded forwards to make the task easier for him, but the hull gunner was expected to depart through the turret. This was little more than tiresome during training, but dangerous and potentially fatal in action. However, the tank's two-man turret, which had seven, evenly spaced pistol ports around the sides, matched by protected vision slits around the cupola, was regarded as the worst vulnerability if the tank was to be used as a cruiser, which in terms of firepower and protection it virtually was.

Both commander and gunner were expected to stand at their work since there was nowhere for them to sit. According to the explanation usually given, the commander, for whom a fairly large cupola was provided on top of the turret, had to abandon his commanding position to act as loader for the gunner; although from other sources it is clear that the commander took on the role of gunner so that he had the cupola directly behind him and the driver in front, whom he could kick if he wanted the tank to turn or halt in a hurry. To make matters worse, when the turret was traversed (a manual operation since there was no power traverse system) both gunner/commander and loader had to remember to step over the driveshaft that ran from the engine at the back to the transmission at the front, and effectively split the fighting compartment in two. Still worse, the traversing handwheel was situated on the far side of the turret, out of the reach of the tank gunner who needed it most.

Another M2A4 which has been named *Al Capone* – an unlikely hero. It is here seen in British service in a workshop. The offside sponson-mounted machine gun can be seen. It also carries the protective armour around the recoil system of the 37mm gun.

Things were made slightly easier by the fact that the gun mounting gave the gunner a limited amount of free movement, some ten degrees either side of the centre line, before there was any need to traverse the turret. In addition to the 37mm gun, which was shortened by about 5in (to reduce its vulnerability in thickly wooded areas, we are told), the tank also mounted five .30-calibre Browning machine guns: one co-axially with the main gun; another in a ball mounting in the hull front for the use of the hull gunner; two more fixed guns in the hull sponsons on each side that were fired by the driver; and the fifth attached externally to the side of the turret for the commander to use from his cupola.

Those tanks that were sent to Britain were attached to the 9th Royal Lancers while the regiment was in Britain, although the tanks never saw active service at any time. The side-mounted machine guns appear to have been removed after a while, as was the external weapon for the commander. Likewise the four that went to Egypt appear only to have been used for training and familiarization, although it has been claimed that some or all of them were sent to Burma in 1941. If this is true they could have served with the 7th Queen's Own Hussars or 2nd Royal Tank Regiment during the retreat to India. Having at first been reluctant to take American tanks and then only in a very limited way, the British authorities ultimately decided to acquire 200 more, only to discover that production had ceased and no more were available. However the Americans sent their latest model, the Light Tank M3 instead.

An M2A4 light tank in British service, photographed here with the 9th Royal Lancers, with the crew attending to the engine. Note the raised rear idler and the strip along the side of the hull designed to protect the pioneer tools.

CHAPTER 1

M3 LIGHT TANK: THE STUART

The M3 and M5 family of light tanks were the culmination of American tank development of the 1930s. By the time of the outbreak of World War II, they were approaching obsolescence, as tank forces in Europe were shifting from light to medium tanks as the main element of their armoured forces. First entering combat in the autumn of 1941 in the Western Desert with the British Army, the Stuart quickly showed that it was inadequate in tank fighting. But the Stuart tank was available in such large numbers that rather than withdrawing it, it was moved to secondary missions such as reconnaissance.

COMBAT CAR AND LIGHT TANK

Following World War I, the US Army's short-lived Tank Corps was subordinated to the infantry branch. Given the prevalent isolationist sentiment in Congress, US doctrine was based on the premise that the US was unlikely to fight in a European war again. Military operations in the Philippines or along the US border were considered more likely scenarios, and tanks were not viewed as important to such missions. The combination of low priority and the parsimonious US inter-war defence budget meant that US tank development laboured under minuscule budgets. Although the infantry was responsible for tank development, the cavalry's role as the army's mobile force inevitably led to interest in tanks as a substitute for horses. In the 1930s, a peculiar situation arose under which the infantry fostered the development of 'light tanks' as the infantry tanks were called, while the cavalry funded 'combat cars', since they were legally prevented from acquiring tanks. This situation was all the more farcical as the design of both types of vehicles shared a number of features and they were both designed and manufactured at the army's Rock Island Arsenal in Illinois.

The most influential tank design of the inter-war years was the British Vickers six-ton export tank. After obtaining a Vickers tank for trials, a rough analogue, the T1E4 light tank, was developed and tested. In the meantime, the cavalry branch

had been experimenting with alternative designs including the T1 combat car, better known as the Christie tank. In early 1933, the Secretary of War ordered that future combat cars and light tanks be limited to a maximum weight of seven-and-a-half tons. Based on the new directive and other design requirements from the army, the Rock Island Arsenal completed the T2 light tank and T5 combat car in 1934. With a number of common features, they were the direct ancestors of the M3 light tank. The T5 combat car was substantially redesigned before series production was undertaken from 1935 to 1937 as the M1 combat car. These tanks were armed with a .50-calibre heavy machine gun, a separate .30-calibre machine gun in a single turret, and a .30-calibre machine-gun in the hull. In the mid-1930s, the US Army considered the .50-calibre heavy machine gun to be an effective anti-tank weapon, since it could penetrate the armour of most foreign tanks of the period. The M1 combat car also evolved during production, with a new slab-sided turret on later production vehicles.

The Stuart family is best remembered for its role in the desert fighting in North Africa in 1941 and 1942. Popularly called the 'Honey' for its pleasant driving characteristics, it equipped the 4th Armoured Brigade of the 7th Armoured Division during Operation *Crusader* in November 1941. This is a classic view of Honeys of the 8th King's Royal Irish Hussars on training in Egypt before the battle.

Alongside the cavalry's efforts, the infantry's T2 light tank entered production in 1935 as the M2A1 light tank. The hull bore a strong resemblance to the M1 combat car, but the M2A1 light tank was fitted with a smaller, one-man turret with a .50-calibre heavy machine-gun. After only ten were produced, the infantry switched to twin-turreted tanks on the presumption that such a configuration would have more combat value for infantry support, since the turrets could independently direct fire at two targets simultaneously. The twin-turreted M2A2 light tank was produced in 1935–7 and was by far the most common version in the 1930s.

The original ancestor of the Stuart family was the T5 Combat Car developed for the US Cavalry at the Rock Island Arsenal in 1934. It shows many of the features that would become characteristic of the Stuart light tanks, notably the hull design and the vertical volute suspension bogies. (US Army MHI)

LESSONS OF THE SPANISH CIVIL WAR

The first major tank combat since World War I took place during the Spanish Civil War which began in the autumn of 1936. Most of the tank fighting occurred in 1937, when the Soviet T-26 light tank of the Republican forces was pitted against the machine-gun-armed German PzKpfw I and Italian CV.3/35 light tanks of the Nationalist forces. The reports of US Army attachés in Spain made it clear that the cannon-armed T-26 was clearly superior to the machine-gun-armed tanks. The dominant lesson was the vulnerability of light tanks to anti-tank weapons such as the German 37mm gun. These lessons were of considerable interest to the US Army, as US light tanks and cavalry cars were based on the Vickers six-ton tank, which also formed the inspiration for the Soviet T-26. Studies in 1938 concluded that future US tanks should be armed at least with a 37mm gun, and that the vehicle armour had to be increased from the existing level of ⅝in (16mm) as this could be easily penetrated by a 37mm gun from any realistic combat range.

As a short-term expedient, the existing light tanks could be modestly upgraded. However, incorporation of enough armour to defend against a 37mm anti-tank gun would require a much more elaborate effort. The infantry's new M2A3 light tank entered production in 1938 having benefited from some of these lessons. The hull was lengthened and suspension bogies spaced further apart to accommodate the heavier armour, with the frontal armour increasing from 16mm to 22mm. A modified engine, the Continental W670-9, was introduced and there were numerous other improvements. Most of these features were incorporated into the cavalry's parallel M1A1 combat car which also entered production in 1938. While the Spanish Civil War was the catalyst for

The later production batches of the M1 Combat Car used a slab-sided turret instead of a round turret. This is the combat car of the commander of the 13th Cavalry, marked prominently with the white command guidon with the regimental crest in the guidon and repeated on the rear side panel. (US National Archives)

the US Army's development of new medium tanks, it did not provoke any serious questions about the viability of light tanks on the modern battlefield. This would not have mattered, as defence budgets in 1938–40 would not permit the complete transition of the army from light tanks to medium tanks. However, the shift to medium tanks was well underway in Europe, most notably in the Soviet Union, France, and Germany.

This is an M2A2 light tank of the 28th Tank Company during summer wargames in New York state in 1940. In contrast to the M2A1 light tank, the M2A2 light tank had its armament in two separate turrets. The initial production series used rounded turrets as seen here. (US National Archives)

The cavalry branch largely ignored the Spanish Civil War lessons and its 1940 production plan focused on the M2 combat car, still armed with a .50-calibre machine-gun. In December 1938, however, the infantry authorized the construction of the improved M2A4 light tank, fitted with a single large turret with a 37mm gun, and protected with thicker 1in armour. Other important improvements included the incorporation of radio receivers in all tanks, and radio transmitters in command tanks. By the time the M2A4 light tank was ready for production in May 1940, war had broken out in Europe. The US government recognized that its isolationist foreign policy was likely to change, and with it the need for a substantially enlarged and modernized US Army. As a result, tank production was shifted from the small government arsenals to larger commercial plants to permit a surge in production if war broke out. M2A4 light tank production began at the well-known railway manufacturer, American Car & Foundry in Berwick, Pennsylvania, in May 1940.

The final production batches of the M2A2 light tank used slab-sided, welded turrets as can be seen in this overhead view of a tank on manoeuvres at Fort Belvoir, Virginia, on 22 November 1940. (US Army MHI)

1
2
3
4
5
6
7
8
9
10
11
12
13
14
15
U.S.A.
DIABLO
33
34
35
36
37
38
39
40
41
42
43
44
45
46
47

M3, 1ST BATTALION 1ST ARMORED REGIMENT, 1ST ARMORED DIVISION, TUNISIA, NOVEMBER 1942

(Art by Jim Laurier, © Osprey Publishing)

Key

1 Stowage bin
2 Tow cable
3 Armoured cover for fuel filler cap
4 Radio aerial
5 Continental W670-9A radial engine
6 Engine muffler
7 Protectoscope pistol port
8 Browning .30cal. machine-gun
9 .30cal. machine-gun ammunition box
10 Gun mount protective cage
11 Gunner's periscope
12 Firewall
13 37mm M6 gun in M22 combination turret
14 Co-axial .30cal. machine-gun
15 Gun mantlet
16 Turret lifting ring
17 Gun elevation wheel
18 Turret traverse wheel
19 .30cal. sponson machine-gun
20 Gunner's seat cushion
21 Driver's Protectoscope view port
22 Driver's seat
23 .30cal. machine-gun tripod
24 Driver's controls
25 Synchromesh transmission
26 Headlight
27 Headlight brush guard
28 Transmission housing cover
29 Towing shackle
30 Foot step
31 Glacis plate
32 .30cal. bow machine-gun
33 Rubber track block
34 Ammunition bin
35 Track end connector
36 Drive sprocket
37 Vertical volute spring
38 Transmission tunnel cover
39 Assistant driver's seat
40 Return roller
41 Rubber-rimmed road wheel
42 Windshield stowage box
43 Vertical volute suspension bogie
44 Trailer idler wheel assembly
45 Sponson machine-gun mount
46 Sponson machine-gun ammunition
47 Engine air filter

The effectiveness of anti-tank guns during the Spanish Civil War made it clear that more armour would be needed for tanks to survive on the battlefield. To accommodate the weight of added armour, the suspension bogies on the new M2A3 light tank were spaced further apart. This M2A3 is on exercise with the 66th Infantry (Tanks) at Fort George Meade, Maryland, on 14 November 1939. The triangular marking identifies this as a battalion headquarters tank. (US Army MHI)

Following the shock of France's defeat in June 1940, the US Army decided to expand its tank units and a new Armored Force was created on 10 July 1940, consolidating the cavalry combat cars and infantry light tanks under a single command. The M1 and M1A1 combat cars were redesignated as the M1A2 light tank, and the M2 combat car became the M1A1 light tank. The fall of France forced the US Army to recognize its backwardness in armoured vehicles. Instead of low-intensity colonial or border conflicts, it was growing likely that it would face a high-intensity conflict in Europe. The US Army responded by forming its first armoured divisions in the summer of 1940 which would need modern medium tanks, but until US industry was ready to manufacture medium tanks, light tanks would have to suffice.

THE M3 LIGHT TANK

Although the M2A4 light tank was a substantial improvement over the previous light tanks and combat cars, it had technical and design problems. Work began on the new M3 light tank in July 1940. The added weight of armour caused mobility problems on the M2A4, and was partly resolved by a shift to the enlarged rear idler of the M2 combat car which increased the area of ground contact. The long recoil mechanism of the M5 37mm gun in the M20 combination mount projected far outside the M2A4 turret, making it difficult to protect. A modified design was produced, the M5 37mm gun with a new short recoil mechanism in the M22 combination mount.

Like the infantry's M2A3 light tank, the cavalry's M1A1 combat car also was up-armoured and had the spaced bogies. This M1A1 combat car was part of C Troop, 1st Cavalry during the May 1940 manoeuvres. (US National Archives)

Finally, the existing 1in armour was deemed inadequate to protect the tank from contemporary anti-tank guns, but a frontal protection of 1.5in of armour was all the chassis could bear, even though it did not offer proof against 37mm anti-tank guns at normal combat ranges. The M3 light tank entered production at American Car & Foundry in March 1941. It was the most numerous US tank at the outbreak of the war, and would be the principal US type to see combat in the first year of the war.

The creation of the Armored Force in 1940 led to a major expansion of US armoured units. This is the original version of the M3 light tank with the riveted D37812 turret. Similar to the turret of the M2A4 light tank, it used a new type of external pistol port flap, and the gun was fitted in a new mount. The 37mm gun was installed by government arsenals after the tank was manufactured, and during the 1941 wargames, some tanks were hastily put into service before their guns were fitted like the vehicle in this photograph with a dummy gun. This tank from the 1st Armored Division is seen crossing the Catawba River on a pontoon bridge during the November 1941 Carolina manoeuvres. (US National Archives)

The original production batch of 100 M3 light tanks was fitted with the D37812 riveted turret similar to that on the M2A4 light tank, but with a new pattern of pistol port. Trials had shown that heavy machine-gun fire could dislodge the interior head of the rivets, however, sending them careering around the turret interior and injuring the crew. As a result, the new D38976 welded turret, made from face-hardened armour, was authorized in December 1940 and the first tank with the new feature was completed in April 1941. The M5 37mm gun was replaced by the improved M6 37mm gun which had a tube 5in longer than the M5, and an automatic breechblock. The original M3 light tanks had the 37mm gun in the M22 combination gun mount which used a shoulder stock for elevating the gun. This was replaced by the M23 combination gun mount which used a more conventional elevation gear, an improved shell deflector and other changes.

The M3 light tank was an adequate, if uninspiring design which reflected US neglect of tank development in the years leading up to World War II. It was comparable or superior in terms of armour, fire-power, and mobility to older European designs of the late 1930s such as the Soviet T-26, the Polish 7TP, and the Czech/German PzKpfw 38(t). However, the Spanish Civil War experience had been interpreted very differently in Europe, reinforcing a trend to larger, more heavily armoured and better-armed tanks. Prior to the outbreak of World War II, most European armies had abandoned the light tank as the basis of their armoured forces, favouring medium tanks that were larger and more than five tons heavier. In France, this produced the Somua S.35 and Char B1 *bis*, and in Germany the PzKpfw III and PzKpfw IV. The most radical solution was attempted in the Soviet Union, where the Spanish Civil War inspired the T-34 design which would replace both their infantry's light tanks and the cavalry's cruiser tanks. While the main influence in tank design in the 1920s and 1930s came from Britain and France, Soviet and German innovations dominated the wartime experience.

During the early war years, the US Army was strongly influenced by their more experienced British allies in tactics and technology. Unfortunately, British tanks were no longer in the forefront of design technology. A combination of a lack of maturity in US Army tactical doctrine, and a concentration on production quantity over quality, meant that US tank design consistently lagged behind Germany throughout the war. The US Army began to shift its emphasis to medium tanks in 1941 with the clumsy M3 medium tank, but medium tank production did not begin to exceed light tank production until December 1941. A truly modern medium tank, the M4A1 Sherman, did not appear until the spring of 1942. Though the M3 light tank compared badly with its European contemporaries, it fared better in comparison to its likely rivals in the Pacific, the Japanese Type 95 *Ha-go* light tank and Type 97 *Chi-ha* medium tank.

THE M3 STUART GOES TO WAR

While the United States was ostensibly neutral through 1940 and 1941, President Franklin Roosevelt was convinced that his country would eventually be dragged into the war, and took steps to prepare for this eventuality. With Britain as the lone defender against Germany and Italy, Roosevelt began to assist in arming the British forces. This culminated in the March 1941 Lend-Lease Act. British officers in the United States had little to choose from in American tanks, just the M2A4 light tank and M3 medium tank. But in the desperate circumstances of early 1941, they ordered whatever was available. The first order was for 100 M2A4 light tanks, and the first 36 arrived in June 1941; 32 were shipped to the UK and four to Egypt. The further supply of the M2A4 was halted once the improved M3 light tank became available.

The two new American tanks shared a confusing similarity in nomenclature, the M3 light tank and M3 medium tank, and so Britain instituted its own system for American tanks using the names of American Civil War generals. The M3 light tank was called the General Stuart, after the Confederate cavalry general J.E.B. Stuart, and the M3 medium tank was named the General Lee, after the legendary Robert E. Lee. To add some balance, the M3 medium tank with a new British turret became the Grant, and the new M4 medium tank became the Sherman after the two Union generals. None of these names were sanctioned by the US Army, nor were they commonly used by US troops during the war. However, the names did become popular in the United States after the war, and are still widely used.

The Stuart tank did not conform to British design or tactical concepts. Although an infantry tank by US standards, it was lightly armoured compared to British infantry tanks such as the Matilda. Nor did the Stuart have the range deemed necessary for a cruiser tank, being capable of only about 75 miles on firm ground and about 45 miles in rough desert conditions. However, in technical terms it was closer to the cruiser tanks than to the infantry tanks, and so was used as such when first issued to units in the Western Desert in 1941. In terms of armament, its 37mm gun was similar to the standard British 2-pounder in anti-armour penetration at usual combat ranges, but had the advantage of also firing a high explosive round which was useful in engaging targets other than tanks such as anti-tank guns and infantry.

In August 1941, a programme was started to modify the Stuart to adapt it to British practices. By October 1941, the list had grown to more than 26 changes, and to further complicate matters, the modifications carried out in Middle East workshops did not coincide directly with those carried out

The M3 light tank saw its baptism of fire during Operation *Crusader* in Libya in late November 1941. This is *Crossbow* from the 3rd RTR, 7th Armoured Division, knocked out by a hit to the turret. Prior to the fighting, the division's Stuarts were fitted with 'sunshields' which were a frame assembly with cloth covering designed to make the tank look like a lorry to enemy reconnaissance aircraft. This was part of an elaborate deception scheme intended to surprise Rommel's Afrikakorps. Although most tanks had the sunshields removed, some tanks like this one left on the lower portion. (US Army MHI)

in the UK. The most noticeable external changes were the addition of sand-shields, a water container rack, a ration box, a blanket box and a cooking set box, blanking plates over the sponson machine-gun ports, and a folding frame to make it easier to close the turret hatch while standing in the cupola. The Stuart had a total of five .30-calibre machine guns: two fixed in the hull, one flexible in the hull, one co-axial with the main gun and one on an external mounting on the turret roof. This was deemed excessive by British tank specialists. The fixed sponson machine guns were normally deleted in favour of more internal stowage. There were extensive internal changes affecting both mechanical details and stowage. By 1941, the Stuart was a mature design, and was more durable and dependable than the British tanks of the day, leading to its nickname of 'Honey' in the 7th Armoured Division.

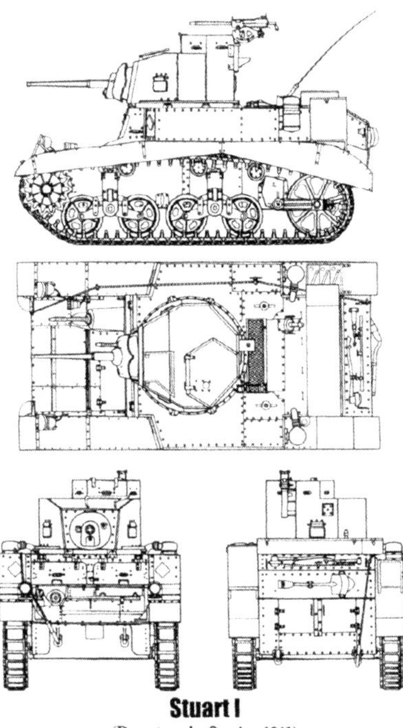

Stuart I
(Desert mods, October 1941)

ABOVE The second production version of the M3 light tank introduced the D38976 welded turret which was essentially similar to the earlier riveted type except for the construction technique. This tank of the 2nd Armored Division at Fort Benning, Georgia, on 18 December 1941 shows all the crew, ammunition, parts and supplies that were crammed into this small vehicle. Although not apparent from this angle, the M3 light tanks of the 2nd Armored Division were mainly the diesel engine version at this time, a type that was not popular because of the difficulty in getting the engine started, especially in cold weather. (US Army MHI)

DESERT DEBUT

The first large shipment of 84 Stuart tanks arrived in Egypt in July 1941. By the autumn of 1941, enough Stuarts had arrived to equip the three tank regiments of the 4th Armoured Brigade, part of the famous 'Desert Rats', the 7th Armoured Division. These units would first see combat in the November 1941 Operation *Crusader*, an attempt to re-capture Cyrenaica and relieve Tobruk. The units equipped with Stuarts were the 8th King's Royal Irish Hussars, the 3rd and the 5th Royal Tank Regiment, which had a total of 165 Stuarts on hand at the start of the operation. The 7th Armoured Division's other two brigades were equipped with cruiser tanks, Crusaders for the most part, numbering a further 287 tanks, for a grand total of 453 tanks. There were additional tanks in other units, with the British forces operating about 700 tanks at the beginning of the offensive, plus a substantial reserve. The Afrikakorps' two panzer divisions (15. and 21.Panzer Division) had 260 tanks at the start of *Crusader,* including 77 light PzKpfw II, 145 PzKpfw III and 38 PzKpfw IV, plus about 135 M-13/40 tanks with the Italian Ariete Division and no reserves.

The first combat use of the Stuart took place on 19 November 1941 in a sharp battle between the 8th Hussars and Kampfgruppe Stephan of Pz.Rgt.5 of the 21. Panzer Division near Gabr Saleh. The 8th Hussars lost 20 Stuarts, while the Germans lost two PzKpfw III and one PzKpfw II light tank. Heavy fighting by all three Stuart regiments took place the following day, and only 98 Stuarts were operational by the end of the day's combat. The Stuarts later took part in the intense fighting for the Sidi Rezegh airfield. The 4th Armoured Brigade was committed to the battle on the afternoon of 22 November. During the night of 22/23 November, tanks of I./ Pz.Rgt.8 of 15.Panzer Division stumbled into the night leaguer of the 8th Hussars and the 4th Armoured Brigade head-quarters. In the darkness and confusion they overwhelmed the unit, capturing the regiment's commander, 167 troops and 35 Stuart tanks. Only seven Stuart tanks managed to escape the debacle.

By Sunday 23 November 1941, the 7th Armoured Division was in a desperate situation, having suffered heavy tank losses in the preceding days, and now facing the full weight of both panzer divisions. By the end of the fighting on 23 November, the 7th Armoured Division had been reduced to about 35 Stuarts and 40 cruiser tanks. Having shattered the most powerful British formation, Rommel decided on a rash gamble, and on 24 November directed his forces to a race to the Egyptian frontier, hoping to snatch a quick victory. In the end, the Afrikakorps had suffered too many losses and was too exhausted to conduct so bold a venture. In December 1941, the Afrikakorps was forced to withdraw and Tobruk was relieved.

Following the heavy losses of Operation *Crusader*, the latest models of the Stuart were shipped to Egypt as part of the Lend-Lease programme. This Stuart of the 7th Armoured Division has the new round turret fitted out at the workshops in Egypt in March 1942. It is from the original production batch of this turret, lacking the forward cupola view-slits. Some innovations had been added after *Crusader*, including the addition of smoke mortars on the turret, and a reinforced bracket for the sunshield deception devices. (US Army MHI)

The decimation of the 7th Armoured Division in the initial fighting at Sidi Rezegh had more to do with tactical deficiencies than with technical problems. The German armour units were able to overcome their more numerous opponent with superior tactics, including a skilled use of tanks in co-ordination with the highly effective 50mm PaK 38 anti-tank gun and the legendary 88mm gun. Rommel remarked to a captured British officer, 'What difference does it make for me if you have two tanks to my one? You send them out and let me smash them in detail. You presented me with three brigades in succession.'

British workshops in Egypt made many modifications to the M3 light tank before issuing them to the troops. This included the addition of sand-skirts over the suspension, mounting brackets for sunshields, and additional stowage containers. This is *Bellman*, a tank from the 8th King's Royal Irish Hussars, knocked out during the initial skirmishes with Panzer Regiment.5 during Operation *Crusader*.

The fighting showed that the Stuart and Crusader tanks were barely adequate for tank fighting. This was not simply a matter of gun and armour. Although many accounts of the desert fighting suggest that the German tanks were better armoured and had longer-range guns, this was not the case. The 30mm superstructure front armour of the PzKpfw III Ausf. G could theoretically be penetrated by the Honey's gun at 1,500m, while the PzKpfw III Ausf. G's 50mm gun could penetrate the Honey's 38mm superstructure front at similar ranges. Most engagements took place at closer ranges where both tanks were vulnerable to each other's fire, and shots were often fired against the side armour of opposing tanks, where there was no clear advantage to either side.

The German advantage was in less appreciated factors such as tactics, training, command and control, and fightability of the tank. The PzKpfw III was better laid out for tank fighting than the Stuart, having a turret crew of three: commander, gunner and loader. The commander could concentrate on directing his tank, and co-ordinating its actions with those of neighbouring tanks. The German tank periscope was superior, using an early form of stadiametric rangefinding. Gun elevation was geared, so that after firing the first shot, the German gunner could adjust his fire with precision.

In the M3 light tank, the commander had to double up as gunner. This seriously distracted him from his function of observing enemy actions and made the tank almost blind in combat. When operating the gun, the commander had no means of vision other than the tank's telescopic sight, or a small pistol port. The British realized this shortcoming, and as an expedient, shifted crew functions. During combat, the commander moved to the rear of the turret, while the redundant hull co-driver moved into

The Afrikakorps made use of captured Stuarts on numerous occasions. This M3 light tank with the third type round turret was later recaptured by US forces at Cheylas, south of Tunis, in 1943. It was originally captured from US forces in 1943, repainted, and remarked in German insignia. (US Army MHI)

STUART I, 8TH KING'S ROYAL IRISH HUSSARS, 4TH ARMOURED BRIGADE, 7TH ARMOURED DIVISION, OPERATION CRUSADER, NOVEMBER 1941

Stuarts at the time of Operation Crusader were still finished in the Caunter scheme, a disruptive pattern developed by a former 4th Armoured Brigade commander, Brigadier J. A. L. Caunter. Like the dazzle painting of World War I warships, the pattern was an attempt to confuse the enemy regarding range, and direction of travel. This scheme has seldom been accurately depicted, and the first complete details were published in 1997–8 in a series of articles by Mike Starmer in the journal *Tankette*. The base colour of the pattern was BSC No. 64 Portland Stone. The two other colours were BSC No. 28 Silver Grey and BSC No. 34 Slate, although the 'New Service Colour', Khaki Green 3, was given as an alternative to Slate. A major tactical problem in the desert was vehicle identification, and prior to Operation Crusader, a white/red/white identity marking, inspired by World War I tank marking, was adopted for British tanks. Coloured pennants were also used on the aerials or special poles for the same purpose, in this case in yellow. This regiment had a tradition of using famous racing names for identification. Headquarters used race-horse names beginning with H, such as the commander's 'Hurry On', with the squadrons using names starting with the company letter. B Squadron used the names of hounds, such as Boxer, Beacon, and Bellman as seen here. The B Squadron square tactical sign was in yellow, as is the vehicle name, though the square has been partly covered. (Art by Jim Laurier, © Osprey Publishing)

the turret and served as gunner. To accommodate the tank commander, an armoured car-pattern sling seat was added under the turret cupola. In October 1941, plans were underway to substitute a rigid folding seat, shaped like that on a motorcycle, but it is not clear how many tanks, if any, received this modification before the battle began. In view of the small size of the Stuart turret, this change led to extremely cramped conditions. The gunner and loader lacked traversing seats, and had to clamber over the transmission tunnel running through the centre of the fighting compartment.

Another unusual feature of the Stuart was the location of the turret traversing wheel on the right (loader's) side of the turret, which British workshops changed to the left side. As a result of these features, Stuart crews tended to fight with the turret pointed directly forward, steering the tank towards the target and using the limited traverse of the M22 mount for precision aiming rather than the turret traverse. The 37mm gun in the early Stuart was usually elevated using a shoulder brace, and so in the event of a miss, the gunner could not adjust the succeeding shot with any precision. The M5A1 telescopic sight lacked a ranging feature. The British workshops in Egypt added a Philips internal communication set, enabling the commander to talk to the crew. British doctrine of the time still recommended firing from the move, but Stuart crews found that the most effective tactic was to close on the enemy as quickly as possible, make a quick halt, and then fire the main gun.

Although the Stuart was not equal to the PzKpfw III, it did not fare badly in comparison to British cruiser tanks of the period which were also decidedly inferior in durability. According to the 4th Armoured Brigade commander, only 12 Stuarts were lost due to mechanical breakdown during Operation *Crusader*. Indeed, it was the basic automotive reliability of the Stuart that helped keep the Desert Rats in the field in the later stages of the battle. Its main problem was its poor range: undamaged tanks were sometimes abandoned, and the need for frequent refuelling stops restricted the mobility of the brigade. A number of intact Stuarts were recovered by the Germans in 1941 and more were captured in early 1942. By the time of the Gazala and El Alamein fighting, ten or 12 were in German service and they were sometimes designated as PzKpfw M3 747(a).

The Stuart continued to see combat in the January 1942 fighting. But following *Crusader*, shipments of the more powerful M3 Lee and Grant medium tanks began to arrive. As a result, the armoured regiments began reorganizing, and gradually shifted to a composition of one squadron of Stuarts and two squadrons of Grants. By the time of the Gazala battles and the defence of the Alamein line in the spring of 1942, 12 of the armoured regiments still included Stuart squadrons. Many of these were the new intermediate production type with the round homogenous turret and new vision ports. The role of the Stuart continued to decline as more modern equipment became available. As the new M4A1 Sherman medium tank began to arrive in the summer of 1942, the Stuarts were shifted out of the line squadrons, and transferred to reconnaissance. By the time of the Alamein offensive in the autumn of 1942, the Eighth Army was operating 128 Stuarts, about 11 per cent of its force.

COMBAT IN ASIA

Following their victory in Malaya in February 1942, the Imperial Japanese Army (IJA) struck into Burma, spearheaded by three tank regiments. Britain dispatched the 7th Armoured Brigade consisting of two tank units hastily withdrawn from the North African campaign, the 2nd RTR and 7th Hussars. The 7th Hussars were equipped with Stuart light tanks and fought a series of costly rearguard actions, including several against the Japanese 14th Tank Regiment. By the time the survivors of the unit reached British lines in India, only one Stuart remained in action. But the Japanese advance had been brought to a halt short of India.

An M3 Stuart of 7th Armoured Brigade in Burma. Not the easiest tank to fight, and prone to running short of fuel at crucial moments, it was at least a match for any Japanese light tank it might come across. The tank was photographed near Taukkyan, on 8 March 1942.

7

By the end of the North Africa campaign, the Stuart was obviously no longer capable of facing Axis armour. The one theatre where the Stuart continued to play a frontline role was in Burma. US and Chinese troops formed the jointly manned Provisional Chinese Tank Group with four battalions of M3A3 Stuarts and two of M4A4 Shermans. They took part in the Chinese offensive along the Burma Road and into southern China. Most British units taking part in the 1944–45 fighting had been re-equipped with Lee or Sherman medium tanks. However, the Indian armoured force still used the Stuart in some numbers. The first Stuarts had arrived in India in 1941, though the conversion of cavalry regiments to armour did not take place in earnest until 1942–43. Of its 18 armoured regiments, at least three Indian regiments were equipped mainly with the Stuart in early 1943: the 7th Light Cavalry, the 18th KEO Cavalry and the 45th Cavalry. The 7th Light Cavalry was the first Indian armoured unit to see combat in March 1944. As part of the 254th Indian Tank Brigade, the unit took part in the Imphal and Kohima campaign, and participated in the retaking of Burma in 1945. The 45th Cavalry of the 50th Indian Tank Brigade took part in the later stages of the Arakan campaign in February 1945.

OPPOSITE Australia began receiving Stuart light tanks via the British Lend-Lease allotments from the autumn of 1941. Before being introduced to combat in New Guinea, the vehicles were modified in Australian workshops, with the addition of a protective ring around the base of the turret to prevent the Japanese infantry from jamming it. This is a Stuart of the 2/6th Armoured Regiment during operations near Popendetta, New Guinea, on 19 May 1943. It uses the third turret type. (US National Archives)

THE STUART IN NORTHERN EUROPE 1944–45

Although the Stuart was no longer ideal for infantry support or tank operations, it could still be employed for other tasks. So many Stuarts were available that there was never any real thought of abandoning them, in spite of their shortcomings. In 1943–44 alone, the US supplied 5,300 Stuarts via Lend-Lease, mainly to Britain. In turn, these were passed on to Commonwealth forces such as Canada, Australia, New Zealand and South Africa, as well as to other Allied forces equipped from British stockpiles, such as Polish troops. The United States also provided more than 530 M3A3 and M5A1 light tanks to de Gaulle's Free French forces. After the M7 light tank failure, a second Stuart replacement was begun in March 1943, emerging as the M24 Chaffee light tank. The M24 light tank was better armed than the M5A1 with a 75mm gun, and it was a thoroughly modern design. Production began in April 1944, but the first vehicles did not appear on the battlefield until December 1944. Few saw service with British forces.

Britain was one of the main recipients of the M3A3 light tank, where it was known as the Stuart V. By this stage of the war, it was used primarily as a reconnaissance tank. Prior to the Normandy landings, they were fitted with deep wading trunks for amphibious operations as seen here.

By the time of the 1944 Normandy invasion, the M3A3 and M5A1 light tanks were widely used throughout the Allied forces. In the US Army, each tank battalion had a company of M5A1 light tanks, a total of 17 M5A1 light tanks, 53 M4 medium tanks and six M4 105mm howitzer tanks. During the Normandy campaign, at least two separate GHQ tank battalions, the 744th and 759th, retained the light tank configuration. US armoured divisions had 77 light tanks each, 17 each in the three tank battalions, 17 in a cavalry reconnaissance squadron, and nine in headquarters companies. Other specialized units also used the M5A1, including non-divisional cavalry reconnaissance squadrons. By September 1944, the US 12th Army Group had seven armoured divisions, 16 separate tank battalions and eight cavalry groups operational in north-west Europe, with a combined organizational establishment of over 1,110 M5A1 light tanks. The French Army also followed US organization but used both M3A3 and M5A1 light tanks.

The M5 light tank was used most intensively in the first months after the Normandy landings. Patton's Third Army, for example, lost 308 M5A1 tanks during the 1944–45 fighting, of which nearly half were lost in August and September 1944 alone. A similar pattern was repeated in Hodge's First Army which suffered the majority of its light tank casualties in June-September 1944. The heavy casualties in the light tank companies led tank commanders to exercise caution in employing the M5A1 light tank, and the diminishing casualties in later months was due in no small measure to restricting the missions of the light tanks to reduce their vulnerability.

By September 1944, the heavy losses suffered in the fighting in Normandy led the Armored Section of Gen. Bradley's 12th Army Group headquarters to request that all M5A1 light tanks be replaced as soon as possible by the new M24 light tank. The War Department in Washington did not concur, citing shipping and logistics problems. As a result, a policy was established to replace the M5A1 in the most vulnerable units, namely the corps' cavalry and the armoured divisions' reconnaissance squadrons where the M5A1 light tanks did not have the support of M4 medium tanks. The only armoured division to replace most of its M5A1 tanks in the tank battalions was the 7th Armored Division.

In addition to its recognized vulnerability to German tanks and anti-tank guns, the M5A1 light tank faced a new foe in north-west Europe: German infantry rocket anti-tank weapons such as the Panzerfaust. These weapons accounted for about 15 per cent of M5A1 losses, while tank and anti-tank guns caused 55 per cent, and mines about 25 per cent. The poor armour protection of the M5A1 resulted in a higher rate of crew casualties than in medium tanks, with a medium tank crew having about a one-in-five chance of becoming a casualty when their tank was knocked out, compared to a one-in-three chance in light tanks. A report to Gen. Dwight Eisenhower from the 2nd Armored Division in 1945 concluded: 'The M5 light tank is obsolete in every respect as a fighting tank…The light tank is being used for working with the infantry. We subject it to direct fire just as little as we can, for it is realized that the armor will not turn the German fire or the 37mm gun damage the German tanks or SP guns.' In total, the US Army lost 777 M5A1 light tanks in combat during the campaign in north-west Europe, and 424 in Italy.

The most common use of the Stuart tank in British and Commonwealth formations was in the reconnaissance troops of armoured units, which had 11 Stuarts each. Although most British units in north-west Europe used the Stuart V (M3A3), some recce troops still had the older Stuart III (M3A1) or the Stuart VI (M5A1). Polish and Czech armoured units followed British organizational practice, and their vehicles were provided from British Lend-Lease sources. The Poles received about 110–130 Stuarts of various versions for the 1st Armoured Division in north-west Europe and the 2nd Armoured Division in Italy. The Czechoslovak Independent Armoured Brigade operated about 30 M5A1 light tanks. Besides their use as reconnaissance vehicles, turretless Stuarts were widely used as armoured ammunition carriers to supply forward tank units. For example, of the 259 Stuart III and Stuart VI tanks in service with the Canadian 1st Army in north-west Europe at the end of the war, 109 (42 per cent) were ammo carriers.

STUARTS IN THE MEDITERRANEAN THEATRE

Besides operations in north-west Europe, Stuarts remained in widespread use in the Mediterranean theatre with British and American forces in 1944–45. Since it was mainly intended for reconnaissance, some British recce troops modified the Stuart by removing its turret, a practice first started in the Western Desert. The lighter weight made the vehicle faster and more nimble than turreted Stuarts, and these features were sometimes judged more valuable than the firepower of the 37mm gun. These were dubbed 'Stuart Recces' and varied considerably in detail. Stuarts were also used as ammo carriers in this theatre.

In 1944, Britain assisted in the formation of the Yugoslav 1st Armoured Brigade, which was equipped with a single M3A1 Stuart III and 56 M3A3 Stuart V light tanks. They were landed on the Adriatic coast, and took part in the liberation of Yugoslavia. Even the Yugoslavs found the firepower of the Stuart to be deficient, and upgunned some of their tanks with captured German 75mm PaK 40 anti-tank guns, or quadruple 20mm FlaK 38 anti-aircraft guns.

The M3 light tank underwent continual incremental upgrades during its production. The new D39273 rolled homogenous turret was introduced from October 1941. This round turret used Protectoscopes, a type of armoured viewing device for the turret. This is from the standard production batch, which had four viewing ports added to the cupola. The 2nd Armored Division at Fort Benning was the first unit to receive this type in large numbers, seen here on 20 February 1942. (US Army MHI)

IDENTIFYING THE M3

One quite striking development which makes these vehicles instantly recognisable from the outside was the adoption of a new, larger-diameter trailing idler in contact with the ground. This increased the length of track in touch with the ground and improved stability, although this was not entirely new. It had been introduced on certain light tanks of the M2 series which had been fitted experimentally with diesel engines and was intended to support the greater weight. On the M3 and subsequent tanks, however, it permitted an extension of the rear hull which formed a cowl that expelled used air and exhaust fumes downwards at the back.

Early examples of the M3 series featured the octagonal turret composed of face-hardened armour plate but rather obviously riveted, as was the tank's hull. The rivets stood proud from the armour, unlike on the M2A4 and earlier light tanks and combat cars, whose riveted hulls and turrets had most of the rivets flush with the surface of the armour, making them look smooth, almost welded. Likewise the pistol ports that had characterized the turret of the M2A4 tank had been replaced by just three, with hinged armoured covers which incorporated a Protectoscope vision device.

THE M3 IN BRITISH SERVICE

Over 4,500 Stuarts were made, of which Britain received nearly 2,000 including 50 of the diesel-powered version. Petrol-fuelled M3s were designated Stuart I in British service while the diesel version was known as the Stuart II.

To begin with, the news that British armoured regiments were to receive American tanks was met with a great deal of dismay and there was the inevitable groaning in the ranks. But once crews got used to them they behaved as good soldiers should and made the best of them. The reliability of the radial engine was commented upon by a number of British regiments, despite the agonizing spluttering that it made, which seemed to indicate imminent failure but rarely did. However, its fuel capacity and range had not been improved over the M2A4. Although experiments were being conducted in Britain and the United States to develop auxiliary fuel tanks, Stuart tanks are invariably seen without them. In fact, in desert conditions crews were lucky to manage 45 miles on a full tank, and preferred to refuel after about 20 miles in order to have some petrol in reserve for manoeuvring in action. At best, refuelling slowed progress so that in a pursuit the faster Stuart was unlikely to catch up with the slower, but longer-legged German tanks; at the worst, refuelling often seemed to be required when action was imminent, which was inevitably inconvenient.

An early Stuart with all the British modifications including an extra stowage box on the offside, masking the location of the redundant sponson machine gun. The turret armament is all covered, to keep the sand out. Note also the supporting brackets for the lid of the commander's cupola, otherwise it was almost impossible to close without outside help.

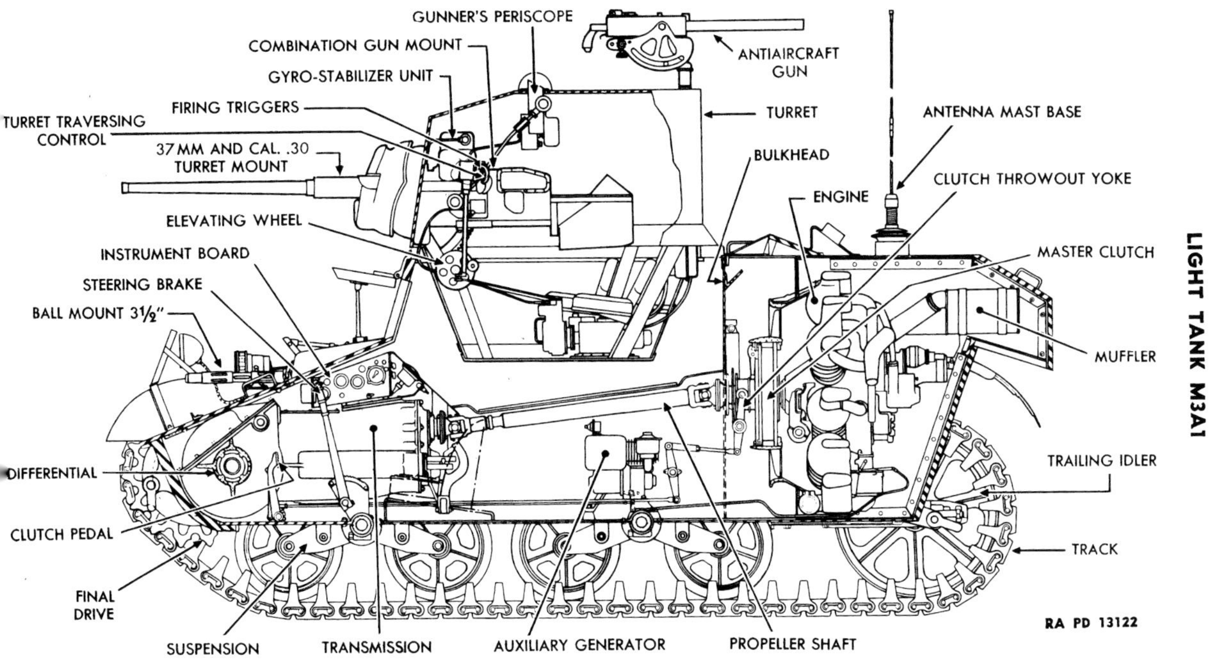

Figure 4 — Cross Section of Light Tank M3A1

A side elevation section drawing of an M3A1 light tank showing the cramped turret basket above the driveshaft.

It was also discovered that the cupola hatch and the driver's armoured visor could only be closed with outside assistance, so an elevated rest was provided for the former and levers for the latter so that they could be closed from the inside. Even so, it was the fighting arrangements that came in for most criticism. Vyvyan Pope, who had been Royal Armoured Corps advisor to the British Expeditionary Force and later commander of the Royal Armoured Corps in the Middle East was one of the most critical. He abhorred the idea of a two-man turret, although this would be a feature of some British tanks before long, and he invested a good deal of time devising seating arrangements for the turret crew, which never came to anything. Indeed, a canvas sling seat was the best that could be fitted and that had the disadvantage that the commander had nowhere to put his feet, and he swung to and fro with the motion of the tank.

Although the 37mm gun was the same shortened version that was fitted to the M2A4, it had been redesigned for the M3 and no longer had a protruding recoil system at the front that required armouring. Most of the solutions to the fighting difficulties came from units in the field who had the most pressing reasons to solve them. For instance, given the difficulties of traversing the turret and trying not to trip over the driveshaft in the process, the usual practice was to aim the entire tank at the target. For the same reason, crews reversed out of action, so that the gunner was always firing forwards, even after British workshops had field-modified the location of the traversing handwheel from the right side of the turret to the left, within reach of the gunner. Although the M3 used the existing 37mm gun M5 it was now fitted into the M22 mounting, which retained the 20-degree free movement of the gun considered essential for fine laying with a manually rotated turret. It also proved just possible to fit a three-man crew into the turret by adding a wireless operator/loader

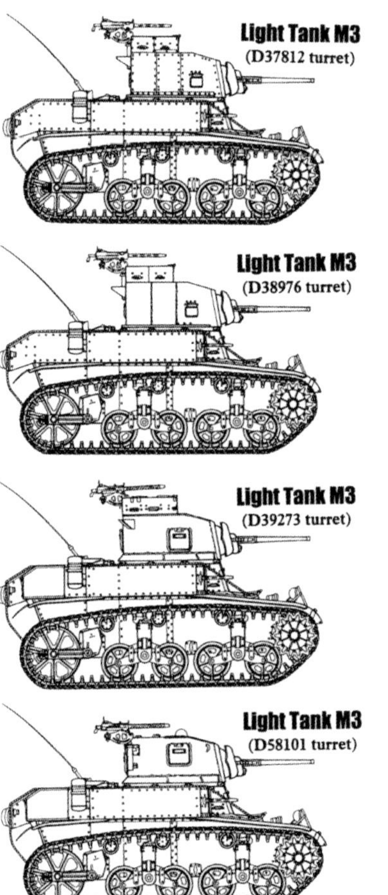

so that the commander stayed in his cupola, in desperate need of an effective tank periscope to enhance his view in action. In order to conform to British practice each tank also had to be fitted with a pair of 4in smoke grenade dischargers on the right-hand side of the turret exterior, fired by triggers on the inside, linked to each weapon by Bowden cable.

When a new M3 Stuart tank arrived in the Middle East it had to go into the workshops to be prepared for service in the desert, not only by fitting sand guards and so on, but it had to undergo at least 17 modifications, some almost trivial, others long-winded and vital, some of which have been mentioned above, before it could be sent forward to a fighting regiment.

Notwithstanding that a letter on the subject of Freezing of Designs had been sent by US Assistant Secretary of War Robert Patterson to the Chief of Ordnance on 26 August 1940, upholding a British complaint that modifications to tank design resulted in delay and increased costs, some changes, resulting from experience and the ongoing need to improve, were inevitable over time. An excellent example in connection with the light tank M3 was the riveted turret. Tests in Britain and in the United States revealed that a 37mm round that struck a riveted turret without penetrating still loosened the armour plates from the structural steel frames underneath. If the rivets themselves were struck, even by rounds from a .50-calibre heavy machine gun, they were forced through the armour at such velocity that they were a danger to the turret crew. Welding the turret instead was recommended, and the modification was approved by the Ordnance Committee on 27 December 1940. The work seems to have been undertaken by American Car & Foundry without any undue disruption to production. The advent of welding meant that the internal framework mentioned above could now be dispensed with, although the front turret plate, through which the 37mm gun obtruded, was still bolted in place. This was done, ostensibly, to make it easier to remove the gun itself, but when it was pointed out that this was not necessary this part was also, later, welded in place. The welded turret did not replace the riveted one in British service. Older tanks with riveted turrets are seen alongside newer ones with welded turrets, although the latter appear to predominate.

In March 1941 the Americans initiated another redevelopment of the M3 Light Tank with another new turret. This was formed from homogenous steel armour plate 1.25in thick. It was an all-rounded turret, except at the front where the gun mounting was flat, and flared out at the bottom to cover a new forged steel ball race ring. The cupola was retained but was now of rounded design with two small hatches instead of one big one, making it much easier to open. A round hole in one of the flaps was intended to take a periscope, although one was never fitted and the hole was plated over. Other aids to vision were the three hinged pistol ports with Protectoscopes around the turret; four protected vision slits in the cupola; and modifications to the hinged plates in front of the driver and hull gunner so that, in addition to Protectoscopes, both men were provided with protected vision slits.

Later production M3 tanks were fitted with the longer M6 version of the 37mm gun with a semi-automatic breech, fitted in the M23 mounting. A gyro-stabiliser was fitted which worked in elevation, but required a lot of skill and additional training so it was invariably disconnected. In a manually rotated turret the M23 mounting, which still retained independent movement through a narrow arc, was provided with a screw-operated traverse of its own. Otherwise, in terms of the hull the tank was still a Light Tank M3, although a welded hull was later introduced, with armoured covers over the fuel caps.

British pressure to improve fighting conditions inside the Stuart led to investigations into the possible development of a rotating turret basket for the crew but in the meantime, in order to introduce some of these improvements in existing tanks, a fourth version of the M3 entered production, the last of the series. This version featured the rounded turret, without the cupola but with a rotating periscope for the commander. It had no turret basket yet, or a power traverse system, yet in some of the tanks the M23 mounting had already had the limited arc for fine adjustment deleted – a feature required in a manual turret, but not in a powered one. So, with the main traversing handwheel in the wrong place as far as the British were concerned, the gunner, with his eye pressed against the sighting telescope, had to rely on the loader to traverse the gun but was unable to do the fine laying that placed the gun on target. This effectively made the tank unfightable until the main traversing handwheel was moved over to the gunner's side. Such tanks were designated Stuart

OPPOSITE An M3A1 viewed from above with an auxiliary fuel tank located behind the turret. Notice the elimination of the turret cupola and its replacement by two turret hatches and the commander's rotating periscope. It is in fact virtually impossible to tell an M3A1 from a Stuart Hybrid, many of which were also sent to Britain and had to be modified to make them fightable.

Although no longer in use as a tank, the British Army continued to use the Stuart in secondary roles after the war: this Stuart VI (M5A1) is used as an artillery tractor for a 17-pounder anti-tank gun.

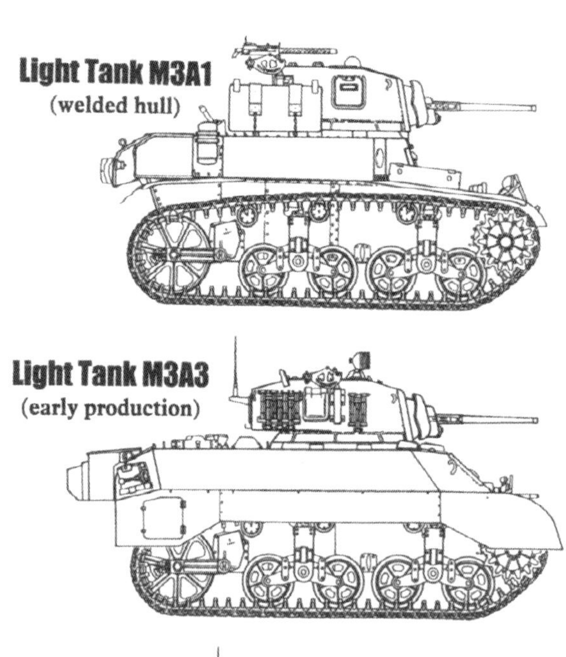

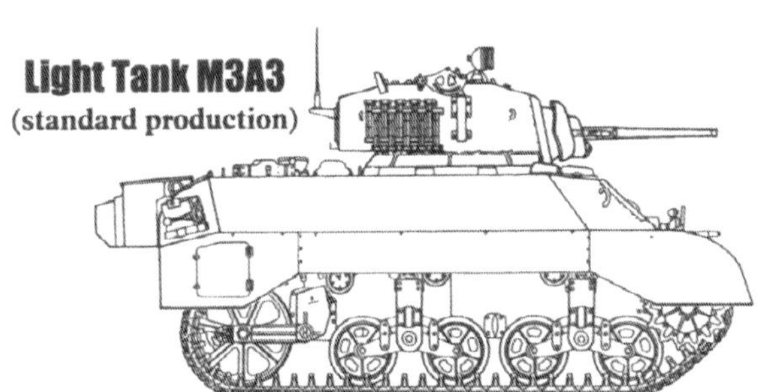

Hybrids by the British and it is virtually impossible to tell them apart from an M3A1 from the outside.

It is not known how many of these Stuart Hybrids were built, or where they went, but New Zealand received 292 and there cannot have been very many more of them. Some, including possibly some with diesel engines, were also delivered to Australia.

THE LIGHT TANKS M3A1 AND M3A3

In May 1942 production began of yet another version of the M3 Light Tank although this one, now with power traverse and a rotating turret basket for the fighting crew, was effectively regarded as a new tank and given the designation M3A1. Outwardly it looked very similar to the Stuart Hybrid, with the same rounded turret without a cupola, but inside it was quite different.

Experiments had been carried out on M3 series tanks before the final layout had been decided. For instance, fitting the Oilgear mechanical traverse system into an ordinary M3 proved that, under power, the turret now rotated too rapidly for the crew to keep up with it, since their movement was restricted by the central driveshaft. Clearly if it was to be adopted a rotating basket would have to be provided for the turret crew so that they could travel round with the turret. But even the installation of a basket brought its own problems. For instance, the hull gunner's usual exit route through the tank was up and out through the turret hatch, but unless the basket stopped in exactly the right place, enabling him to get through, he was trapped.

The M3A1 carried the longer M6 version of the 37mm gun in an M23 mounting. In this respect also it was identical to the earlier Stuart Hybrid, except that independent traverse of the gun was no longer necessary since the tank had power-operated traverse under the control of the gunner. Also, under certain circumstances the M5A1 telescopic sight, on the left of the 37mm gun, proved impossible to use, so as an alternative the gunner was provided with an M4 periscope sight in the turret roof instead. A gyro stabilizer, working in elevation only, was also part of the gunnery system, although not always used. Since the gyro stabilizer, radio and other equipment placed considerable demand upon the tank's battery a petrol-driven charging set was installed behind the driver's seat.

Although it was better than the earlier arrangement, with the turret crew standing upright in a manually traversed turret, the rotating basket was uncomfortably cramped, since the basket still had to clear the main driveshaft, and the tank

An M3A3, again fitted with deep-wading gear including inlet and exhaust trunking. Notice the sloping front of the hull and the angled corners.

commander, without a cupola to provide elevated vision, relied on an M6 periscope in the turret roof for all-round observation. The tank had the same engine as other tanks in the M3 series, even though there was a threatened shortage of air-cooled radial engines, and it still suffered from a very limited fuel capacity. The Guiberson T-1020 air-cooled radial diesel was also available although the Americans had decided to use only petrol-engined vehicles in the interests of simplified fuel supply. Even so diesels were still popular elsewhere and the British named the M3A1 with the petrol engine as the Stuart III, while the diesel-powered version was the Stuart IV.

According to one source the Light Tank M3A3 project was initiated by the US Armored Force in April 1942 but there is good reason to believe that it was inspired by the British authorities. American sources claim that they required an M3 tank with a hull like the M5 – which it isn't, but it does have the increased fuel capacity that the British had been crying out for and a longer turret with room at the back for a radio set, which seems to have been an exclusively British requirement. Britain acquired about two-thirds of the total number built, designating them Stuart V, and used them in Italy and north-west Europe. M3A3 tanks were also supplied to the French forces in North Africa and to the Chinese. Only a few remained in American hands and some of them were used for experimental purposes.

An M3A3 or Stuart V, suitably marked. Note the sloped sides of the hull and the style of 37mm turret, as fitted to the M5A1 light tank.

The most distinctive feature of the M3A3 was the use of sloped armour at the front and on both sides, formed from homogenous steel armour about 29mm thick. This allowed more room inside the tank for the driver and hull gunner who were each provided with a hinged hatch above their heads, each with a rotating periscope. At the sides the extra room allowed space for more fuel tanks, which effectively doubled the road range of the tank but increased its weight from 14 to 16 US tons, and required a revised ratio of gears in the final drive. The turret was still rounded and of welded construction, but extended backwards to form a box-like bustle that housed the radio set, while a mounting was also provided on the back for a wireless aerial. Two large square hatches were provided in the roof of the turret; the commander's on the right featured a fully rotating periscope, while the gunner's hatch alongside it was blank, with the gunner's periscope sight in front of it. A new gun mounting designated M44 was fitted, which appears to have held the 37mm gun more firmly, and since the turret had power rotation, it was not necessary to move the gun itself. The rotating turret basket had seats for two but, because it had to stay clear of the driveshaft, was particularly cramped. On the outside, at each side, there was room to stow track grousers and on the right side was a mounting for a .30-calibre Browning machine gun for the commander to use as an anti-aircraft weapon. Otherwise, in terms of engine and suspension it was the same as other M3-series tanks, although there was no diesel version. It appears to have been the best tank of the M3 series and at this late stage it reverted to its true Light Tank role in British service – as a reconnaissance machine, not a substitute cruiser tank.

TURRETLESS RECONNAISSANCE TANKS

The history of the 4th Queen's Own Hussars contains an interesting piece of history. After the battle of El Alamein in November 1942, the regiment took part in the initial pursuit, almost to the other side of Libya, by which time most of its Stuart light tanks were worn out and the rest were handed over to another regiment to continue the pursuit, while the survivors of 4th Hussars went back to Egypt. Here they learned that they would be sent to Cyprus in January 1943, where for the next six months they defended the island against an invasion that never came, in a mixture of equally worn-out Crusader and Valentine tanks.

They returned to Egypt in June 1943, and after some months they learned that they would now become an Armoured Reconnaissance Regiment, and that the regiment would be armed half with Sherman tanks and half with Stuarts (or 'Honeys' as they knew them then). Then the blow fell, as their history tells it:

> The 1st Armoured Division, of which the regiment was now part, though it was inconveniently located at Algiers, decided that the turrets of the Stuart tanks must be removed. The regiment, who knew their Honeys well, resisted this strenuously. The division held that the removal of the turret would improve the efficiency of the tank for reconnaissance and reduce the silhouette when in contact with the enemy; in theory they were valid arguments. The regiment, pleading from experience in battle, claimed that without the turrets the crews would be perilously vulnerable and that the tanks would be completely unarmed. The man with the biggest stick won, of course, and the turrets were removed. It was a poor consolation to the regiment to be able to prove in Italy that they had been right by the fact that 80 per cent of their casualties were suffered in the turretless Stuart tanks.

Of course, one imagines that the order to remove turrets from Stuarts was passed down from some higher authority. Although they were most common in Tunisia and

Italy, there is also evidence of them operating in north-west Europe: a turretless M3A3 was photographed in Bethune, France, in 1944, and another serving with the 23rd Hussars in 1945. But since normal turreted versions of earlier Stuarts are also seen there, the tank may have been one brought with its regiment from Italy. Some were also seen in Palestine in 1946; in at least one case a turretless M3A3 was armed with a .50-calibre heavy machine gun.

An M3 turretless light tank in the desert, laden with stowage and with a .30-calibre Browning mounted. In reality these vehicles were no more capable than enlarged Universal Carriers.

Turretless Stuarts were, in reality, little more capable than enlarged Universal Carriers with much superior performance. At most they were usually armed with an extra .30-calibre Browning machine gun. They certainly had a lower silhouette than a turreted tank, which should have been an advantage on reconnaissance missions although, as the 4th Hussars suggested, the crew were much more vulnerable. In Italy they seem to have been used as supply carriers, often seen carrying ammunition up to the front line, where the protection they still had to offer would be appreciated. The conversion appears to have been carried out on all versions of the M3-series light tanks, including the M3A3. One of the latter, photographed with a folding, waterproof hood over the crew compartment, appeared to be jeopardising its low silhouette on reconnaissance missions.

Perhaps taking a leaf out of the British book, the Americans introduced two versions of the reconnaissance tank by removing the turrets from M5 Light Tanks. Styled T8 and T8E1, they were not adopted for service, although similar vehicles were used as command tanks by senior officers in armoured divisions. A turretless version of the M5 was photographed carrying Brigadier General George Read of the 6th Armored Division in north-west Europe. Turretless M5 tanks appeared in Britain after the war as tractors for the 17-pounder anti-tank gun and some stayed on for years as general-purpose runabouts on firing ranges.

Different regiments had different names for their turretless tanks. To the 8th Hussars for instance, they were 'Jalopies', while the 10th Hussars called theirs 'Runnies'. The 9th Lancers described them as 'a tremendous improvement on the Daimler Scout Car', which hardly seems a very fair comparison. Obviously, with the removal of the turret all gunnery problems went as well, while the automotive performance was improved by the reduction in weight. Indeed, by the time they reached Italy even the matter of increased vulnerability was somewhat doubtful since armour protection on the early Stuarts was minimal anyway. Men exposed above the hull top would be in danger from enemy machine guns or even rifles but one could always duck down out of harm's way when bullets started flying around.

THE M5/M5A1 LIGHT TANK

In 1941 a shortage was perceived for the seven-cylinder radial engines for aircraft and tanks, so in June a programme was initiated to install in an M3-series light tank a pair

A turretless M3A3 in Italy, complete with a folding hood but no sign of a machine gun, even in the front of the hull.

of Cadillac V8 car engines, Model 42, each direct-coupled to a Hydramatic automatic transmission system. A pair of driveshafts carried the drive forward, but much closer to the hull floor than the driveshaft from the radial engine. Both driveshafts entered an automatic transfer box at the front of the tank, direct-coupled to the controlled differential steering system in the transmission at the front.

Some experts feared that unequal running by the two engines and differences in the automatic transmission would lead to problems, but this does not appear to have happened. The new arrangement was experimentally installed in a modified M3-series light tank that was designated M3E2, and later M3E3 when it was fitted with a sloping armoured plate at the front and enlarged engine compartment in the back to house two radiators, since the Cadillac engines were water-cooled.

Initially standardized as the Light Tank M4, it was quickly changed to become the Light Tank M5 to avoid potential confusion with the new Medium Tank M4 (the Sherman), and production began in April 1942 at the Cadillac plant in Detroit. The M5 Light Tank mounted the M3A1 turret with power traverse along with the 37mm gun M6 in the M44 mount. In addition to the regular hull machine gun in its flexible mounting, which was fired by the hull gunner who sat to the right of the driver, early examples featured a fixed machine gun in the centre of the glacis plate that could be fired by the driver (although this was eliminated when production began). The hull gunner was also designated assistant driver and he had a duplicate set of steering levers

An M5A1 of the Scots Guards in 6th Guards Tank Brigade with an interesting selection of other vehicles.

and a floor-mounted accelerator pedal so that he could take over in an emergency.

In November 1942 a new version of the tank with an enlarged turret entered production as the Light Tank M5A1. The new turret, which was developed at the same time as that for the M3A3, was lengthened at the back to accommodate a radio set and had two large hatches on top; also like on the M3A3, the external machine-gun position was moved to the side of the turret, and on later versions was fitted with an armoured shield behind which it could be stowed. As might be expected the hull layout of the M5 and M5A1 were more or less identical although the M5A1 had an escape hatch in the hull floor, located behind the hull gunner's seat. In fact this feature was introduced on late models of the M5. As originally built, the turret on the M5A1 had a hinged pistol port on each side, equipped with a Protectoscope vision device. This was later welded shut and on late production tanks was eliminated altogether.

Both the M5 and M5A1 were designated Stuart VI under British nomenclature although there is no evidence that the M5 Light Tank ever saw service with the British Army. Britain received 1,131 M5A1 Light Tanks under the Lend-Lease agreement.

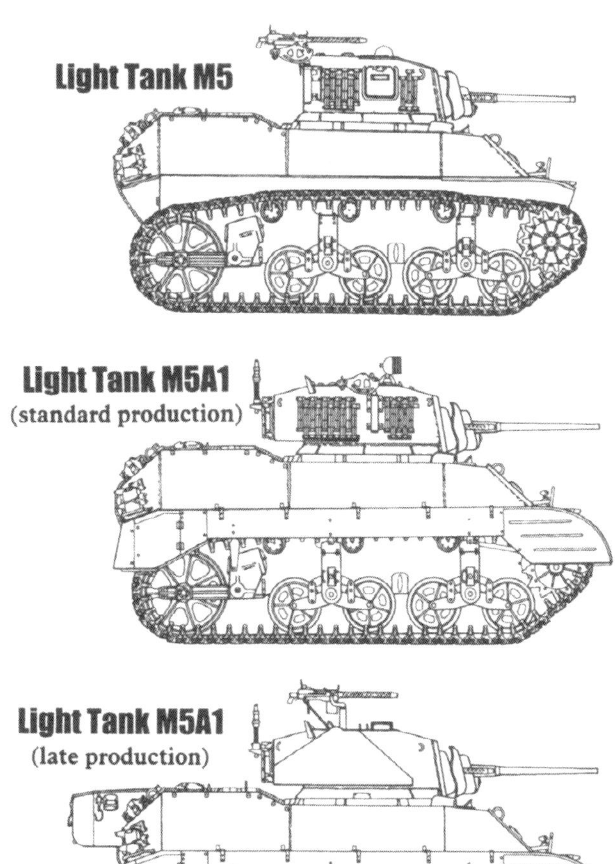

An M5A1 in British service. Points to note are the slab sides to the hull and the way that the rear engine deck is raised to accommodate the two Cadillac V8 engines.

CHAPTER 2

M3 MEDIUM TANK: THE GRANT AND LEE

The M3 medium tank was rushed into production in 1941 as a stop-gap to satisfy the desperate need for a medium tank in the US and British tank forces. Its design was a messy stew of outdated inter-war design features and time-saving short-cuts. To its credit, it was one of the best-armed tanks of its day and was based on a sound automotive design. The Grant was a godsend to British armoured divisions in the spring and summer of 1942 because of its good armour and heavy firepower. The Lee/Grant entered combat at the turning point of the war against Germany in North Africa. It was used by the British Eighth Army in the 1942 battles at Gazala, Alam Halfa, and El Alamein, and later took part with both British and US tank units in the final defeat of the Afrika Korps in Tunisia in 1943. By the time production reached full stride in early 1942, the more mature M4A1 Sherman tank was entering production, which quickly replaced the M3 on the assembly lines. While the M3 disappeared from the tank role in the European theatre by mid-1943, it continued to serve in more distant theatres, such as Burma. Its chassis also formed the basis for a number of specialized armoured vehicles, such as the widely used American M31 tank recovery vehicle.

MEDIUM TANK GENESIS

The lack of medium tanks in the US Army in the 1930s was the result of both budget shortages and doctrine. The lingering effects of the Depression and the small size of the pre-war army undermined any attempts to procure medium tanks in quantity. In addition, the presumed role of the US Army to conduct homeland defence and limited military operations in the overseas possessions such as the Philippines did not warrant such expensive weapons. The outbreak of war in Europe in September 1939 forced the United States to rethink its military plans, and funding for army modernization rapidly increased.

An M2 medium tank of Company B, 1/69th Armored Regiment (M), 1st Armored Division, on manoeuvres at Ft Knox in 1941. The angled turret on this type proved too cramped and was enlarged on the M2A1. (MHI)

A company of M2A1 medium tanks of the 69th Armored Regiment, 1st Armored Division, conduct a demonstration at Ft Knox in the summer of 1941. One of the older M2 tanks with the early turret can be seen in the background. (MHI)

The US Army had sponsored some experimental medium tank designs in the 1930s, building five T3E2 medium tanks in 1934, and a further 19 T4s and T4E1s in 1936–37. These medium tanks were armed only with machine guns, and offered few advantages over contemporary light tanks that were half the price. Such shortcomings led the Ordnance Committee to recommend the development of the T5 medium tank in May 1936, a design that was the ancestor of the later M3 and M4 medium tanks. The T5 was essentially a scaled-up M2 light tank, but with a 37mm gun as its principal weapon. Like many inter-war US designs, the T5 had a profusion of machine guns – there were four .30-calibre machine guns in barbettes around the superstructure, two fixed forward-firing machine guns in the bow, and provision for several anti-aircraft machine guns. This was a reflection of the contemporary doctrine that saw the medium tank primarily as an infantry support weapon, and the presumption that a large number of machine guns would add to the value of the tank in combat. This concept continued to influence later designs such as the M3 medium tank, though there was little evidence that so many machine guns could be employed effectively in combat.

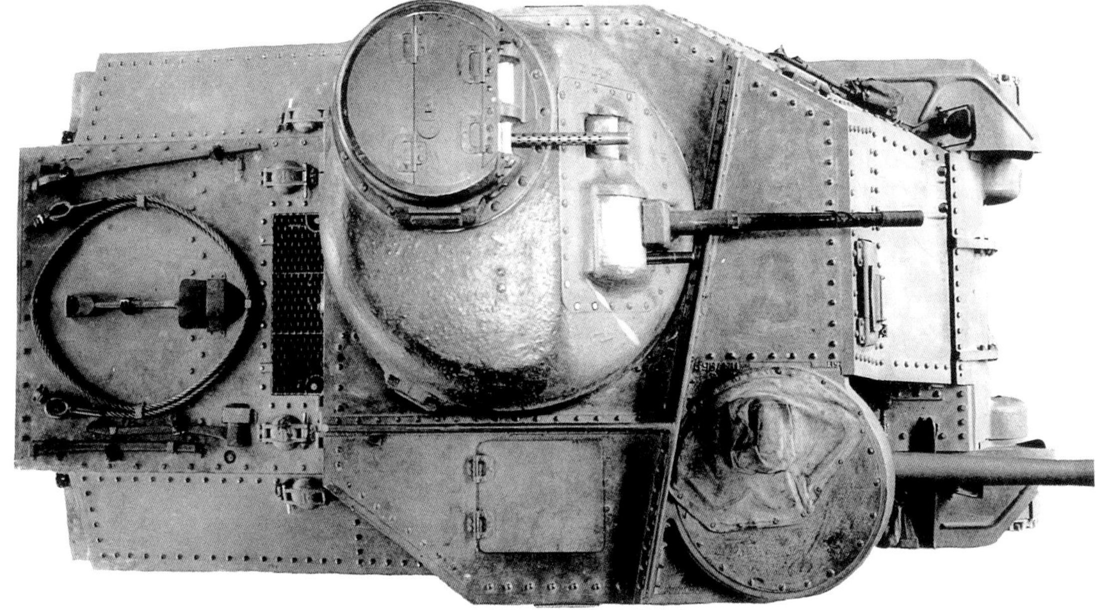

A fine overhead shot shows the distinctive layout of the M3 medium tank with its right-side sponson gun, turret and turret machine-gun cupola. (NARA)

The T5 Phase I pilot was completed in February 1938 and was shipped to Aberdeen Proving Ground (APG) for trials. One dubious innovation added during the trials was a pair of bullet-deflection plates on the rear of the tank, which permitted the barbette gunners to hit enemy infantry lurking in trenches behind and below. The T5 was accepted for service in the summer of 1938 as the M2 medium tank, the first US medium tank to be standardized in the 1930s.

A significant new influence on American tank design was the Spanish Civil War. The fighting there in 1936–39 suggested that modern anti-tank guns such as the German 37mm gun would be the primary nemesis of the tank. The M2 had been restricted to a maximum 15 tons weight because of engineer bridge limits, but this limited the thickness of the armour plate to a level insufficient to resist the 37mm gun.

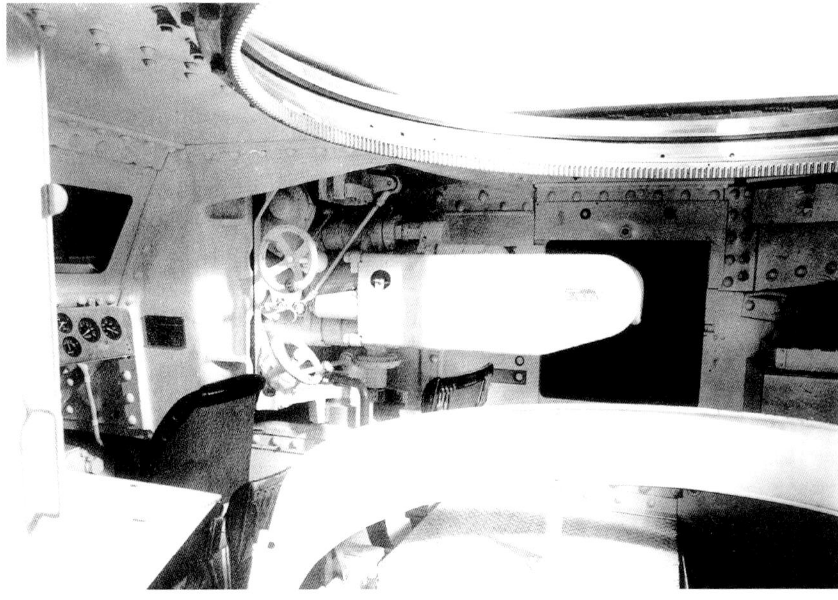

This interior view of an M3 without its turret shows the driver station to the left and the 75mm gun station in the centre. (NARA)

As a result, a more thickly armoured variant with the weight limit raised to 20 tons, called T5 Phase III, entered trials in the late autumn of 1938 at APG. Besides the thicker armour, there were many other changes, such as a cast turret and a more powerful engine. The infantry was somewhat concerned about the limited high-explosive firepower of the 37mm gun, and noted that European medium tanks such as the French Char B1 *bis* and the German PzKpfw IV were using short 75mm howitzers for more potent fire support. As a result, the T5 Phase III pilot was rebuilt into the T5E2 configuration by mounting a 75mm howitzer in the right sponson and replacing the gun turret with a new turret fitted with a stereoscopic rangefinder for better long-range accuracy. Trials of the T5E2 at APG from April 1939 to February 1940 were successful and the design served as a forerunner for the later M3 medium tank.

While testing of the T5 Phase III took place, the first serial production of the M2 medium tank began at Rock Island Arsenal in the summer of 1939. A total of 18 were completed. Testing of the initial production vehicles prompted the army to prematurely end M2 production in favour of the upgraded M2A1 medium tank based on the T5 Phase III. The M2A1 introduced a new, more spacious turret, automotive improvements and thicker 1.25in (32mm) armour.

The stunning defeat of the French Army in June 1940 sent shock waves through the US Army. The central role played by the panzer divisions forced the US Army to begin a crash programme to raise its own tank divisions, and a modern medium tank was clearly needed. In the summer of 1940, the army consolidated its scattered infantry tank units and cavalry mechanized units into the new Armored Force, and Congress provided funding for 1,500 medium tanks. Rock Island Arsenal did not have the capacity to build so many tanks, so the army turned to industry. The presumption was that locomotive plants would be best suited to manufacturing large armoured vehicles such as medium tanks. In addition, the army decided to create a specialized tank plant near Detroit, and Chrysler was given the contract to manage this facility. Chrysler received a contract for 1,000 M2A1 tanks on 15 August 1940, to be delivered in a year's time. The ink on the contract was hardly dry before the army reconsidered its plans. The M2A1's appalling design was a sad reflection on the

A column of M3 medium tanks of Company C, 1/69th Armored Regiment, 1st Armored Division, taking part in the Carolina manoeuvres in November 1941. These are from the initial production series lacking the gyrostabilizers for the gun, as is evident from the lack of gun counterweights. (MHI)

M3 MEDIUM TANK

(Art by Hugh Johnson, © Osprey Publishing)

Key

1 Hull glacis plate
2 Siren
3 Counterweight for 75mm gun stabilization system
4 75mm gun
5 Driver's seat
6 Gunner's seat
7 75mm gun elevation wheel
8 Protective guard for 75mm gun breech
9 Periscopic sight cover for 75mm hull-mounted gun
10 37mm gun
11 37mm gun stabilization counterweight
12 37mm gun sighting port
13 Turret cupola .30-cal. machine gun
14 Turret machine-gun cupola
15 Armoured visor for turret cupola
16 37mm gun ammunition stowage
17 Stowage box
18 Idler tensioning tool
19 Radio antenna pot
20 Armoured fuel cap
21 Idler wheel
22 Turret basket
23 Tank radio transceiver
24 Stowed .30-cal. machine-gun tripod
25 Suspension bogie
26 Drive sprocket
27 Headlight
28 Two forward-firing .30-cal. machine guns
29 Transmission armoured housing
30 Final drive armoured housing

14
15
16
17
18
19
20
21
22
23
24
25
26

backward state of US tank design in general, and it was painfully evident to the US Army that the M2A1 was already obsolete. The 1940 France campaign made it clear that a medium tank needed at least a 75mm gun comparable to the French Char B1 *bis* or German PzKpfw IV. As a result, the Chrysler contract was modified on 28 August; instead of 1,000 M2A1s, Chrysler would provide the same number of the new M3 medium tank armed with a 75mm gun. Production of the M2A1 returned to Rock Island Arsenal, and between December 1940 and August 1941, 92 of these dismal tanks were manufactured. Their combat potential was so questionable that in April 1942, Ordnance recommended that the 110 M2 and M2A1 medium tanks should be limited to training use. Thus they were never deployed in combat and were declared obsolete in October 1942.

BIRTH OF THE M3 MEDIUM TANK

In June 1940, the chief of infantry recommended that, based on the recent campaign in France, US medium tanks should incorporate at least 2in (52mm) armour on the front. The characteristics for the new tank were drawn up in mid-June 1940 and standardized on July 11, 1940, as the M3 medium tank, even though the design was far from complete. In August 1940 the head of the new Armored Force, General Adna Chaffee, met with Ordnance officers to discuss the M3 medium tank requirements. On being presented with some sketches of an M2A1 derivative with a multitude of gun barbettes and a sponson gun, Chaffee made it clear that he wanted a tank with thicker frontal armour and a 75mm gun in a fully rotating turret. Ordnance officials warned Chaffee of their lack of experience in designing a turret, turret ring, and gun mounting sufficient for a 75mm gun, and, given the extreme urgency of the requirement, recommended an interim medium tank patterned on the T5E2 with a sponson-mounted 75mm gun supplemented with a turreted 37mm gun. The original design was modified by deleting the machine gun barbettes, but Ordnance remained infatuated with an excess of machine guns, including two fixed forward-firing machine guns and another in a cupola on top of the turret. Design of the M3 began in September 1940

The M3A1 medium tank differed from the other variants in using a cast hull. This is an intermediate production example with the splash strip at the base of the turret and the stabilized 75mm gun, and is seen serving in one of the driver companies of the Armored Force School at Ft Knox in 1942. (NARA)

and the first pilot was completed in March 1941. The Armored Force remained very unhappy with the M3 design and wanted its production run limited to about 360 tanks to cover the gap until the 75mm gun tank was ready. In the event, this limit was ignored because of the urgent need for medium tanks.

The urgency for rushing the M3 into production was increased by the arrival of a British purchasing commission in the United States in 1940. After heavy tank losses in France, the British Army wanted to purchase 3,650 cruiser tanks in the United States, preferably based on British designs. Neither the US government nor industry was interested in manufacturing British designs, and British tank officers were not keen on the M3 design after being shown early mockups. Part of the problem was that the US and British armies had fundamentally different views about the tactical role of armoured divisions, with the US favouring the traditional cavalry mission of an exploitation force rampaging through the enemy's rear areas after the breakthrough had been accomplished by the infantry, while the British conception focused on the need to defeat the panzer divisions. The US doctrine implied a tank with a dual-purpose gun, with an accent on high-explosive firepower, while the British doctrine favoured a cruiser tank with a gun oriented toward anti-tank firepower. With little bargaining power, the British purchasing team reached an agreement under which a variant of the M3 medium tank with a different turret and other modifications would be built for the British Army. In particular, British doctrine favoured placing the tank radio in the turret near the commander, which required a bustle on the tank turret that the American M3 design lacked. Initially, the British government contracted with four American railroad plants to manufacture a total of 2,085 M3 tanks and with the Montreal branch of the American Locomotive Company (ALCO) for a further 1,157 cruiser tanks based on the M3 chassis. The US government placed parallel contracts for 2,220 M3 medium tanks later in the year with the same plants. When the Lend-Lease Act was passed by Congress in March 1941, this provided a legal basis for US arms sales to Britain while retaining the pretence of neutrality, and the US government took over the British contracts for the M3 tanks.

Besides the existing contract with the new Detroit Tank Arsenal, additional contracts went to the American Locomotive Company (ALCO), Baldwin Locomotive Works, Lima Locomotive Company, Pullman Standard Manufacturing Company,

An M3 of Gardiner's 2/13th Armored Regiment in action on February 20, 1943, after the costly fighting near Sbeitla. (NARA)

The M3A5 used a riveted hull and was powered by the GM 6046 diesel, as is evident from the engine deck. This is the 28th production tank on trials at APG on November 26, 1941. (NARA)

and the Pressed Steel Car (PSC) Company. Ultimately, all Pullman and PSC M3 production went to Britain, along with some of the Baldwin production.

The design of the M3 medium tank was influenced by the T5E2 layout as well as foreign designs such as the French Char B1 *bis*. Instead of the short 75mm howitzer, the more potent M2 75mm gun was mounted in the right sponson. The M3 also had a turret-mounted gun, the same 37mm gun used in contemporary light tanks such as the M3 Stuart. Two turrets were designed, one at Rock Island Arsenal for the American M3 medium tanks, and one by a British team led by L.E. Carr. Detail design was finished in January 1941 and the first pilot was completed at Rock Island Arsenal on 13 March 1941. Production quickly followed at the plants, starting with the Detroit Tank Arsenal, which completed its first model in April 1941. Although the production tanks were supposed to be fitted with the newer and longer M6 37mm gun in the turret, shortages led to the use of the shorter M5 37mm gun in some tanks until the supply situation improved.

Plans were under way in 1941 to extend M3 production to an ALCO subsidiary in Canada, the Montreal Locomotive Works. However, British and Canadian officers were not pleased with the awkward M3 configuration and opted instead for a cruiser tank better suited to British doctrine. Since the Montreal plant was already producing components for the M3, the suspension and powerplant of the M3 formed the basis for the 'Modified M3 Cruiser Tank,' which was subsequently named 'the Ram.' The M3A6 designation was reserved for a Ram variant with a riveted hull that never materialized. The Ram cruiser tank, like the forthcoming M4 medium tank, had its main armament in a cast turret. Instead of the dual-purpose 75mm gun of the M4 medium tank, the Ram was to be armed with the British 6-pounder (57mm). The first batch of 50 Ram Mk. I tanks began production in December 1941. These had only a 2-pounder gun because of delays in receiving the intended guns, but the definitive Ram Mk. II with the 6-pounder (57mm) gun entered production in January 1942 shortly before M4A1 production in the US. Ultimately, the Ram never saw combat in its battle-tank version. By the time that the Ram was available, the British Army had changed its opinion on tank guns after having used the Grant in combat in the desert, and now appreciated that the 75mm dual-purpose gun was a more versatile weapon than the 6-pounder, especially for dealing with enemy anti-tank guns. In reality, the Ram was an M3 derivative, but the US Army subsequently designated it as the M4A5 medium tank, as it was produced in Canada in parallel with the M4 Sherman series.

Total production of the basic M3 medium tank and British Grant I tank amounted to 4,924 tanks or about 79 per cent of eventual M3 series production. This was a substantial industrial accomplishment considering the past US record in tank production.

THE M3 DESCRIBED

The nine-cylinder Wright-Continental air-cooled, radial petrol engine was mounted upright at the back, driving forwards to a five-speed synchromesh gearbox at the front linked to a controlled differential steering system with steering brakes and drive sprockets on the ends of the output shafts at the front. The suspension was a vertical volute spring design, created by Harry Knox, and consisting of three bogies on each side. Above that the hull was of riveted construction, a maximum of 2in thick, but

An M3 medium tank and its crew of Company F, 2/13th Armored Regiment, near Souk al Arba in Tunisia on November 23, 1943. This is an intermediate production tank with the gyrostabilizers and gun counterweights. (NARA)

with the 75mm gun behind a casting on the right side. This gun had an arc of fire of 30 degrees (15 degrees either side of its centre line), with a vertical range between 20 degrees elevation and minus 9 degrees depression. Above the 75mm was mounted a small, cast-steel turret on a 54.5in-diameter turret ring with hydraulic traverse carrying a 37mm gun and co-axial Browning machine gun. Above that again was an independently rotating commander's cupola, also armed with a Browning machine gun that had some anti-aircraft potential. The machine-gun cupola was a feature deemed foolish by the British.

In its original form the tank had a crew of seven: in addition to the driver there was a gunner and a loader to serve the 75mm gun, and a radio operator joined them in the hull; plus the tank commander, a gunner, and a loader for the 37mm gun, who were all stationed in the turret.

THE BRITISH TURRET

The British, needless to say, did not like the new tank when they first saw it. Major General Douglas Pratt saw the full-size wooden mock-up and described it as 'high as the Tower of Babel'. But at the time the British were still pushing to have American factories build British tanks, particularly the A12 Matilda and the A15 Crusader, and were only slowly coming to realize that this was never going to happen. The British were generally very uncertain of the dependability of American automotive components, they did not like the mechanical layout of their vehicles, and they had reservations about the American suspension. Regarding the M3 Medium they were particularly unhappy with the fighting arrangements in general and specifically they objected to the location of the radio set. In fact there was little about the tank that they did like. In the end it was only American agreement that the British might have some concessions, like the design of the turret and some modest changes to the fighting compartment that tipped the balance – that and the fact that there was really no alternative.

M3 Medium Grant and Lee tanks photographed side by side. The different turrets are the main visual difference from this angle.

As part of the concession to British reservations the Americans agreed that M3 medium tanks designed for British use should have a different style of turret, more suited to British requirements. It would mount the same weapons, the 37mm M6 gun and a co-axial Browning .30-calibre, air-cooled machine gun, but was slightly lower and a little wider than the American turret and extended at the back to contain the wireless set. The British turret did not carry a machine-gun cupola on top, but instead featured a two-piece hatch on an independently rotating ring, with a periscope for the commander in one of the turret flaps. The British version managed with a crew of six rather than seven since the radio operator in the hull was not required; instead, the 37mm

A tank transporter recovers Grant tank number 9 of C Squadron, 3rd RTR, 7th Armoured Division, following the Gazala battles in May 1942. Judging from the damaged sand-shield and lost track, it may have been the victim of a mine. (MHI)

loader in the turret doubled as the radio operator, as he did on most British tanks.

The deletion of the cupola not only reduced the overall height of the vehicle, but was in keeping with the contemporary British attitude to cupolas. To the Americans the complex shape of the British turret incorporated too many potential shot traps compared with their own design, although British troops who used the M3 in action do not mention this as a problem. The design of the turret, which was quite a complex shape for a single-piece casting, was entrusted to Mr L.E. 'Ted' Carr. Carr, who had been a member of the Mechanisation Board in Britain, is said to have designed the turret casting for the Matilda infantry tank before the war. He had subsequently been sent over to Canada to help with tank production there and ultimately travelled down to the United States.

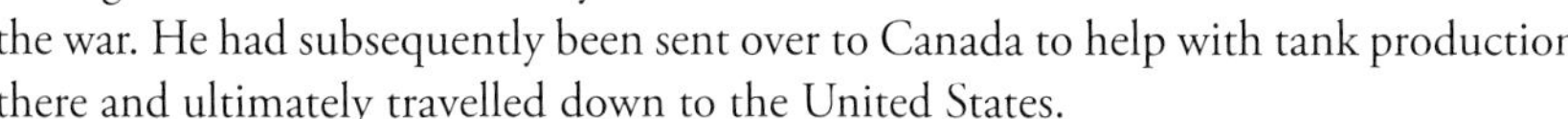

'Ted' Carr's turret for the M3 was created as a one-piece casting by the General Steel Castings Company, associated with the Baldwin Locomotive Works of Eddystone, Pennsylvania. Tanks fitted with this turret were known as the M3 Medium Grant. Other differences included a periscope for the driver, set into the hull roof, forward of the turret, and the elimination of the interior mounting for the American wireless set, along with the seat for the wireless operator. Instead a British No. 19 set was installed in the back of the turret, with its two aerials located on top of the turret in keeping with British requirements. Tanks for service with the US Army carried the SC 508 radio, the aerial for which was set in a special mounting at the rear of the superstructure. One thousand Grant tanks were ordered for the British, 500 of each to be constructed by the Pressed Steel Car Company and the Pullman Standard Car Company, while a further 295 appear to have been built by the Baldwin Locomotive Works.

The first of the M3 tanks with the British turret were completed in July 1941. Improvements were gradually made to the Grant during production, including the addition of full sand-skirts over the suspension and the new WE-210 rubber-block track. Production of the custom-built Grant I tank could not meet the British need for tanks caused by high casualty rates in the desert campaign, so Britain also acquired the American version of the M3 medium tank, which was known locally as the General Lee I.

Baldwin also produced 12 M3A2 tanks with welded hulls, but still with the Wright-Continental radial engine, and subsequently 49 M3A3 tanks with welded hulls and 185 M3A5 tanks with riveted hulls, both fitted with the 410hp General Motors Model 6046 diesel that was based on a pair of six-cylinder Model 6-71 lorry engines. Most of these tanks – ten of the welded-hull M3A2 and most of the diesel M3A3 and M3A5 tanks with Grant turrets – ultimately went to Australia. The diesel-engined tanks were known as Grant II in British service. One of the latter, T24027, was used by General Montgomery as a command tank in the desert and has survived to be preserved. Britain also acquired 1,347 M3 medium tanks with the American turret which were classified as Lee Mark I.

This M3A5 (Grant II) is said to have been used by General Montgomery and is now preserved. Notice that it is still armed with the old M2 75mm gun.

It is as well to remember that when first designed the M3 was regarded as an infantry tank and that the hull-mounted 75mm gun (initially the M2 version with a 31.1-calibre barrel length), with limited traverse, was seen primarily as a gun for firing high-explosive rounds. Some armour-piercing shells were provided but they were traditional solid-steel rounds that tended to break up when they struck the face-hardened armour of German tanks. In addition, the original sight was of a telescopic periscope type that did not always function in harmony with the gun, no matter what kind of ammunition it was firing. Some modern sources as well as contemporary user comments refer to the inaccuracy of the 75mm gun, especially when firing anti-tank rounds, and the periscope sight appears to be the main reason. The 37mm gun in the fully rotating turret on top was regarded as the primary anti-tank weapon, but its relatively limited range and poor penetration meant that, like the British 2-pounder, it was rapidly ceasing to have any value as an anti-tank weapon.

Both the British and American types of 37mm turret were provided with a hydraulic power traverse system which seems to have been reasonably reliable. Both guns were stabilized in elevation only, and both guns had to carry additional counterweights to provide the balance required for the stabilizer to work properly. On the 37mm this took the form of a cylindrical weight fitted directly beneath the gun, but it appears more commonly in photos of American tanks because British crews seem to have had an aversion to stabilizers and tended to disconnect them and even throw them away. Counterweights fitted to the 75mm gun took the form of collars, two of which were clamped around the muzzle of the M2 barrel in order to

A new Lee tank on display in India in 1942. The Lee was used to equip a number of Indian armoured units and later served in the campaign in Burma. This is a later production tank with the long M6 75mm gun.

A Lee tank named Cossack of C Squadron, 150th Regiment RAC with troops of the 19th Indian Division advance on Ft Dufferin in Burma on March 10, 1945. (NARA)

get the balance right. They were not required on the longer M3 gun because the extra length of the barrel was sufficient weight in itself to provide the balance.

For the British, of course, the 75mm was the ideal weapon. It fired an effective high-explosive round, the perfect antidote to emplaced anti-tank guns, and if a better armour-piercing round could be obtained it would also make a very acceptable anti-tank weapon. The acquisition of a better anti-tank round came about in a most unusual way. Among a vast cache of German ammunition found during operations around Tobruk by the Allies was a lot of explosive, capped armour-piercing 75mm rounds for the short-barrelled 75mm gun on the Panzer IV. An Australian officer, Major Northy, serving with the Royal Army Ordnance Corps, reckoned that with some modification this could be mated with the American 75mm cartridge, and with the backing of an American officer, Colonel G.B. Jarrett, his suggestion was accepted. The main modification involved reducing the size of the driving band on the German ammunition. The German fuse was activated by the rotation of the projectile but turning it in a lathe was not sufficient to arm it. This improvised ammunition, added to the extra range of the 75mm gun, at last gave the Allies the advantage that they desperately needed. It was only because the location of the 75mm gun made it impossible for the tank to adopt the ideal hull-down position that the M3 was somewhat vulnerable in a tank-versus-tank battle.

The 75mm gun on the M3 was developed from the famous French 75mm of World War I, the legendary *Soixante Quinze*. As a medium artillery piece it was second to none, yet the gun mounted in the tank was not supplied with a clinometer for firing accurately at longer ranges. It seems that tank crews were not regarded as intelligent enough to cope with such a sophisticated piece of equipment. British tank gunners therefore took to marking the elevating handwheel for this purpose when firing high-explosive rounds.

Later on an improved version of the 75mm gun with a 40.1-calibre barrel was issued for the tank. This was the Model M3, which had a slightly greater range than the M2 and a similar increase in armour penetration. The new gun started to appear in the summer of 1942, and it was seen on some of the M3s that served in Burma.

M3 TANK VARIANTS

As more American plants became involved in tank production, the US Army tried to simplify manufacture. One alternative was to employ a single casting for the hull superstructure instead of the complicated riveted design. This version was designated as the M3A1 in October 1941 and a total of 300 were manufactured by ALCO starting in February 1942. In spite of the short production run, there were numerous changes to the cast-hull M3A1 design, including an added protective lip around the turret race on the intermediate production vehicles, and the revision of the upper roof hatch on the final production series with the hinges at the base of the door, not the top. The M3A1 also underwent other changes occurring more broadly in M3 production, including the removal of the hull side doors and the addition of more armoured ventilation covers to the roof of the superstructure and turret in the final production batches. A total of 28 of these were completed with the Guiberson T-14090-2 diesel engine instead of the usual Continental radial engine, but the diesel programme was cut short because of the unreliability of the engine.

Another alternative in hull construction was the use of welded-plate construction instead of riveted construction, prompted in part by the threat of rivets flying into the crew compartment if the exterior of the rivet was hit by small-arms fire. The short-term solution to this problem was to seal-weld the rivet heads, which was ordered in March 1942. The Carnegie-Illinois Steel Corporation built a welded M3 hull for Rock Island Arsenal in May 1941 and tests concluded that it was superior to the riveted construction. The first of the welded-hull versions was the M3A2, which was otherwise identical to the basic M3 medium tank. Production of the M3A2 began at Baldwin in January 1942, but was suspended in March when it was decided to switch to the diesel-powered, welded-hull M3A3. The decision to move to the diesel engine was due to the bottlenecks in engine supplies, since the Continental radial engine used in the M3, M3A1, and M3A2 was also used in aircraft manufacture. The engine selected for the M3A3 was the General Motors Model 6046, which combined two 6-71 diesel bus engines. The hull rear was reconfigured to accommodate

Rarest of the rare: a Grant III in service with C Squadron, 2/9th Armoured Regiment, Australian 1st Armoured Division. Only a dozen M3A2 chassis were built, and this is one of the few examples with the Grant turret. (NARA)

The rare welded-hull M3A2 can be mistaken for the welded-hull M3A3 except in rear views like this that show the characteristic rear-engine arrangement of the Continental radial engine tanks. This shows the early configuration with the cylindrical air filters. (NARA)

the air intake and exhaust systems. When mounted in a welded hull, the tank was designated as the M3A3, while those manufactured with a riveted hull were designated as the M3A5. Production was undertaken at Baldwin in January–December 1942, with a total of 322 M3A3 and 591 M3A5 tanks being manufactured.

The third engine option for the M3 was the new Chrysler A57 multi-bank engine, which was created by combining five bus engines at the base to create a star-shaped engine offering 425hp. Although complex, the A57 used available machine tools, so it could be put into production rapidly. This required a lengthened hull, and production of the M3A4 was undertaken from June 1942 to August 1942 at the Detroit Tank Plant with some 109 tanks completed. There were some later efforts to improve the M3 powertrain, such as the experimental M3E1 and M3A1E1 with the Ford V8 engine and the M3A5E1 and -E2 with new transmission. However, with M4 medium tank production underway and M3 production concluding, these did not reach production.

PRODUCTION

The British Grant turret was fitted to most hull types, including the M3, M3A2, M3A3, and M3A5. It does not appear to have been fitted to either the M3A1 or M3A4 hulls, even though the British allotted designations to such variants. In total, about 1,660 tanks were completed with the Grant turret, or a bit more than a quarter of the total production.

During the course of production, a variety of incremental improvements were undertaken across the entire M3 family. British reports indicated that the side doors were susceptible to spall damage, so an escape hatch was added to the belly and the hull doors welded shut. In the final production runs, the hull doors were completely absent.

Tests also showed that there was an excessive build-up of fumes inside the turret and hull when the guns were repeatedly fired, so more ventilator fans were added on the hull and turret roof. Starting in January 1942, Ordnance began to make improvements on the M3 and M4 medium tanks in parallel, since they both shared so many common components. This first affected new tracks, which were

GRANT CRUISER TANK, 22ND ARMOURED BRIGADE, GAZALA, MAY 1943

The Grant tanks taking part in the Gazala battles were mostly camouflage-painted in a simple scheme of Light Stone (BSC No. 61), a light tan colour. The white registration number on the hull side was originally painted on the olive drab delivery scheme, and rather than re-paint it, as often as not it was left in white on the original olive drab background. Tactical markings were in the usual style, the circle indicating C Squadron and the red colour indicating the brigade's senior battalion/regiment. This marking was usually carried on either side of the turret, but photos taken after the fighting show some tanks with it in non-standard positions such as on the front left corner, and sometimes on the curved portion of the left front sand-shield. No arm of service markings or other unit markings are evident. Some Grants of the 3rd and 4th County of London Yeomanry began carrying an elaborate camouflage pattern developed by Captain Dick Sutton, which utilized local cement dyed brown, black and white, and applied like paint, but photos after the battle would suggest that this was far from universal at the time. (Art by Hugh Johnson, © Osprey Publishing)

A new M3 Grant, just arrived in the United Kingdom and fitted with all the required equipment, including an extra fuel tank. A team of significant civilians is posing on and around it.

GRANT CRUISER TANK, C SQUADRON, 3RD RTR, 4TH ARMOURED BRIGADE, 7TH ARMOURED DIVISION, GAZALA, MAY 1943

Unit commanders were given some discretion in the application of camouflage patterns in early 1942, and the 3rd RTR adopted a pattern of Light Stone over the lower portion of the tank, leaving the upper surfaces in the original olive drab. To break up the Light Stone, blotches of Purple-Brown were sprayed on. The turret tactical numbers are in yellow in the usual fashion. Many tanks in the unit had cartoon characters painted on the hull side, although this tank does not appear to. (Art by Hugh Johnson, © Osprey Publishing)

interchangeable between the two types. One of the final production changes on the M3 medium tank was the introduction of a new reinforced suspension bogie with more robust volute springs and a trailing return roller mounted behind the bogie to accommodate the springs. By the time that this new bogie was ready in mid-1942, production of the M4A1 medium tank had already begun, so this feature was introduced in parallel on the M3 and M4A1 medium tank production lines.

Production of the M4A1 medium tank started in February 1942 at the Lima Tank Plant and gradually expanded to the other tank plants throughout 1942. Since this was a far more satisfactory design than the M3 medium tank, production of the M3 gradually trailed off in the latter half of 1942, finally ending in December as available sub-assemblies were used up. The M4 medium tank was essentially the same as the M3 medium tank in its hull, suspension, and powertrain. Indeed, the M4 series was based on the same powerplant solutions first developed for the M3, with the M4 and M4A1 having the same Continental radial engine and welded/cast configuration as the M3/M3A1, the M4A2 corresponding to the M3A3/-A5 diesel and the M4A4 corresponding to the M3A4 with its Chrysler multi-bank engine. The only new family in the M4 series was the M4A3 with the Ford V8 engine, first tested in the M3E1. With the M4 tanks arriving in growing numbers, the M3 medium tanks were declared limited standard in April 1943.

COMBAT DEBUT IN EIGHTH ARMY

The Grant tank saw its combat debut in the cruiser-tank role with British armoured units in the desert campaign in the spring of 1942. Unlike the US Army, with its light and medium tanks, the British Army categorized tanks by two principal roles: the cruiser tanks in the armoured divisions and brigades oriented toward defeating panzers, and infantry tanks oriented toward close support of the infantry. The first Grant tanks arrived in the Middle East in November 1941 and were first used for trials and training. Shipments were slow to arrive, and the first unit equipped, the 5th Royal Tank Regiment (RTR), had only 32 at the beginning of February 1942. The Grants were a welcome addition to the British arsenal after the serious losses endured during Operation *Crusader* in November 1941, and continuing problems with British tank designs. British armoured division doctrine focused on the defeat of German panzer divisions, and, as a result, British cruiser tanks were armed first with the 2-pounder and later the 6-pounder guns. Both of these had excellent anti-armour performance, but did not offer a high-explosive punch. This became a serious drawback in the desert war, where the German Afrika Korps used combined-arms tactics to circumvent their own weakness in panzers. Rommel was often able to overcome larger British tank forces with numerically inferior panzer units by skilfully employing anti-tank guns with the panzer force. These guns, such as the PaK 38 50mm anti-tank gun, were small targets and nearly impossible to knock out by tank guns firing armour-piercing shot. Likewise, the 88mm flak gun, used in an improvised anti-tank role, had greater range than British tank guns and so could stand off at a distance and still wreak havoc with the British tank forces. The Grant offered an antidote to the anti-tank gun threat, since it could fire an effective high-explosive projectile that had a much greater chance of disabling an anti-tank gun even without a direct hit. The Grant's 75mm gun was also effective in the anti-tank role, and was supplemented by the 37mm gun in the turret, which offered performance similar to the British 2-pounder tank gun. A gunnery instructor with the 3rd RTR recalled that 'the crews were overjoyed to be able to fire a large 14-pound shell at the Panzer tanks.'

The Grant's other significant advantage was its automotive reliability. At the time, British tank regiments in the desert were receiving the new Crusader cruiser tank, which suffered from engine reliability problems that resulted in serious mechanical attrition in

A Lee tank at the ordnance school near Cairo in the spring of 1942 in an improvised desert camouflage scheme. (MHI)

A Grant tank in its original olive drab finish arrives in Egypt on a tank transporter in the spring of 1942. (MHI)

combat until technical improvements were made. Overall, the Grant was well received. A tank officer recalled 'it was fairly fast with a possible road speed of about 25mph, well-armoured, and considered capable of out-shooting an enemy tank or anti-tank gun except the 88mm. The Grant crews also found their new tank and armament ideal and we looked forward to meeting the panzers more or less on even terms.'[1]

The Grant had its share of problems, however. The configuration of the sponson-mounted gun was far from ideal because it offered only limited traverse. The dual 37mm/75mm armament was a distraction to the commander because it was difficult to concentrate on more than one target at a time. The silhouette of the tank was high, which was both a blessing and a curse. In some conditions it offered the commander a better vantage point for spotting enemy targets in the flat desert wastes. But as often as not, it simply presented a larger target to the enemy. The location of the 75mm gun made it difficult to take advantage of hull-down positions, using terrain to protect the bulk of the tank.

By March 1942, there were about 340 Grants and Lees in Egypt along with American liaison teams to provide training and maintenance assistance. British units seldom distinguished the Grant and Lee, generally labelling both types as 'Grants' regardless of the turrets. Although the majority of the M3 medium tanks arriving in the desert were the radial-engine M3, some diesel-engine M3A5s (Grant IX) were also deployed. Efforts were made to better adapt the tanks to desert conditions. Sand shields were fitted to tanks at workshops in Egypt, starting in January 1942, and the US plants began adding these in the factory. Other changes were authorized in January 1942, including improved exterior stowage and a cloth mantlet cover for the 75mm gun to reduce the intrusion of sand. Later in the month, workshops began plugging up the fixed-hull machine-gun ports, as this armament was judged to be useless, and the 75mm ammunition stowage was raised to 80 rounds and put in armoured bins. In February 1942, there were a number of modifications made to the suspension to improve its durability. Some units made their own local improvements, such as sun-hoods to shade the periscopes, markings on the 75mm elevator wheel to improve their use at longer ranges, improvements to stowage, and various types of

1 Major Bill Close, *A View from the Turret: A History of the 3rd RTR in the Second World War* (Dale & Bredon, 1998).

LEE CRUISER TANK, C SQUADRON, 3RD CARABINIERS, BURMA 1944

In early 1943, SCC13 Jungle Green was adopted for AFVs in the Far East, a dark, drab olive green. Tanks in Burma often carried large white Allied stars, but photos suggest that they were either overpainted with a slightly darker colour or smeared with dirt or oil to reduce their visibility. The 3rd Carabinier Lees had a number of local modifications, such as the removal of the machine-gun cupola, additional rear stowage bins, and a screened frame over the engine deck to protect against Japanese hand-emplaced antitank mines. (Art by Hugh Johnson, © Osprey Publishing)

blade sights to permit the commander to rapidly slew the guns toward the target.

At the time of the Gazala battles in May 1942, British units had 167 Grants and Lees with the 1st and 7th Armoured Divisions, with more in Egypt equipping other units or being used for training or reserve. This made it the second most common tank type in the armoured divisions: there were 257 Crusaders and 149 Stuarts. At the time, the Grant represented one of the best tanks in the desert, offering better anti-tank punch than the 50mm gun on the PzKpfw III and better armour protection. Generally, the Grants and Lees were not deployed in homogenous formations but with either Crusader or Stuart squadrons. In the 1st Armoured Division and the 9th and 22nd Armoured Brigades, the regiments typically had 36 Crusaders and 12 Grants, while in the 7th and 10th Armoured Divisions and the 1st Armoured Brigade, the regimental mix was typically 24 Grants and 20 Stuarts.

A useful view of an intermediate production M3A5, serial 1465, at APG in December 1942 showing some of the improvements, such as the gun counterweights, welded side doors, added ventilators, and grouser stowage boxes. (NARA)

In spite of the new Grant tanks, the May–June Gazala battles went badly for the Eighth Army. The problems were not technical, but tactical. The Afrika Korps continued to display greater combat effectiveness, principally better combined-arms tactics, in spite of technical and numerical shortcomings. Rommel's offensive succeeded in pushing the Eighth Army back into Egypt to El Alamein. The performance of the Grant during the battle was

LEE CRUISER TANK, C SQUADRON, 150TH REGIMENT RAC, BURMA 1945

By 1945, Lees operating in Burma had additional local modifications, notably appliqué armour in the form of spare track links on the hull front and various welded plates on the hull side and sides of the engine compartment to protect against lunge-mines. The markings here are fairly typical, including a white Allied star, a vehicle name, and the usual tactical insignia at the 5 and 8 o'clock positions of the turret rear. On many tanks of the regiment, a yellow tiger was painted to the side of the driver's front visor, derived from the York and Lancaster's badge. (Art by Hugh Johnson, © Osprey Publishing)

good, and its 75mm gun proved an unpleasant surprise for the Germans in numerous encounters. A staff officer who inspected the several knocked-out tanks from the 22nd Armoured Brigade afterwards commented that 'it is apparent that the Grant tank can take a great deal of punishment'. One Grant had been hit no fewer than 31 times, with the only damage being caused by two 50mm hits on the front visors and a rear hit by a 37mm gun. Another had been hit 12 times with no penetrations. Larger-calibre artillery was particularly lethal, with two of the inspected tanks penetrated and burnt out by 105mm howitzer hits and another by an 88mm round that set off an internal fire.

Tank losses at Gazala were heavy on both sides, and July was spent rebuilding for the next encounter. The August fighting at Alam Halfa again saw the Grant as one of the mainstays of the British armoured force, with 164 Grants and Lees among the 713 tanks in the forward-deployed units. The battle was fought from defensive positions, and the Grants were often emplaced with the help of engineers and bulldozers to reduce their high silhouette. On the German side, the Alam Halfa battle represented the arrival of the long-barrelled 75mm gun on the PzKpfw IV Ausf. F2 tank, an echo of the arms race taking place on the Russian Front since 1941. Of the British casualties of the battle, 31 of 67 were Grants, but 13 were repairable. Alam Halfa was the last of Rommel's offensives against the Eighth Army. With British command rejuvenated by the arrival of a dynamic new leader, Lieutenant General Bernard Montgomery, the initiative shifted to the British side, with preparations for an offensive at El Alamein.

The second battle of El Alamein started on 23 October 1942. Montgomery began methodical preparations for the offensive in the late summer, and Churchill

An M3 Lee on public display in India. The name General Lee painted on the side is incorrect; Winston Churchill decreed that only the surname should be used to avoid confusion with any serving generals. This tank has the longer M3 75mm gun.

pressured the US government to speed the shipment of new tanks, especially the new M4A1 Sherman. At the time of the battles, Lend-Lease tanks made up the backbone of the British armoured forces, with 270 Shermans and 210 Grants. Britain received priority for the new M4 tanks and the US 1st Armored Division remained saddled with the older M3 medium tank. The Grant was still a viable battle tank in the autumn 1942 fighting, since the Afrika Korps still had few of the long-barrelled PzKpfw III Ausf. L or PzKpfw IV Ausf. G. Losses up to 10 November included 53 Grants, of which 30 were complete write-offs. In total, 350 Grants and Lees were lost in combat in 1942. El Alamein was the high point of the Grant's career in the desert war, but gradually the Sherman became the preferred replacement. It had all of the advantages of the Grant, including its 75mm gun and its automotive dependability, and none of its vices, such as the awkward gun configuration or excessive silhouette. The Grant remained in service as a battle tank through to the end of the Tunisia campaign in May 1943, but in dwindling numbers.

M3 MEDIUM IN ASIA

Although the M3 medium tank is best known for its role in the desert campaign of 1942–43, it was also widely used by British and Commonwealth forces in Asia. Even in the summer of 1942, at the height of the desert campaign, nearly a third of the Grants and Lees had been diverted to Asia.

BURMA

The British Army in Burma drew most, if not all of its tanks from India, and a ramshackle lot they were to begin with. In due course, after some Royal Armoured Corps regiments had been reconverted back into infantry, at least five British armoured regiments were equipped with what was known in administrative shorthand as Lee/Grants – a term that has been mistakenly used by a number of authors since to describe M3 medium tanks in the Far East. In fact the distinction is quite clear and it was the Lee, the American version of the M3 Medium, which dominated in Burma, albeit with the machine-gun cupola removed from the turret, replaced by a two-piece hatch, and a pair of smoke-grenade dischargers on the outside.

Two regiments, both converted infantry battalions incorporated into the Royal Armoured Corps as 146 and 149 RAC, operated two squadrons of Grant tanks each. A squadron of 146 RAC took part in amphibious operations against Ramree Island, off the Burmese coast, in January 1945 while earlier 149 RAC had employed its two squadrons of Grants at Kohima in 1944.

A Lee tank of the 3rd Carabiniers crosses the Irrawady River in Burma on February 26, 1945, during the 33 Corps advance on Meiktila. (NARA)

Although this particular tank was regarded as outdated in the West by this time, it continued to operate in Burma until the end of the war and found itself fighting in a way that reflected its original purpose. The Japanese did not use tanks extensively in Burma and on the few occasions they were encountered, they were easily dealt with by the M3's guns. But fighting tenacious Japanese infantry gave these big American tanks the opportunity they had been waiting for. The 75mm hull gun, firing a succession of armour-piercing, high-explosive and smoke rounds, proved to be the perfect tool for tackling the camouflaged, defensive bunkers so popular with the Japanese, while the 37mm turret gun, firing canister, could be used against trees and other foliage concealing enemy troops. This is not to say that the Japanese were devoid of anti-tank weapons, although most of them required the attacker to get suicidally close to the tank they wanted to disable, so the tanks relied on escorting infantry to keep them at bay.

M3 VARIANTS

NIGHT-FIGHTING TANKS

A scheme to mount high-intensity searchlights on tanks to permit night-time tank attacks was first attempted in the 1930s, and the British Army conducted trials in June 1940. The concept proved so promising that the production of 300 turrets was authorized and the entire effort cloaked in a veil of intense secrecy. The War Office felt that such a scheme would be most effective if used as a surprise weapon. The project was given the cover name of Canal Defence Light (CDL). A formation of CDL tanks would illuminate the battlefield with intense beams of light, blinding the German defenders while making their positions evident to the attacking force. To further confuse the defenders, the searchlights could have their beams emitted in a flickering pattern, and colour filters could be used to confuse anti-tank gunners about the actual range of the attacking CDL tanks. The original plan was to mount the turrets on the Matilda tank, but they were later transferred to the Grant, as this permitted the tank to retain a 75mm gun and operate the turret at the same time. In 1944, Grant CDL tanks were deployed in the three regiments of the 1st Tank Brigade

CANAL DEFENCE LIGHT, 1ST TANK BRIGADE, 79TH ARMOURED DIVISION, 1944

The 79th Armoured Division's CDL tanks were finished in the usual SCC 15 olive drab, which was adopted in April 1944 to avoid the need to repaint US Lend-Lease equipment. The markings here are typical and include the divisional emblem, the tank name, and the A squadron tactical insignia. The specialized CDL brigade was disbanded in October 1944 and the regiments (11th, 42nd, 49th RTR) returned to normal tank status. A few CDL tanks were later operated by B Squadron, 49th Armoured Personnel Carrier Regiment (formerly 49th RTR). (Art by Hugh Johnson, © Osprey Publishing)

with 'Hobart's Funnies', the 79th Armoured Division, which concentrated the British specialized armour under a single command.

The US Army was shown the CDL tank in October 1942 and decided to form six special tank battalions equipped with a US copy. The US effort was codenamed 'the Cassock Project', and the American CDL tanks were given the cover name of T10 Shop Tractors and the codename 'Leaflet' for operational use. Most Leaflet tanks were based on the M3A1 cast-hull tank instead of the riveted-hull M3 Grant/Lee used on the British CDL tanks. By the spring of 1943, the M3 was out of production, so a contract was given to ALCO to re-manufacture and convert the tanks. A total of 497 Leaflets were converted from June 1943 to early 1944. These incorporated some changes that were intended for final-production M3 medium tanks, such as the splinter shield around the 75mm gun.

Although the CDL concept held great promise, the intense secrecy around the project proved to be its undoing. Senior commanders were not aware of the programme and its potential, and use of the tanks was encumbered by an agreement under which the British and American sides agreed to coordinate their actions before any were put into use. By the autumn of 1944, the US Army was so short of tank battalions in Europe that all six Leaflet battalions were converted to normal tank battalions or mine-clearing battalions. Likewise, the units of the 1st Tank Brigade were reorganized in October 1944. However, some far-sighted officers realized that the CDL tanks might still have some use, and a number were brought forward in the spring of 1945 to help defend bridges over the Rhine from German night attacks. The US Leaflet tanks saw a handful of combat engagements in the final months of the war in this role, and B Squadron of 49 APC Regiment also employed the British CDL tanks in the Rhine and Elbe operations.

TANK RECOVERY VEHICLES

The British converted redundant Grant and Lee tanks to the Grant ARV I (armoured recovery vehicle) by removing the turret and fitting various tools, including a small jib crane that could be fitted to the front of the vehicle. This recovery vehicle was much simpler than the M31, and the British Army obtained 104 M31 and M32 through Lend-Lease, which they called the Grant ARV II. The Red Army was sent 127 M31 in 1943–44. France received a number of M31s outside Lend-Lease channels in armoured units of the French First Army, part of the US 6th Army Group. Australia conducted its own ARV conversion, which fell somewhat between the M31 and ARV I in complexity, having a large rear spade to assist in winching, but without a large heavy-duty crane.

COMBAT ENGINEER VEHICLES

The British Army used the Grant as the basis for one of the early mine-clearing tanks, the Grant Scorpion III. This had a flail device mounted on the front of the tank, and it was first put into operational use in Tunisia in 1943. It was subsequently used in later campaigns in Italy but gradually gave way to devices mounted on the Sherman tank.

The US efforts at mine clearance focused on mine exploders using rollers rather than flails. The T1 mine exploder was tested on an M3 medium tank at APG in early 1943. The device had many shortcomings but evolved into the T1E1 Earthworm mine exploder employed with the M32 TRV. There was at least one field expedient mine-clearing system mounted on an M3 by the Fifth Army Engineer Training Center (FAETC) in North Africa in 1943, which was a Rube Goldberg contraption using a rotating crane that dropped explosive charges in front of the tank to clear a path. The programme was continued later in the US in a modified form on the M4 tank as the Pancake device, but never proved practical. Curiously enough, records of the 1st Armored Division in Tunisia indicate that the 16th Engineers had six M3 medium tanks with 'mine crushers' in late April 1943 during the fighting around Mateur, and these may have been Scorpions borrowed from the British.

The South Africans used a venerable M3 Grant as a command tank in Italy, albeit with the hull gun eliminated and a much larger dummy gun in the turret so that it would look like a regular Sherman – at least from a distance. Notice the chair in front of the turret.

CHAPTER 3

M4 MEDIUM TANK: THE SHERMAN

DESIGN AND DEVELOPMENT

The development of American tanks, in the engineering sense, was undertaken by the Ordnance Department. However, Ordnance was limited to initiating design studies unless a formal requirement was issued by the user service, in this case the Armored Force, and production decisions required the approval of Army Ground Forces (AGF) headed by Major General Lesley McNair. The AGF was responsible for formulating Army tactical doctrine, and came heavily to reflect the opinions and biases of McNair, an artilleryman with prodigious administrative skills but no combat experience. McNair felt that tanks had no business jousting with other tanks, and that this task should be left to his pet service, the Tank Destroyers. Tanks were envisaged as infantry support weapons (in the case of those belonging to independent tank battalions) or as tools for rapid 'cavalry' exploitation of breakthroughs in the case of those of the armoured divisions. The breakthrough would be secured by the infantry divisions with local support from the independent tank battalions to soften up particularly tenacious defensive positions, and any sallies by enemy tanks would be greeted by towed or self-propelled tank destroyers. With a gap secured, the armoured divisions would pour through to wreak havoc in the enemy rear, destroying reinforcements, disrupting the command structure and forcing the enemy infantry to flee or be destroyed. This American approach was in distinct contrast to German doctrine, which viewed the Panzer divisions as a vital mass of mobile firepower, central to the securing of the breakthrough against both armoured and unarmoured opposition, as well as to the rapid exploitation of success.

The basic fallacy of the American doctrine was the inability of the tank destroyers to deal completely with enemy armour. The McNair doctrine presumed a certain amount of concentration of German armour, since a single tank destroyer battalion could hardly be expected adequately to cover an entire divisional front. But with Allied air superiority, concentration of armour by the Germans became extremely risky except on a small scale

Condor, an M4A2 of 'C' Company, 2nd Marine Tank Battalion, was one of a handful of Shermans successfully landed on Tarawa on 'D-Day', 20 November 1943, marking the operational debut of the M4 in the Pacific. *Condor's* combat career was short-lived as it was inadvertently bombed by a US Navy plane which had not been informed that there were Marine tanks ashore, and presumed it to be Japanese. The US Marines were the only significant American users of the diesel M4A2, most being supplied to Britain and others via Lease-Lend. (USMC)

for local counter-attacks. Tanks were, inevitably, obliged to deal with German tanks, usually without tank destroyer support. Moreover, the tank destroyers were not particularly useful armoured vehicles. They were essentially under-armoured tanks with slightly bigger guns, and could not slug it out on even terms with their heavily-protected German adversaries. Since they were open-topped they were very vulnerable to overhead airbursts, mortar fire and even dedicated infantry attack. They were adequate weapons for ambush or fire support; but since the 1944–45 campaign was a string of unbridled offensive drives, they did not fulfil the needs of the US Army. As a First Army report bitterly complained, what was needed was not tank killers, but killer tanks.

The Ordnance search for the killer tank was stymied by the smug complacency of the AGF, and by a major failure in the Army as a whole to appreciate the growing shift within the Wehrmacht towards even heavier and better-armed tanks. The Sherman had proved capable of dealing with the PzKpfw III and IV on equal terms, but its hopeless showing against the Tiger was brushed aside by unfairly blaming the heavy losses at Faid Pass on the inexperience of the troops, and by assuming that the Tiger would be encountered in small numbers and could therefore be dealt with by artillery or tank destroyers. These attitudes were summed up in an AGF policy statement to the Chief of Staff in November 1943 opposing the production of the excellent new T26 (M26 Pershing) heavy tank:

> The recommendation of a limited proportion of tanks carrying a 90mm gun is not concurred in for the following reasons: The M4 tank has been hailed widely as the best tank on the battlefield today. There are indications even the enemy concurs in this view. Apparently, the M4 is an ideal combination of mobility, dependability, speed, protection and firepower. Other than this particular request – which represents the British view – there has been no call from any theatre for a 90mm tank gun. There appears to be no fear on the part of our forces of the German Mark VI (Tiger) tank

Hurricane, an M4 of 'H' Company, 66th Armored Regiment, 2nd Armored Division, has its Whirlwind engine removed with the aid of an M1 Wrecker. Like most of the tanks of 2nd Armored Division, this M4 was camouflage-painted shortly after landing in Normandy with a pattern of Earth Brown over the usual Olive Drab. This repair work was being done near Le Teilleul, France, on 17 August 1944. (US Army)

> There can be no basis for the T26 tank other than the conception of a tank-vs-tank duel – which is believed to be unsound and unnecessary. Both British and American battle experience has demonstrated that the anti-tank gun in suitable numbers and disposed properly is the master of the tank… There has been no indication that the 76mm anti-tank gun is inadequate against the German Mark VI tank.

The contemptuous view of British opinion on this subject was widely shared in the US, and stemmed from the abysmal quality of British tank design in the early years of the war. Yet the combat-wise British liaison officers appreciated what their American counterparts had failed to understand through their own inexperience – that German tank design was not stagnant. Driven by the need to surpass excellent Soviet tank designs like the T-34, there was a constant escalation of German armour and firepower. The British had witnessed the leap from the 20mm and 37mm guns of 1940, to the 50mm and short 75mm in 1941, and finally to the long 75mm of the PzKpfw IV Special (Ausf.F) and the 88mm of the Tiger in Tunisia in 1943. The same improvements had taken place in tank armour as well. The British had every expectation that they would face an even more dangerous adversary in France in 1944, and saw their fears borne out when liaison teams in Moscow reported in July 1943 that the Russians had captured a new 45-ton medium tank called the Panther, with excellent sloped armour and a potent new long-barrelled 75mm gun. To deal with this threat the British had developed a special mounting for the excellent 17-pounder anti-tank gun that could be crammed even into the small turret of the 75mm gun Sherman. This fine weapon was offered to the Ordnance Department in the autumn of 1943, and was ignored. The Sherman with 17-pounder gun, called the Firefly, was issued to British and Commonwealth tank troops initially on the basis of one vehicle per troop, to deal more effectively with the new German tanks. The American tankers would not be so lucky.

Part of the resistance within the US Army to a heavy tank like the T26 to supplement the Sherman was a legitimate concern over logistics. American tanks had to be shipped thousands of miles to distant battlefields in Europe and the Pacific, and every extra ton of tank was a ton less of other vital supplies. The T26 weighed nearly 50 per cent more than the Sherman and would require elaborate new training, new spare parts and new ammunition. The Army was not convinced of the need for this tank, anyway. To some extent this concern over logistics was exaggerated. The Soviet Union, whose heavy industries were stretched far more thinly than those of the US, managed to provide the Soviet Army with excellent heavy tanks throughout the war without insuperable logistics problems. As a compromise, the AGF agreed to up-arm the M10 tank destroyer with the T26's 90mm gun, resulting in the M36; and agreed to allow the limited production of up-armed Shermans with a 76mm gun which Ordnance had been pushing since 1942. The 76mm gun was chosen rather than a different and more potent weapon since it fired the same ammunition already in use by the M10 and M18 tank destroyers. It was a short-sighted move, as this gun was barely capable of defeating existing German tanks like the Tiger I, and provided no leeway for newer tanks with even better armour. This development was greeted with ambivalence by the Armored Force. While a better tank gun was desired, the M1A1 76mm gun chosen was only marginally better than the 75mm gun in anti-tank performance, while lacking the advantage of the 75mm gun's excellent HE round for general support. On this subject, the Armored Force summarized its position in September 1943:

> The 76mm gun M1 as a tank weapon has only one superior characteristic to the 75mm gun M3. This superior characteristic is in armor penetrating power. The 76mm gun will penetrate on an average of 1in more armor than the 75mm gun M3 at the same range. The high explosive pitching power of the 76mm gun is inferior to the 75mm gun. The 76mm HE shell weighs 12.37lb and has a charge of .86lb explosive. The 75mm HE shell weighs 14.6lb and has a charge of 1.47lb explosive. The exterior ballistics of the 76mm gun are generally less satisfactory for a general purpose Medium Tank weapon than the 75mm gun. The 76mm gun has an extremely heavy muzzle blast, such that the rate of fire when the ground is dry is controlled by the muzzle blast dust cloud. Under many conditions this dust cloud does not clear for some eight to thirty seconds. The presence of this heavy muzzle blast makes the sensing of the round

Tanks of 'E' Company, 66th or 67th Armored Regiment, 2nd Armored Division advance along a hedgerow near Champ du Bouet, France during the bocage fighting in Normandy, 10 August 1944. The lead tank, an M4A1 (76mm) W, was among the original batch of new 76mm gun tanks to arrive in France. Although originally scorned, the 76mm gun tanks were much sought-after following the first encounters with Panthers. (US Army)

> extremely difficult for the tank commander and gunner... The characteristics of the complete round of the 76mm gun makes it possible to stow only approximately 70 per cent as many rounds of ammunition in the Medium Tank M4 for the 76mm gun as can be stowed for the 75mm gun M3. The great length of the 76mm round slows the loader and somewhat slows the rate of fire... If the 76mm gun as adopted for all Medium Tanks in a division then insofar as the attack of all targets except enemy armor is concerned a handicap has been imposed on the Medium Tank. . . It is believed that a fairly good percentage of 76mm guns should be included in a Medium Tank unit for the purpose of giving it a sufficient share of the additional penetrating power obtainable with the 76mm gun.

The Armored Force recommended that about one-third of the Shermans be armed with the 76mm gun, but none were available for the armoured divisions until after the landings in Normandy.

That the Sherman was so successful is all the more surprising given such barren roots. Tank development in the US in the 1940 languished under the restrictions of a parsimonious Congress and an antiquated tactical doctrine that were not overcome until the staggering defeat of France in 1940. Production and design facilities in the US were hardly more elaborate than those of a small European state like Sweden or Poland, yet Roosevelt's commitments to Britain in 1940 necessitated rapid expansion to production levels in excess of those of the major European powers. In the summer of 1940 the US Army was about to adopt the M2A1 medium tank, a pathetic symbol of the depths to which Ordnance Department designs had sunk, armed with a tinkertoy assortment of machine guns and a single paltry 37mm tank gun. Reassessments forced on the Army by the French defeat made it horribly clear that the planned production of 1,000 M2A1s would be foolish in the extreme.

Fortunately the Army could depend on a vigorous and mature steel industry and some of the best automotive and locomotive factories in the world. While the redesign of the M2A1 was undertaken, plans were laid for quantity tank production. It was evident that it would be at least a year before casting facilities would be ready to handle turrets capable of mounting a 75mm gun, so a stop-gap design was completed carrying a 75mm gun in a sponson mount, and a 37mm gun in a small turret, in much the same configuration as the French Char B1 tank. This began to roll off the assembly lines in June 1941 as the M3 medium tank. It formed the backbone of the newly-formed armoured divisions, and was supplied to British tank units fighting in the Western Desert through Lend-Lease. Although well-accepted by its British crews, the peculiar gun arrangement and the resultant excessive vehicle height doomed the M3 to a short production life of only 15 months.

Using virtually the same chassis and powertrain as the M3 Medium, the new M4 was designed around a large cast turret capable of mounting an M3 75mm tank gun. The initial production model, the M4A1, used a cast-armour hull, and first rolled off the assembly lines in February 1942. Since there were not enough casting facilities to provide hulls in the quantities anticipated, the M4 welded-hull version was developed, and became available in July 1942. In 1942 the initial US Army plans called for 60 armoured divisions, and Roosevelt announced a suitably ambitious production programme for 45,000 tanks in that year alone. This would have entailed manufacturing as many tanks every four days as had been manufactured in the US in the previous ten years! Clearly a major stumbling-block was going to be engine production. The M4 and M4A1 were both powered by the Wright-Continental

To help break out of the hedgerows Shermans were fitted with the so-called Cullin Devices, better known as 'Rhinos', which consisted of old 'Rommel Asparagus' beach obstructions cut up to make prongs. This helped the Sherman to dig into the hedge and crash through it without 'porpoising' and exposing the thinner belly armour. This M4A1 of the 741st Tank Battalion is fairly remarkable in that it was still fitted with the 'Rhino' on 9 March 1945. Most of these prongs were dropped immediately after the conclusion of Operation 'Cobra'. (US Army)

R-975 Whirlwind radial aircraft engine, which unfortunately was also in demand by the Navy and Army Air Force. To supplement these, Ordnance decided to adopt the GM Twin 6-71 diesel, which consisted of a pair of bus engines joined at the flywheel end by a clutch and transfer unit. Although the new Armored Force entertained the notion of using exclusively diesel engines in all its tanks, this idea was dropped in 1942 when Quartermaster Corps complained about the logistic difficulties of supplying armoured units with both diesel fuel for tanks and petrol for motor transport.

The diesel-powered M4, designated M4A2, became available in April 1942 and was earmarked for Lend-Lease. The only significant combat use of the M4A2 by American forces was its employment in Marine tank battalions; diesel-powered tanks were preferred by the Navy since they used the same fuel as small craft. The Ford GAA engine was also adopted in 1942, with the first of these M4A3 tanks being manufactured in June 1942. Although not produced in the quantities of the M4 or M4A1, it was the preferred variant of the US Army. The final engine type developed for the M4 was the Chrysler A-57 multi-bank which consisted of four car engines mated together; it was so long that it required a lengthened hull, and was manufactured as the M4A4, almost exclusively for the British forces although there was some US training use. Regardless of the enormous production capacity of American heavy industry, the drain on steel production by the shipbuilding industry whittled down the President's ambitious tank production programme to more manageable levels.

M4A4 SHERMAN

(Art by Peter Sarson, © Osprey Publishing)

Key

1. Radio bracket
2. M3 75mm gun
3. Browning .30-calibre machine gun
4. Co-driver/machine gunner's seat
5. Ventilator
6. Co-driver/machine gunner's hatch
7. Gyro stabiliser pump & motor
8. Main gun firing pedal
9. Ammunition stowage compartment
10. Turret basket
11. Oilgear hydraulic turret traverse mechanism
12. Browning .30 cal ammunition
13. Gyro-stabiliser control
14. Periscope
15. Indirect sighting device
16. Periscope
17. Browning .50 cal anti-aircraft machine gun mount
18. Ventilator
19. Commander's seat
20. M3 gun gyro-stabiliser
21. Co-axial Browning .30 cal machine gun
22. Periscope
23. Radio aerial
24. Fuel cut off
25. Synchromesh
26. Driveshaft
27. Transmission oil cooler
28. Chrysler A57 multibank engine
29. Fuel filler cap
30. Fire extinguisher
31. Air vent
32. Fuel tank
33. No.2 carburettor air cleaner
34. Auxiliary generator
35. Fire extinguisher
36. Generator
37. Parking brake
38. Gear selector
39. Driver's seat
40. Steering levers
41. Drive sprocket
42. Breather
43. Powertrain (final drive & brake system)
44. Towing ring

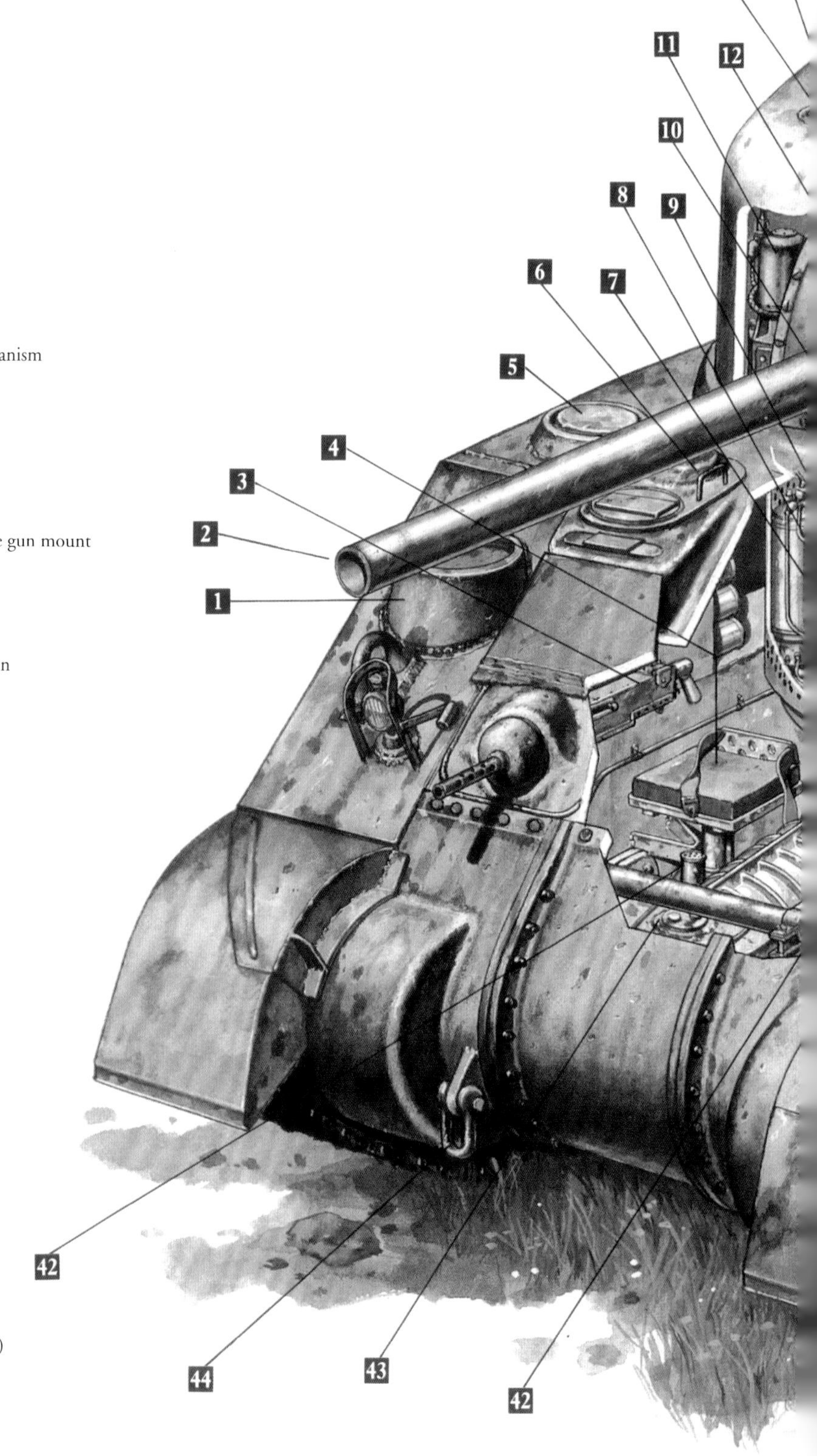

17
18
19
20
21
22
23
24
25
26
27
28
29
30
31
32
33
34
35
36
37
38
39
40
41

US VARIANTS

The principal types of Shermans in US Army service in 1944 were the M4 and the M4A1. They were identical internally, both being powered by the Continental Whirlwind radial engine, but the M4 had a welded hull and the M4A1 a cast armour hull. Some units preferred the M4A1, feeling that the rounded surfaces warded off enemy projectiles better; but in at least one tank battalion, the 73rd, the troops became convinced that the cast armour was inferior to that on the M4, and avoided using M4A1s in combat. Most units could see no difference between the two types, though the welded hull version did have a bit more interior. space. By August 1944 more M4A3s were becoming available, and the troops soon took a liking to them because of the greater horsepower, greater torque at low speeds and better reliability of the engine. Otherwise, the M4A3 was very similar in appearance to the M4 except for the engine grille-work and a different air-filter configuration at the rear.

The layout of the Sherman was conventional. The engine was mounted in the rear behind a firewall, and the powertrain passed under the turret basket to the clutch and transmission in the front of the tank. Due to the use of a radial engine in the initial Shermans the powertrain was mounted quite high in the hull, resulting in a tall silhouette for the tank. This made the Sherman a more conspicuous target, but on the positive side it provided more interior space, allowing more ammunition to be stored than in most tanks of its day. The crew consisted of five men: the driver in the left hull front, the assistant driver/bow machine gunner beside him in the right hull front, and a turret crew of three: the tank commander in the right-rear of the turret, the gunner immediately in front of him, and the gun loader in the left side of the turret.

A pair of M4s await further orders in the battered town of Coutances, 31 July 1944. The lead tank is armed with a 75mm gun, while the second vehicle mounts a 105mm howitzer. These 105mm assault tanks were used by the HQ companies in tank battalions. The white stars have been overpainted on these tanks, as they provided a conspicuous target for German anli-tank gunners. (US Army)

FIREPOWER

The Sherman was armed with an M3 75mm gun fitted with a gyro-stabilizer for one axis (elevation) stabilization. The standard anti-tank round was the M61 APC, which could penetrate 68mm of armour at 500m and 60mm at 1,000m. The round weighed 20lb of which the projectile was 15lb. The other standard rounds were the M89 White Phosphorus (WP 'Willy Peter') Smoke and the M48 High Explosive. The maximum theoretical rate of fire was 20 rounds per minute, though this was seldom attempted or achieved in combat.

The turret was traversed from the gunner's or commander's position by a hydraulic and electric unit, and the gunner had a manual traverse wheel as well. The Sherman had a very fast turret traverse for its day, which was one of the few advantages it possessed over the Panther. In the early Shermans the gunner had a periscopic sight for aiming the main gun, but this proved troublesome as the articulated linkage easily misaligned. A telescopic sight was developed and fielded in 1943. Tanks fitted with the M70 telescopic sight were conspicuous by their use of the wider M34A1 gun mantlet. This was a three-power sight without special filters, and was good out to 1,000m even though it did not have either the optical quality or the power of German sights, and could prove difficult to use if facing into the sun. Ranging was done by the commander or gunner by estimation using ballistic reticules in the sights. The 75mm Sherman was one of the first tanks fitted with a gyro-stabilized gun. Opinions on the value of this feature vary, with most veterans claiming it was worthless and was generally left turned off. It was not fitted in some 76mm tanks. Some tankers who had better luck with it insist that it was rarely used because it took care to keep in adjustment and thorough training to use properly, and most troops did not want to bother with either. As a result, most firing was done from a halt. The M3 75mm gun was flanked by a Browning .30-calibre machine gun. Firing of the main gun was by foot pedal or a button on the turret traverse handle.

Behind the gunner was the commander. In most 75mm Shermans the commander had a two-piece split hatch immediately above him fitted with a single traversable periscope. There was a small vane sight in front of this periscope, and another located forward of the gunner's periscope. These two vanes could be aligned by the commander to 'rough-aim' the gun. They were later replaced by a single 'U'-shaped sight which was easier to use. The commander had very limited sighting from this periscope, and when the 76mm gun was introduced in the new T23 turret an improved commander's cupola was added which had all-round vision blocks giving a much more satisfactory view. Some late production 75mm gun tanks were also fitted with this feature. The commander talked to his crew through a small hand-held microphone. The tank's radio receiver was carried behind the commander in the rear turret bustle, and

Looking like a bit of rather tacky stage decor, this M4A3 105mm howitzer tank of the 751st Tank Bn photographed near Poretta, Italy, in February 1945 has been decorated with white paint and spun glass in a curious attempt at camouflage. The vehicle has been partly dug in at the rear to gain higher elevation for the howitzer. Due to the static nature of much of the fighting in Italy, tanks were more commonly used there in an indirect fire-support role. (US Army)

This interior view of an M4A3(76mm) W was taken from the commander's seat looking forward towards the gunner's position. The gunner's seat is folded down revealing the complex plumbing associated with the Oilgear hydraulic turret traverse mechanism. This particular vehicle has its telescopic and periscopic gunner's sights removed. (US Army)

command tanks had an additional transmitter. Initially three out of five tanks had a receiver only, but by late 1944 the whole platoon usually had receivers and transmitters.

The loader sat or stood in the left side of the turret. The turret had brackets for 12 rounds of ammunition around the lower turret basket wall, and there were eight more rounds in a ready-rack under the gun. Originally the turret basket was heavily shielded by protective screening around most of the lower sides, but this was gradually reduced since it interfered with passing ammunition up from the stowage bins in the hull. There was a stowage rack for 15 rounds in the left sponson at the loader's knee, and racks for 15 and 17 rounds in the right sponson accessible to the commander. The main 30-round compartment was located under the turret basket behind the bow-gunner. This was awkward for him to reach, though the practice in some units was for the bow gunner to move his seat back, swing around backwards, and pass the rounds up through gaps in the turret basket wall. The main bin was a constant source of complaints since it was very hard on the hands unless an 'ammunition puller' tool was used. As this was often misplaced, a screwdriver became a popular tool for prying the rounds out. Some crews became frustrated and tore out the bin's innards, simply stacking the ammunition like a pile of logs in the cardboard packing tubes it came in. The belly escape hatch was located in front of this bin. Strangely, in some areas this escape hatch became a prized item among local infantry units, who stole them to provide armoured overhead cover for their foxholes! This led to modification orders for chains to be added to prevent such thefts after some divisional commanders complained that they had tanks out of service missing this part.

There never seemed to be enough space for ammunition in the Sherman. It was common practice in most units to store additional rounds in every nook and cranny. In some cases this was the result of crew anxieties that they would not be adequately resupplied, but in some divisions in Patton's Third Army it was policy. American tank tactics in France stressed 'reconnaissance by fire' (that is, attacking likely targets where anti-tank guns or Panzerfaust teams might be lurking), the feeling being that it was cheaper in men and tanks to squander ammunition than to risk surprise attacks. Many a French church belfry fell victim to 'prophylactic fire'.

Probably the worst aspect of the loader's position was that he had no escape hatch and had to crawl under the gun to exit through the main (commander's) turret hatch. This led to a higher casualty toll among loaders than there need have been. Eventually a small oval hatch was added above the loader's position, though in the interim some units modified the protective guard around the back of the gun with hinges so that it could be swung out of the way to speed the loader's exit.

A typical firing sequence went as follows:
Commander to driver: 'Driver … STOP'
Commander to gunner: 'Gunner … TANK'
Commander to loader: 'AP'
Commander to gunner: 'Traverse left… Steady-on… One thousand'
Gunner to Commander: 'Ready!'
Commander to gunner: 'FIRE!'

The crew of an M4 of 37th Tank Battalion, 4th Armored Division, commanded by Sgt. T. Dunn, prepare to bed down for the night after a lull in the fighting near Chateau Salinas, 26 September 1944. This particular tank has the wider M34A1 mantlet that permitted the use of a new telescopic aiming-sight for the main gun. (US Army)

Besides the main gun, the Sherman had a coaxial .30-calibre Browning machine gun used to shoot-up enemy vehicles or infantry, and there was another in the right hull front in a ball mount operated by the bow-gunner. It was a reliable weapon, if a bit hard to change barrels. On the commander's cupola was a .50-calibre Browning, ostensibly placed there for anti-aircraft fire, but more often used to reach out to targets beyond the range of the .30-calibre Brownings. It was rather awkwardly placed, obliging the commander to expose himself to aim it properly, but it was a very destructive weapon against targets such as trucks or wooden buildings. When not in use it was stowed in clips on the rear of the turret with the barrel removed.

An M4A3(76mm)W clanks through the mud near Riedwihr, France, on 31 January 1945 in support of the 75th Infantry Division during the destruction of the Colmar Pocket. This view clearly shows the large hatch added over the loader's station in the left of the turret on the 76mm gun version after complaints about the difficulty of the loader escaping when the tank was hit. The small square port on the turret side was used to dispose of spent shell casings.

The 75mm gun tanks began to be supplemented by the newer 76mm gun tanks in July 1944. They made up as much as one-third of some battalions, and by 1945 some battalions had nearly half their complement armed with 76mm guns. The new vehicles, first the M4A1(76mm)W and later the M4A3(76mm)W were easily identifiable by the new, larger T23 turret and the long barrel of the gun. There were other less apparent changes such as the larger driver/bow-gunner hatches, and the one-piece 47-degree hull front on the M4A3. Internally, the vehicles had 'wet stowage' – see below.

The M1A1C 76mm gun fired the same ammunition as the M10 and M18 tank destroyers. There were two rounds commonly available for it: the M42A1 HE weighing in at 22.6lb, and the M62 APC-T round which weighed 25lb with a 15.5lb projectile. Less common, and in great demand, was the T4 HVAP-T round weighing 19lb with a 9.4lb projectile. Called 'souped-up AP' or 'hyper-shot', this

M4A3(76mm) Ws of the 25th Tank Battalion, 14th Armored Division take up firing positions outside Huttendorf, France, 11 February 1945. The lead tank still has sandbags on the front hull, but they are missing from the side cage. The turret lacks sandbag protection and is camouflage-painted with thin, rolling stripes. (US Army)

tungsten-cored round was always in short supply in tank battalions as it was reserved for tank destroyers. Seldom were there more than two or three rounds available for each 76mm gun tank before 1945, when a lucky outfit might have as many as five. It was saved for dealing with Panthers and Tigers. At 500m the standard APC round could punch through 98mm of armour, compared to about 150mm for HVAP, and at 1000m it was 90mm against 132mm.

Some Shermans had a small single-fire smoke mortar mounted in the turret. Opinions on this device vary; some units did not use them, as they found that when they were fired to provide cover the Germans tended to spray the smoke cloud with machine gun fire, much to the consternation of infantry accompanying the tank. The WP smoke round was a preferred means of concealment in many units, even though considered too small and slow.

PROTECTION

OPPOSITE A column of M4A3Ws of the 14th Armored Division passes by three Shermans disabled by mines near Barr, France, 29 November 1944. These particular vehicle are very late-production 75mm gun tanks with all-around vision cupolas and wet stowage. What appears to be a white sheet on the disabled tank to the right is in fact the cerise air identification panel commonly carried on American and British tanks to prevent Allied fighter-bombers from strafing them. (US Army)

The hull armour on the Sherman was 51mm thick in front and 38mm on the sides. The turret had an 89mm gun shield, and the turret armour ranged from 76mm at the front to 51mm on the side. On the late production welded-hull models the armour was raised to 63mm on the hull front. The Sherman's armour could be penetrated at most ordinary combat ranges by any of the tanks and self-propelled guns commonly in Wehrmacht service in 1944, with the minor exception of older types like the PzKpfw III, which were infrequently encountered. For example, the PzKpfw IV Ausf. H, which was one of the more common types in service, could penetrate the frontal armour with AP rounds from ranges in excess of 2,000m, or the sides from over 4,500m. The Sherman had been designed to resist the old 37mm PAK 36 which the Germans had started to replace in 1940 after the fall of France. The chassis could not accept too much more armour without sacrificing mechanical reliability, and so this was not seriously considered. This situation was very demoralizing to American tank crews in Europe, since their tanks were regularly knocked out by everything from hand-held Panzerfausts to 88mm anti-aircraft guns, while they watched with utter disgust as the shells from their own guns bounced harmlessly off Panthers and Tigers.

An all too common sight in the drive across France: in the distance, a Sherman burns while a medic races to aid the wounded crew. In the foreground, a medic waits by the side of a crewman wounded when his tank was hit. Bayon, France, 12 September 1944. (US Army)

The Sherman, besides being thinly armoured, also had the reputation of a firetrap. This was popularly attributed by many in the US Army to the decision to use petrol engines rather than diesels. This view was sparked by the Tank Destroyer command's pitch to its troops about the supposed advantages of the diesel engines (used in some of the M10s) over the petrol engines used in most US Army Shermans. A popular initiation rite for new troops in these TD units was to order them to the engine deck of a diesel M10 and tell them to determine how full the fuel tank was.

When the 'rube' admitted being unable to see anything in the dark interior of the fuel tank, his tormentor would strike a match and hurl it into the open pipe. Not being familiar with diesel fuel, the 'rube' would assume that the match was about to ignite a major conflagration and would hurl himself to the ground in a most unseemly fashion, much to the delight of previously initiated onlookers.

New M4A3(76mm) W tanks of the 2nd Platoon, 'A' Company, 13th Tank Battalion, 1st Armored Division, fire their guns near Lorenzana, Italy, on 19 August 1944. The red barrel bands indicated 'A' Company, while the presence of two stripes on the gun tube and the number '2' to the rear of the turret sides indicated 2nd Platoon The second tank, with its half-barrel band, is the vehicle of the company commander. (US Army)

In fact, battlefield experience and Ordnance tests established that the main cause of Sherman fires was ignition of the ammunition propellant. A lesser culprit was the occasional ignition of turret hydraulic oil, personal stowage or sometimes fuel. It was estimated that 60–80 per cent of Shermans penetrated by AP rounds or Panzerfausts burned. This is easy to believe in view of the fact that a penetration from nearly anywhere in the frontal arc would bring a projectile in contact with ammunition, and once the casing ruptured, the HE filler used in many German AP rounds would ignite it. The common practice of storing 30 or 40 additional rounds of ammunition outside the bins and racks only served to exacerbate this problem. Once a propellant fire broke out the crew had little choice but to abandon the vehicle as quickly as possible.

An M4A3E2 'Jumbo' (left) and M4A3E8 of the 37th Tank Battalion, 4th Armored Division pass through Alzey, Germany, on 20 March 1945. The Sherman on the right is an HQ tank and is either Maj. Bautz's tank, 'Tornado', or Col. Creighton Abram's 'Thunderbolt'. The thick turret frontal armour on the Jumbo is very evident in this view. This particular assault tank has been re-armed with a 76mm gun; initially the Jumbos were armed with 75mm guns. (US Army)

Ordnance developed two solutions to this problem. As a short-term solution, plates of appliqué armour 25–35mm thick were added to the hull sides over the two right-hand ammo bins and one left-hand bin to lessen the chance of penetrations at these vulnerable spots. This was reasonably effective against the smaller-calibre anti-tank weapons still encountered in Italy in 1943 and early 1944, but it was ineffective against hits by Panthers, Tigers or Panzerfausts.

In February 1944 some late production M4A3s had 'wet' stowage bins added: these consisted of racks surrounded by water. When the bins were hit by an AP round they poured water over the spilled propellant, either preventing a fire or inhibiting it long enough to allow the crew to escape. The propensity of American crews to pile in added ammunition meant that even this improvement could not be totally effective, but a study done by the US Army in 1945 found that only 10–15 per cent of the 'wet' stowage Shermans burned, as compared to 60–80 per cent of the 'dry' stowage Shermans. The wet stowage was used on M4A1s and M4A3s fitted with the 76mm gun, and on a small number of late M4A3s with the 75mm gun.

During the fighting in the bocage, where all travel was channelled down narrow tracks, Shermans became sitting ducks for concealed anti-tank guns. This led to some US units using Shermans fitted with 'dozer blades as lead vehicles. The 'dozer blades were raised up, and sometimes sandbags were added for further cover. The practice was eventually discouraged since the added weight damaged the front bogie springs, and usually led to heat blistering on the front rubber wheels that could cause the solid rubber tyre to separate from the metal hub after 20 or 30 miles of driving on a hot summer day.

Ordnance had developed a more practical solution in the form of the M4A3E2 Jumbo assault tank. The Jumbo was an up-armoured M4A3 with extra plates 38mm thick added to the hull front and sides; a new 140mm-thick differential housing; and a new turret similar in appearance to the 76mm gun T23 turret, but 152mm instead

OPPOSITE Mines are always a constant threat to tanks, and this danger led to bizarre counter-measures. Here a T1E3 of the 738th Tank Bn (Special) prepares to clear a stretch of road near Beggendorf, Germany, on 11 December 1944. About 200 of these 'Aunt Jemima' mine-rollers were built; while effective on roads, they were less popular with the troops than the flail-type mine detonators as they easily bogged down on soft terrain. (US Army)

A close-up look at a PzKpfw V Ausf. G Panther hit by eight rounds of 76mm APC near Saverne, France. The gouges of six of these rounds are evident, only the hit on the lower left corner of the glacis plate causiug a minor penetration. The 76mm gun could only get penetrations against the front of the Panther by using the scarce HVAP ammunition, or by firing from a dangerously close range. (US Army)

of the 63mm of the standard production model. Only 254 were built, but they were very popular with the troops when they entered service in the autumn of 1944. The added weight led to decreased road speed, but the added protection more than compensated for this in the eyes of the troops. These tanks were used to lead columns down roads likely to be protected by concealed anti-tank guns. They were initially armed with 75mm guns but were subsequently retro-fitted with the 76mm, and some had hull flamethrowers added as well. Production was curtailed when the decision was made to proceed with the production of the M26 Pershing heavy tank. Unfortunately, due to the AGF's previous foot-dragging, only a handful of M26s reached Europe before the end of the war, and so the Sherman continued to bear the full brunt of tank fighting long after it should have.

Following the climactic battles during the breakout from Normandy and the resultant annihilation of much of the Panzer force in the Falaise Pocket, German armoured vehicles were not again encountered in such large concentrations until the Ardennes counter-offensive. While German tanks were still met with frequency in small numbers, anti-tank rockets like the Panzerfaust and Panzerschreck became an increasing threat to the Sherman. These weapons were difficult to use effectively unless fired from very close ranges, but their shaped-charge warheads could easily penetrate the armour of a Sherman, and almost invariably started a fire. To provide some added protection against these sort of attacks American tankers began adding various sorts of improvised armour to their vehicles. In some units spare track links were draped over the front hull to provide some 'stand-off' protection. The most common approach was to add a layer of sandbags to the front, and sometimes even to the sides of the hull and turret. This was accomplished by welding an 'I' beam along the hull side to support the weight of the sandbags, then adding a frame of metal rod or thin girders to contain the sand bags. This load usually amounted to about 150 sandbags, which added two to three tons to the weight of the vehicle. Their effectiveness in stopping Panzerfausts was somewhat questionable, as is apparent from this account by a Sherman gunner of the 2nd Armored Division:

> We were attacking in a Sherman with 75mm gun. Visibility was very good. There were Jerries dug in about 40 yards in front of our tank in a line of foxholes. Several were flushed out and moving to the rear when a Jerry bazooka hit the left track and broke it. We were unable to back up when a second shot hit in front of the turret, but did not pierce the turret. The third hit the front of the tank, dislodging all the sandbags, about 40 in all, and cracked the front plate. The fourth hit the same spot and cracked the front slope still wider and set the tank on fire. The fifth shot hit the extra armour plate welded to the front plate of the bow gunner, about 1½in thick, and knocked that off and cracked the front plate.

Even if only occasionally effective, the sandbag armour was a good morale booster for troops who were otherwise anxious about the indifferent quality of their equipment.

Engineers put the finishing touches to a sandbag armouring job by painting the vehicle in Olive Drab and black swathes. When tanks carried so much extra weight, the 'duck-bill' extended end connectors were almost invariably fitted to give better floatation on soft soil. This particular tank belonged to 25th Tank Battalion, 14th Armored Division. (US Army)

Some units, such as 4th Armored Division, discouraged the use of sandbags because of their questionable ballistic value and the adverse effect they had on the weight and therefore the performance of the tank, preferring other methods instead. Besides using spare track shoes, the 4th Armored also cut the armour off disabled Panther tanks and welded it to the front of Shermans to provide additional improvised assault leaders like the E2 Jumbos.

MOBILITY

The Sherman was comparable to its contemporaries in mobility. It was capable of 25mph on a level road, and could be coaxed to 30mph if not over-burdened with sandbags. Some crews tampered with the engine governors to squeeze a little more speed out of it, but this was discouraged as it often led to overstraining the engine. The Sherman performed best on dry terrain because of the narrow width of its track. On mud or snow it compared unfavourably with the later German tanks like the Panther or Tiger, which had been designed with very wide tracks as a result of experience on the Eastern Front. A Sherman driver from the 2nd Armored Division recalled:

'I saw where some Mk V [Panther] tanks crossed a muddy field without sinking the tracks over five inches, where we in the M4 started across the same field the same day and bogged down.'

Complaints of Shermans bogging down in sand in North Africa reached Ordnance in 1943, but there were two factors which

A new M4A3E8 of the 25th Tank Battalion, 14th Armored Division provides a clear view of the extent of sandbag armour additions. Indeed, the improvised armour covers so much of the hull front that the 14th Armored Division frequently painted the 'bumper' unit identification codes on the gun tube. The M4A3E8 was the culmination of Sherman tank development in World War II. (US Army)

An M4A2 of the French 2e Division Blindée passes through Strasbourg on 25 November 1944 on its way to the Rhine. The 2e DB was considered by the Americans to be the best of the French armoured divisions. The rather gaudy markings that adorned the tanks of the 'Division Leclerc' when they first landed in Normandy gradually became more restrained during the course of the fighting in northern France. (US Army)

inhibited satisfactory solutions. Army engineer regulations forbade vehicle widths beyond 124in due to shipping problems. A wider track would anyway have been difficult without a complete redesign of the suspension. As an expedient, in the spring of 1944, extended end connectors-better known to the troops as 'duck-bills'-were made available for attaching to the outer ends of the track. They reduced ground pressure from 14psi to 12psi, but were somewhat fragile and could easily be snapped off. Nonetheless, they were very necessary on overweight vehicles like the M4A3E2 Jumbos, or in very muddy conditions as prevailed in France and Italy in the autumn of 1944. The real solution was the development of new horizontal volute spring suspension (HVSS), which was introduced on the new M4A3E8 entering service in December 1944. Its wide track brought the ground pressure down to 11psi, which put US tanks on a more equal footing with their German adversaries.

Of the three major Sherman types used by the US Army the M4A3 was preferred because of its better engine. Both the M4 and M4A1 were rather underpowered and did not provide as much torque as might be desired at lower engine speeds. A frequent problem with the Whirlwind engine was that the spark plugs fouled excessively during extended idling periods, and the electrodes burned out on long road marches. This was hard to repair, as access to the lower bank of cylinders could frequently only be accomplished by removing the engine. The most vociferous critics of the Whirlwinds were the hapless crews who received reconditioned engines which had their cylinders chromed to replace worn surfaces. These were unreliable, had short lives and guzzled oil. The M4 and M4A1 were more prone to engine fires than the other Shermans due to the propensity of the Whirlwind to leak oil and petrol around the engine case and accessory mountings, and to blow oil out the crankcase breather, covering the cylinders and hot exhaust manifolds after piston rings had started to wear, and creating a blow-by. In spite of these problems, it should be kept in mind that compared to German or Soviet tank engines the Whirlwind was remarkably durable, and it compared rather badly only against other American tank engines.

The Ford GAA engine in the M4A3 was a more powerful engine than the Whirlwind and offered good torque at low engine speed. It was a bit of an oil-guzzler,

An M4 105mm howitzer tank of the 48th Tank Battalion, 14th Armored Division passes through Hochdelden, France, on 25 January 1945. The 105mm howitzer tanks were used by HQ companies to provide indirect and direct fire support for their battalions, and were used in tank units instead of M7 'Priest' self propelled guns, which were too vulnerable due to their open tops. They are bedecked with a winter coat of lime and salt whitewash for camouflage, and the improvised sandbag armour is hardly noticeable on the front of the hull. (US Army)

and could be easily damaged by overspeeding. It took some getting used to after driving the M4 or M4A1 as it would spit or pop back if the throttle was opened too quickly at 500–800rpm, causing a momentary drop in power. It was more reliable and durable than the Whirlwind; and much as American tankers admired the Panther, the rapid drives across France and Germany would have been impossible in such a vehicle given its capricious engine performance.

SHERMANS IN BRITISH SERVICE

THE M4A1

The first production line for the new tank was established early in 1942 at the Lima Locomotive Works in Ohio, and although this first contract was intended for the British, the first production tank to be completed was despatched to Aberdeen Proving Ground in Maryland to be tested by the Ordnance Department before entering service with the US Army. It was powered by a Continental R-975 C1 petrol engine, a nine-cylinder radial, air-cooled and set upright in the back, effectively the same as the Wright R-975 EC2 engine in the M3 Medium; this was regarded as somewhat underpowered for the heavier M4 series tanks. It was the second of these tanks, originally given the number T25190, that was sent across to Britain as a sample.

It has a number of features that are typical of very early Sherman tanks. It mounted the shorter M2 version of the 75mm gun in its turret, linked to a rotor sight on top of the turret, on the right hand side. In addition to a .30-calibre Browning machine gun in a ball mounting at the front of the hull on the right (what in America was known as a lap gun), it also featured a pair of Brownings sticking out the front of the hull, with a limited degree of elevation, that were fired by the driver. This additional machine-gun mounting had also been fitted to M3 Medium tanks but it only appeared on a limited number of early Shermans, after which it was eliminated. The suspension, of the vertical volute type, is also of the earlier pattern as used on the M3 Medium, with the return roller directly above the mounting; the suspension was also later changed.

This tank was one of the first to be fitted with fume-extracting ventilators: one on top of the turret, one at the right of the hull front on the redundant aerial base, and one behind the turret, also on the right. Direct vision slots were also provided for the driver and his mate, which were later replaced by periscopes in front of their roof hatches. When it arrived in Britain the new tank was displayed on Horse Guards Parade in London, and was fitted with a cast brass plate on each side bearing the name *MICHAEL* in honour of Michael Dewar of British Timken, head of the British Tank Mission to Washington. Like all M4A1 tanks (called a Sherman II in British terminology) it had a one-piece cast hull, 2in (about 51mm) thick at the front. The 75mm M2 gun was fitted with a pair of weights, clamped like collars around the muzzle in order to balance the gun so that it could be operated with the gun's automatic stabilizer. Later on the tank was fitted with the longer M3 75mm gun which did not require counterbalance weights. It was subsequently used during trials of poison gas dropped from the air and is now retired to the Tank Museum at Bovington, probably the oldest example of a Sherman tank to survive anywhere.

Named in honour of Michael Dewar, head of the British Tank Mission in Washington, this pre-production M4A1 Sherman, *MICHAEL*, mounts the shorter M2 gun. It is shown half-on and half-off a transporter on Horse Guards Parade in London. Now an exhibit at the Tank Museum, Bovington, it is probably the oldest Sherman tank to survive anywhere.

A cast-hulled M4A1 of HQ 4th Armoured Brigade in Holland, cluttered up with a fair amount of additional stowage.

An M4A1 of 4th Armoured Brigade shortly after landing in Normandy. Note how the rearmost section of skirting has been attached to the rear deck and used for stowage – in this case mostly of extra petrol containers.

Sherman tanks in British service (mostly at this stage the M4A1 and M4A2 types) first saw action at the battle of El Alamein in October 1942. They had started to arrive in Egypt in August and September 1942 but were not able to go into action immediately. First they had to pass through workshops to have various items fitted that British experience in the desert had proved necessary. These included mild steel sand guards along each side and stowage bins fitted to the back of the turret, plus of course a suitable desert camouflage. While the tanks were being modified British crews had to be trained to operate them. In action the 75mm turret-mounted gun gave them an advantage over the majority of German and Italian tanks, although inevitably some Shermans were knocked out, particularly because they were somewhat taller than contemporary British types. This was due to the fact that the driveshaft, from the upright radial engine, was inevitably quite high but still had to pass beneath the rotating turret basket. At the front the transmission was the same as the M3 Medium, and at the risk of repeating ourselves, comprised a five-speed and reverse synchromesh gearbox driving into a controlled differential transmission that provided steering. These features were the same in all marks of Sherman, irrespective of the engine fitted.

Although never as numerous as some types of Sherman in British service, notably welded-hull types such as the M4A2 (Sherman III) and M4A4 (Sherman V), the cast-hulled M4A1 (or Sherman II) remained in service until the end of the war. It served particularly with the Royal Scots Greys, 3rd County of London Yeomanry and 44th Royal Tank Regiment in 4th Armoured Brigade. Indeed the brigade commander, Brigadier Michael Carver, had his own Sherman II command tank when the brigade was operating in north-west Europe.

This is said to be the command tank of Brigadier R.M.P. Carver when he commanded 4th Armoured Brigade. The tank is an old Sherman II (M4A1) but the additional aerials on the turret give it away.

An M4A2, the diesel-powered version, crossing the river Volturno in Italy, with a deep wading air outlet fitted at the back.

THE M4A2

The diesel-powered M4A2 was actually the first Sherman tank to enter production with a welded hull. The degree of welding required on the front of the tank, due to the awkward shape around the driver's and hull machine-gunner's positions among other things, meant that the front, (despite also being around 2in thick) was more vulnerable then it needed to be, due to the welds being weaker than the armour plate. There was no simple solution to this problem, which affected all welded versions of the tank to one degree or another, until the new 47-degree front plate was introduced early in 1944.

M4A2 tanks were assembled by the Fisher Tank Arsenal in Michigan and the Pullman Standard Car Company in Indiana to begin with. The M4A2 was powered by the General Motors Model 6046 12-cylinder, water-cooled diesel (rated at 375hp) which was formed from two six-cylinder General Motors Model 6-71 truck engines mounted side-by-side, as first seen in the M3A3 and M3A5 tanks. It is said that the idea of using a pair of diesel engines derived from evaluation of the A12 Matilda tank *Grampus* that was sent from Britain to Aberdeen Proving Ground in September 1940, but more immediately it was the desire to find an improved source of power for the Sherman tank and to reduce the demand for Wright/Continental radial engines that were also required for aviation purposes.

Diesel fuel was an added complication that the Americans felt they could do without, so it was laid down that the US Army should only use petrol-fuelled tanks in service. Tanks with diesel engines were mainly to be used for training at home or for export to the Soviet Union or the United Kingdom. American troops did use some diesel-powered Shermans in Tunisia and the M4A2 was one of the mainstays of the armoured element of the US Marine Corps.

Robin Hood, a smartly finished M4A2 (late production) of the Sherwood Foresters, making its way along a crowded street. Notice the white-painted interiors to the hatch covers and the additional aerial at the front.

In British service, where no such inhibitions applied, the M4A2 was classified as the Sherman III. It was liked for its improved power over Shermans fitted with the Wright radial petrol engine, and its greater speed. At least with hindsight the

M4A2, or Sherman III, appears to have been the most popular Sherman with British crews, although it was said to be the heaviest Sherman of all at 31.3 tons, presumably due to the power unit. However, one has to remember that most men were biased in favour of the tank they served in, so such opinions may not constitute reliable evidence. The tank certainly saw a lot of service, in North Africa, in Italy and in north-west Europe, although the most convincing evidence of their suitability for service, at least as far as reliability and durability were concerned, was Exercise *Dracula*, held in Britain in the late summer of 1943. It tested the British cruiser tanks Cromwell and Centaur, and the American Sherman tanks M4A2 and M4A4; all were required to cover about 2,000 miles on the roads around Bovington before a gunnery trial at Lulworth. The M4A2 was consistently the best performer with the M4A4 a close second; it had to stop to refuel each day, which the diesel-powered tank did not, while the British tanks demanded a lot of maintenance *en route* – especially the underpowered Centaur. No diesel Fireflies or Crab flail tanks were ever built, and diesel Duplex Drive swimming tanks were not available until after D-Day, as explained in the next chapter.

As time went by the M4A2 was subjected to many of the developments included on other Shermans. These included a one-piece transmission cover at the front, replacing the three-piece bolted type fitted to earlier models, and a revised system of dispersing exhaust gases and cooling air that reduced the amount of dust thrown up behind the moving tank.

THE M4A3

Although generally regarded as an American tank, seven M4A3 tanks (which would have been designated Sherman IV in British service) are said to have been sent over to Britain for examination. It was powered by a Ford Model GAA engine of V8 configuration, petrol-fuelled and water-cooled and rated at 450hp. It was never used in action by British forces. Only samples were shipped over for evaluation.

THE M4A4

Despite the popularity and longevity of the M4A2, the M4A4 or Sherman V is always regarded as the 'British Sherman'. Built by Chrysler Motors at their Detroit

BELOW LEFT An almost overhead view of an M4A3 in the United States with what looks like a T23-series tank beyond. Powered by a Ford GAA V8 engine, the M4A3 was almost exclusively an American tank, only seven sample tanks being supplied to Britain.

BELOW Although M4A3 tanks (Sherman IV to the British) arrived in Britain in large numbers, they were destined for American service. This photo shows a huge tank park, probably in the west of England, but notice that these tanks have their machine guns stored out of sight.

War Admiral was a Sherman V (M4A4) of 1st Canadian Army Tank Brigade near Mileto in Italy.

Tank Arsenal from July 1942 until September 1943, the M4A4 featured the massive Chrysler A57 multibank engine, rated at 370hp. The engine was in fact composed of five Chrysler six-cylinder car engines arranged, radial fashion, around a common crankcase. The result was a 30-cylinder engine, always rather tiresome to service and of such bulk that it filled even the enlarged engine bay, from which it had to be removed in order to service adjacent items. Changes were also made in the size and location of the fuel tanks for the same reason. The bigger engine and enlarged engine compartment also affected the hull of the tank which was 11in longer, which in turn meant that the suspension units were more widely spaced – although this had already been seen in the Chrysler-built M3A4 with the same multibank engine.

Thus the M4A4 was a very distinctive tank, although it was not popular in the United States on account of the engine and was relegated to a training role. Of 7,499 built the majority were despatched under the Lend-Lease agreement to the United Kingdom where they seem to have been tremendously popular, many serving as Firefly, Crab flail or Duplex Drive amphibious tanks. Its longevity and reliability were attributed to the very high standard of maintenance by British crews along with careful driving techniques.

An M4A4 or Sherman V serving with Guards Armoured Division in Holland towards the end of World War II.

Like the M4A2, the Sherman V was somewhat heavier than its siblings in the

Sherman family – 31.1 tons against 31.3 tons for the diesel version. In this case it was probably accounted for by the bulky engine and longer hull, although the spaced-out suspension increased the length of track on the ground and led to an overall reduction in ground pressure. It saw service in north-west Europe, Italy and Burma, where a number were supplied to the Chinese Army.

LEFT An M4 (Sherman I) at a depot in Britain, shortly after it arrived from the United States and still with its American serial numbers at the back.

ABOVE *Fox*, an M4 Sherman of the Royal Marine Armoured Support Group heading a column of Centaurs, inland from the D-Day beaches.

THE M4 AND HYBRID

This was effectively a sister tank to the M4A1, similarly powered by the Continental R-975 C1 engine, but with a welded instead of a cast upper hull. The M4 was slightly heavier, but a little roomier inside which allowed a modest increase in ammunition stowage. Although first built by the Pressed Steel Car Company in the summer of 1942, it did not enter British service until later in 1943 and never saw service with the British Army in the Western Desert or Tunisia. Even so it was classified as the Sherman I in accordance with its American designation, and 2,073 of these tanks were recorded as being in British service by December 1944. By this time the longer M3 gun was the standard 75mm weapon in Sherman tanks, with the M34A1 gun mount that featured a full-width mantlet (or shield rotor as the Americans called it).

In August 1943 Chrysler's enormous Detroit Tank Arsenal had started building M4 tanks and by the end of that month had introduced a new version fitted with a cast hull front, which may have been done to overcome the vulnerability of the welded front. This was known as the Sherman I Hybrid to the British and quite a number were ultimately converted into Fireflies, mounting the big British 17-pounder gun. Although they could be seen on most types of Sherman tank in British or American service, panels of applique armour are often associated with this particular version of the Sherman tank. Usually factory-fitted, the applique armour consisted of three pieces of armour 1in thick, covering areas where ammunition was stowed inside the tank – one panel on the right side and two on the left.

A Sherman I Hybrid photographed near Rauray. While some of the crew watch, infantrymen dig a trench. The line where the cast front is welded onto the rolled side is clearly shown.

Another view of a Sherman I Hybrid. These tanks were built at the Detroit Tank Arsenal from August 1943.

Additional external armour was also added to the front of the turret where internal armour had been ground away to make gun control equipment more accessible, and – on welded tanks only – to the front of the hull, to enhance their protection.

THE 105MM SHERMAN

Although there was a high-explosive round for the 75mm gun in the Sherman the Americans also introduced a 105mm weapon which was installed in a version of the M4 (Sherman I) tank. Production began in February 1944 and was terminated in March 1945. Of the 1,600-odd tanks built around half, completed later, were fitted with wider tracks and the new horizontal volute suspension. The earlier ones, with the old vertical volute suspension, did at least have the new-style hulls with 47-degree sloped frontal armour, enlarged driver's and co-driver's hatches – and without any of the bulges that characterized earlier Shermans. All 105mm gun tanks (including an M4A3 version) were built at Chrysler's Detroit Tank Arsenal.

An M4 with the 105mm gun on the road in Italy, rather overloaded with infantry passengers. The type was not popular in British service because it was said to be too complicated.

They were classified as assault tanks to provide immediate artillery support to armoured formations rather than close-support tanks after the British style. The 105mm howitzer Model M4 was a weapon designed for high-angle, curved-trajectory fire at a relatively low velocity, so although a High Explosive Anti-

Tank (HEAT) round was included in the tank's ammunition inventory it proved very difficult to hit such a target except at minimal range. High-explosive rounds were supplied as two-piece ammunition (projectile and cartridge case) for which a selection (up to seven) of charges were available, depending on the range required. Round and cartridge case were then brought together and loaded in the normal way. To begin with the tanks had only manual traverse for the turret and complaints started to pour in. However, it took longer to develop an Oilgear power traverse for the 105mm turret than had been anticipated, and with the end of the war approaching nothing could be done to improve matters.

Styled 'Sherman IBY', this is a late-model M4 (Sherman I) armed with a 105mm howitzer. It features horizontal volute suspension, a 47-degree angled hull front and pivoting gun cradle. It arrived in Britain as a sample towards the end of the war and now lives at the Tank Museum.

An M4 Sherman with a 105mm howitzer and the insignia of the Gunnery School emblazoned on the turret side, photographed at Lulworth Camp.

ABOVE Sherman IIA (76mm) of the celebrated Snake Troop of B Squadron, 2nd Royal Tank Regiment in Italy; the three tanks were named *Asp, Anaconda* and *Adder.*

ABOVE RIGHT A view of a Sherman IIA (76mm) under test in Italy. Note the absence of a muzzle brake on the 76mm gun and the round commander's hatch on the far side of the new-style turret.

In British service the 105mm Sherman I tank is mostly associated with Italy, although it does not appear to have been particularly popular. The 17th/21st Lancers history, for instance, mentions it as follows:

> A new weapon arrived at this time [c. September 1944] – the Sherman fitted with the 105mm gun howitzer for close support. These were issued to squadrons and Regimental Headquarters in the same role as the old 3in Crusaders in Africa. The 105mm HE (High Explosive) shell was considerably bigger than the 75mm, and the smoke shell was particularly effective. However, it was too complicated a weapon for tank use, since the need to use varying charges at different ranges made the tank commander's task more suited to an artilleryman; and though much research was done to get a simple general-purpose setting, the weapon remained redundant until the end of the war, and then 75mm would have done the task just as well.

Exactly how typical this was of British or other non-American Sherman regiments in Italy is difficult to say, although Americans in Italy and north-west Europe appear to have been able to use it without any difficulty. The writer was wrong in claiming that it was a close-support weapon – it was more a piece of self-propelled artillery mounted in a tank, which is why separate zone charges were supplied.

At least one sample 105mm Sherman went to the Gunnery School at Lulworth for evaluation, but the type was turned down by the British authorities for service in north-west Europe. Even so, 105mm tanks were included with other Lend-Lease shipments anyway. Most of these appear to have been handed over to the Canadians, who proposed converting them into Observation Post tanks for artillery use, although as far as one can tell this was never done. A single surviving M4 (105mm) with horizontal volute suspension, or Sherman IBY in British service, was for some time displayed at the front of the Tank Museum, but now is in store.

THE 76MM GUN SHERMAN

Since the ideal tank, the Sherman Firefly, was always in relatively short supply, Shermans with the new 76mm gun were supplied to regiments in Italy as an alternative. This is not to say that some Fireflies did not reach Italy, and see service with British, New Zealand, South African and even Polish regiments. But there were never really enough of them and so the difference was made up with 76mm gun

The sample Sherman III (76mm) with horizontal volute suspension. This tank is now part of the Tank Museum collection, and in first-class running order.

tanks, even though the performance of the 76mm weapon was inferior to the 17-pounder (76.2mm) of the Firefly, although it was possibly more accurate.

The version supplied to Britain was the Sherman IIA, the M4A1 (76mm) in American parlance. This was fitted with a new-style cast upper hull and new T23 turret; the M1A1 version of the 76mm gun (without muzzle brake); the C4 version of the Continental R-975 engine, which was slightly more powerful; but the old-style vertical volute suspension. It was also the first type of 76mm gun Sherman to enter production, initially by the Pressed Steel Car Company. Probably the most famous of these tanks were those of Snake Troop of B Company, 2nd Royal Tank Regiment, in Italy, with tanks *Adder*, *Anoconda* and *Asp*.

Although the 76mm gun Sherman never entered British service in north-west Europe they did serve (again as the Sherman IIA) with 1st Polish Armoured Division. Britain also received up to five samples of the diesel-powered M4A2 (76mm) tank with horizontal volute suspension, designated Sherman IIIAY in British service, one of which has survived and is now in the Tank Museum collection.

COMMAND, CONTROL AND OBSERVATION POST TANKS

The Royal Armoured Corps converted some tanks into Command, Control or Rear Link roles, some with the main armament removed and replaced by a dummy to permit more space inside the turret. Additional wireless sets were often carried, their presence indicated by extra radio aerials. They were later joined by locally modified Contact tanks, which included a Royal Air Force officer who maintained contact with 'cab rank' fighter-bombers that were called down when necessary. Some tanks were placed at the disposal of Royal Artillery officers for use as mobile observation posts. Indistinguishable at a glance from any other tank in the regiment, Observation Post tanks normally carried no gun (just a dummy barrel), had extra wireless sets inside and were fitted out with map tables and stowage lockers.

T146410

THE FUNNIES

Two of the better known British variations of the Sherman, the Crab flail tanks and the Duplex Drive amphibian, are examined in later chapters. Here we are only going to mention some lesser-known variants, most of which never saw active service. Only tanks that retained their turrets and guns are considered. The Anti-Mine Reconnaissance Castor Roller Attachment (or AMRCRA) was a frame, pushed ahead of a tank, and running on four castoring rollers. The idea was to explore the limits of a minefield with rollers that detonated mines without harming the tank; one version, the No 1A Mark I was designed to be attached to a Sherman tank but apart from a prototype, was never used.

CIRD was the Canadian Indestructible Roller Device which employed heavy rollers on sprung arms which were thrown off-centre by the explosion of a mine and reset by the tank itself. Shermans equipped with CIRDs were landed on D-Day but never used, being damaged. The intention was to use them in conjunction with Crab flails to locate minefields. Either a CIRD-equipped Sherman or a Crab flail was used to test another mine-clearing device called Tapeworm. This was a trailer-mounted hose, towed by the Sherman. Leaving the trailer on the edge of a minefield, the tank proceeded across, pulling the hose behind it. Once across, the hose was pumped full of liquid explosive and detonated to explode more mines. But there is no account of it ever being used.

Conger worked on the same principle. This time the hose was carried in a gutted Universal Carrier, without an engine, towed by a Churchill or Sherman tank. The 2in hosepipe, 300ft long, was launched across the minefield by a 5in rocket. Having been detached from the carrier, which was towed out the way, the hose was pumped full of nitro-glycerine and detonated, exploding adjacent mines by sympathetic detonation. When used once in Holland the whole thing blew up, killing a number of people including nearby civilians, after which it was never used again. Snake was a rigid tubular device composed of sections of Bangalore torpedo joined together. It was transported separately and pushed across a minefield by a Sherman tank using a length of chain slung underneath. Not so lethal as Conger, it was taken to north-west Europe and may have been used operationally.

A Sherman was also fitted with the mine-detecting device Lulu, but this was too fragile and easily damaged so it was never used. Two anti-mine ploughs, normally fitted to Churchill tanks, were also tested on the Sherman. One was the Bullshorn Mark III, as promoted by the 79th Armoured Division. It consisted of a system of ploughshares mounted on a framework, pushed ahead of the tank. The other was the Jefferis MD1 (Ministry of Defence 1) plough, named after the redoubtable Colonel Millis Jefferis who controlled the organization that designed it. Very similar to the Bullshorn device, it was capable of being folded back when not in use, although it never seems to have been adopted despite Millis Jefferis being a favourite of the Prime Minister.

One major modification carried out in Britain involved M4A4 (Sherman V) No. T-148350 being fitted with an experimental suspension by Mr Horstmann of Slow Motion Suspension Ltd of Bath. Although said to have been better for cross-country operation than the existing vertical volute system it was never proceeded with.

Other British modifications that arrived too late included a form of skirting plate to protect the suspension and the British version of the All Round Vision cupola which, by means of an adaptor ring, could be fitted in place of the flush commander's hatch on the Sherman.

OPPOSITE Sherman Vs (M4A4) demonstrating the Bullshorn Mark III plough device for unearthing mines. This device was used in action on D-Day, albeit attached to a Churchill AVRE.

OPPOSITE A Sherman V (M4A4) pushing the Anti-Mine Reconnaissance Castoring Roller Attachment frame ahead of it. As a means of crossing an entire minefield it was of dubious value but for reconnaissance, for discovering the edge of a minefield, it was just about acceptable.

CHAPTER 4

FIREFLY: THE 17-POUNDER SHERMAN

Anyone who studies tank history is, in the end, bound to conclude that the most important feature of any tank is its gun. True, there are other factors. If you're a member of the crew, then protection comes high on the list. Those who conduct battles would favour excellent mobility, while others will be heard demanding greater reliability, improved communications, or longer range. All of these things are important. But when it comes down to it, the gun is what it is all about, and that gun, in the majority of cases, is required to be particularly good at destroying other tanks.

There are reasons why British tank armament failed to keep pace in the early years of World War II. Some of them are justifiable, but the majority are not. In summer 1940, following the dramatic events culminating in the fall of France, MajGen Vyvyan Pope told the War Office that the next generation of tanks would need more powerful guns. The trouble was that the next generation of tanks, particularly the Crusader, had already been designed around the existing 2-pounder gun (see *British Battle Tanks: British-made Tanks of World War II*), and nobody seems to have considered making arrangements for improving things if and when a new gun became available.

That had to wait until a further generation of tanks, typified by the Cromwell, appeared (see *British Battle Tanks: British-made Tanks of World War II*), but this took so long to happen that the tank was already out of date when it entered service, and once again, the designers had failed to build in the ability to improve, should a better weapon appear. Of course, the Cromwell was a special case. Its introduction had been delayed by the need to replace tanks lost in France, and the same was true of its gun, the 57mm 6-pounder. British practice, since the advent of the 2-pounder, was to design a gun to fit a field carriage, and once that was in production, to alter the gun to suit a tank mounting.

Yet production of the 6-pounder was in arrears while the Army's lost stock of 2-pounder anti-tank guns was replaced. As a result, although the new cruiser tank, the Cromwell, was designed to take the 6-pounder, by the time it was considered fit

31 August 1944: a Firefly of Guards Armoured Division crossing the railway at Beaurains. A good deal of foliage, held in place by a net, has been draped over the hull with similar applications over the turret and gun. Spare track links appear on the front of the hull and sides of the turret, but most obvious of all is the Prong device at the front, a variation on Sgt Culin's inspired design. All are suggestive of service in the Bocage country.

for service, the priority had changed. The dedicated anti-tank gun was out of favour for tanks, and in any case, with regular ammunition, the 6-pounder was effectively out of date. Thus, no Cromwell tank ever actually went into action with the 6-pounder, which for other reasons, was something of a pity.

THE 17-POUNDER

The Ministry of Information film *A Date with a Tank*, released in 1944, offered a dramatic portrayal of the design and construction of the first batch of 17-pounder anti-tank guns against a deadline to have some of them in the field before the rumoured German heavy tank, the PzKpfw VI Tiger, put in an appearance. There was an element of truth in this, although the timescale was shortened for dramatic effect.

Thinking in the Royal Artillery was far ahead of those responsible for designing British tanks. This is illustrated by the fact that the very first requirement for an anti-tank gun of about 3in calibre, firing a projectile weighing about 17lb, was being considered as early as 21 November 1940. That was a year before the first 6-pounder anti-tank gun – the weapon it was due to supersede – entered production.

In the meantime, just to confuse the issue, British tank and gun designers had been led away from the true path by unfortunate experience and heretical foreign practice. The experience was Gen Erwin Rommel's habit of intermingling tanks and anti-tank guns, and the latter, being small and inconspicuous, were difficult targets for a gun that only fired a small calibre round of solid shot. The heresy, which came

SHERMAN VC FIREFLY, 21ST ARMOURED REGIMENT, 4TH CANADIAN ARMOURED BRIGADE, 4TH CANADIAN ARMOURED DIVISION, NOVEMBER 1944

The idea that adding surplus track links to your tank could improve the armour protection seems to be universal. It could be found applied to British tanks in Gaza in 1917 and on Challenger tanks in the Gulf in 1991; but it reached a high point in World War II, most particularly among Canadian armoured regiments who in effect covered their Shermans with whatever type of track they could find. A British officer who studied the phenomenon at the time pronounced it totally ineffective. All it did, in his view, was to increase the weight of the tank to an unacceptable level. However, he also recognized that it was a symptom of the crews' lack of confidence in the armour of their tanks. Indeed, he said, crews had firm beliefs in how these track links should be arranged and attached. Some believed that the tracks should be fixed with the outer surface outwards; others insisted that the inner surface should face outwards so that incoming rounds might be deflected by raised portions. Then there were those who welded the tracks to the hull, while others recommended that they should hang loose and absorb some of the impact. Whatever the system, the tracks added a fair amount of weight to a tank that was already overloaded, but they seem to have survived. Markings, of course, were totally obscured. Under the Canadian system armoured regiments were simply numbered, but all had fine traditional titles; 21st Armoured Regiment was the prosaic alternative for the Governor General's Foot Guards. In October and November 1944 they were in action east of Bruges, up to the Scheldt estuary. (Art by Tony Bryan, © Osprey Publishing)

as a package with successive American medium tank designs, was the belief that tanks should be a form of mobile artillery to support the infantry first and secondly, an anti-tank gun, since that role, according to American doctrine, was reserved for something that looked like a tank but wasn't a tank, known optimistically as a Tank Destroyer. Thus an American tank gun of this period was a dual-purpose weapon capable of firing both high explosive and armour-piercing ammunition. It was pounced upon with delight by British tank crews as an antidote to Rommel's anti-tank gun menace, and for a while at least, something that could match German armour in a tank-versus-tank fight. Yet the Germans were soon ahead of the game once more. In summer 1942, they introduced an improved version of the Panzer IV with a long, high-velocity anti-tank gun that opened up fighting ranges even more and placed the British at a disadvantage yet again. It is probably worth remarking at this stage that German schemes to up-gun their existing tanks not only did so without affecting the tank's general performance, but they also involved improvements in armour protection.

SHERMAN IC FIREFLY WITH TULIP ROCKETS, C SQUADRON, 1ST COLDSTREAM GUARDS, GUARDS ARMOURED DIVISION, NEAR BREMEN, 12 APRIL 1945

During the fighting in the Rhineland, over the winter of 1944–45, 1st Battalion The Coldstream Guards acquired some rockets and launching rails normally fitted beneath the wings of Hawker Typhoon fighters for use in the ground attack role. Not having enough to equip the entire regiment, the regimental fitters were told to fit them to the tanks of C Squadron, Fireflies and regular Shermans alike. It was a peculiar thing to do. The rockets with their 60lb warhead were devastating enough but, even when fired from a diving aircraft, were not renowned for their precision or accuracy. Launched from a tank, which had to halt in order to fire, they were wildly inaccurate but most spectacular. In our drawing one of C Squadron's Fireflies has just fired a Tulip, as the rockets were called, and awaits the result. The rockets were suspended from launching rails on either side of the turret, aimed using the tank commander's sighting vane and then fired electrically. With no other velocity behind it the rocket first dips, then picks up speed and races away in the general direction of the target. There is no evidence that a rocket was ever fired at a German AFV, which it probably would not have hit in any case – if it had the results might have been quite impressive. The missiles were usually used against manned road blocks or woods where enemy troops might be hiding and the effect was salutary. Road blocks were simply blown away, while anyone who thought they were safe in a wood invariably changed their minds and surrendered after they had experienced a rocket or two from the receiving end. Whether the attachments were ever worth the trouble of fitting, the risks of carrying them is another matter altogether. (Art by Tony Bryan, © Osprey Publishing)

Clearly, as far as the British were concerned, the time had come to adopt the 17-pounder as a tank gun, although at this time no suitable tank was available. Whose fault was that? Historically, since about 1943, the British have been castigated for their failure to match the Germans in the design of heavy, big-gun tanks. It is only fair to point out that at a Tank Board meeting held in London on 9 December 1941, the idea was discussed of fitting the new 17-pounder into a tank. It has been suggested that this is associated with General Staff specification A29 calling for a 45-ton tank – a large cruiser – with a 17-pounder armament and what are described rather vaguely as 'twin tracks'. This was to be a Rolls-Royce project, which may well be so, but proof is lacking. What we do know is that A29 was dropped in favour of another 17-pounder design, based upon the Cromwell and known as A30 and that work on this tank got under way in 1942. Tanks do not spring out of the ground fully formed, nor grow on trees, and even under the pressures of war there is a long period between the idea of a tank being mooted and its ultimate appearance. This may well explain

TOP Lulworth was undoubtedly the spiritual home of the Firefly, and this VC sports the cannon insignia of the Royal Armoured Corps Gunnery School. It is an early conversion, fitted with brackets for the Houseboat disguise. Note also the patch of armour used to seal off the redundant hull machine gun aperture.

BELOW RIGHT An official photo of another early VC conversion that also has the Houseboat brackets. Compared with the prototype, viewed from more or less the same angle, note the support for the open loader's hatch, the access panels on top of the radio box, and the barrel support in the centre of the rear deck.

the preference for A30, which was largely a modification to an existing design, rather than something entirely new.

Even so, the progress of A30 from concept to finished article was long and wearisome. In the meantime, the Tank Board and the General Staff laid down specifications for two more 17-pounder tanks, the short-term A34, later to become the Comet, and the long-term A41, the future Centurion. Both were proposed in summer 1943, and both would turn out to be excellent tanks of their kind. Yet the former would only be ready in time to see a few weeks' service before the war with Germany ended and the latter just too late to take part at all. What mattered to the Allied tank men was the here and now.

7 June 1944: a Firefly and other Shermans of A Squadron 3rd County of London Yeomanry form up after landing on D+1, inland from their landing point at Mont Fleury. The Firefly in the foreground has a stowage box across the front, a camouflage net on the turret, and a muzzle cover on the end of the gun.

DEVELOPMENTS AT LULWORTH

The credit for initiating the design of what became the Sherman Firefly should probably go to a Royal Tank Regiment major named George Brighty who in 1943 was based at the Royal Armoured Corps Gunnery School at Lulworth in Dorset. Despite the fact that A30, the official Challenger in name and practice, was already undergoing initial gunnery trials at Lulworth, Brighty seems to have been convinced that the Sherman was a better mount for the 17-pounder. But he was stymied by the turret, which was too small and cramped to accept the big gun, and in particular, the substantial recoil system that would be required in a tank. Brighty was almost certainly working on an unofficial basis, and it would be interesting to know how he got hold of a tank, particularly one he intended to butcher in order to prove his case.

This was the stage Brighty had reached when he was joined by an old colleague, another Royal Tank Regiment major named George Witheridge who, as it happened, was also bent on improving the firepower of the Sherman. The difference was that Witheridge had experienced the inadequacy of the firepower of British and American tanks first hand. He was in the Western Desert in Africa, commanding C Squadron of 3rd RTR, when he was blown out of his Grant at the battle of Gazala in May 1942. It was probably no accident that the first Grant tanks to arrive in the Middle East went to 3rd RTR if George Witheridge was with the regiment. The Grant was the tank that first expanded the British experience of tank gunnery, in particular the use of high explosive rounds, which Witheridge seems to have been concerned with at this time.

Although he recovered from his wounds, George Witheridge was not considered fit to return to combat duty. So, based upon his pre-war experience with experimental gunnery at Lulworth, Witheridge soon found himself appointed to the Middle East Gunnery School in Egypt. While there he met Gen Jacob Devers, probably one of the most underrated American armour officers. Devers must have been impressed

SHERMAN VC FIREFLY *BEUTE-PANZER*

It is not entirely clear how many Fireflies fell into German hands in serviceable condition. At least four have been identified from photographs, all M4A4 VC, and of these one is known to have come from 4th County of London Yeomanry at Villers-Bocage. Another appears to have been Canadian. Whether any of them saw combat in the hands of their new owners is unclear but the number would be limited due to the lack of ammunition. It seems more likely that, if they were used at all it would have been as decoys or stalking horses. The tank represented here appears to have been used mainly for evaluation, familiarization and recognition purposes. With surviving black-and-white photographs as the only source of information it would be unwise to attempt any definitive statements about camouflage colours although it is probably safe to say that they would not be as exotic as some representations suggest. On the other hand our subject shows no evidence of British markings so it may well have been over-painted. Photographs show it being tested and examined by German troops and with the eye of faith it is possible to discern patches that could be different colours. However, apart from the German crosses, this artwork only represents one interpretation. (Art by Tony Bryan, © Osprey Publishing)

Naturally, there comes a time when everyone must rest and the gramophone comes out, but where do you stow a gramophone and records on a tank? This Hybrid IC, probably belonging to 5th RTR, is overloaded with stores and heavily camouflaged about the turret.

16 July 1944: a classic view of a 1st Northamptonshire Yeomanry Firefly in the Odon Valley, west of Caen. The Firefly is a IC fitted with the T62 type ribbed-metal track design. The British had a poor opinion of the alternative rubber block track.

because he invited Witheridge to spend some time at Fort Knox, Kentucky, to advise on tank gunnery techniques. The British officer's experience of American tanks in combat would also be seen as a strong recommendation. George Witheridge arrived at Knox on a six-month posting in January 1943.

In June 1943, George Witheridge returned to Lulworth, clearly sold on the value of American tanks, and in particular, the Sherman. For a year or more before the Grant arrived, British tank crews had been crying out for a tank gun that could fire both armour-piercing and high-explosive rounds. While he was in Egypt, we know that Witheridge was concerning himself primarily with the development of high explosive ammunition, and this can only have been reinforced by his time at Fort Knox, where the creed saw the tank more as an infantry support than an anti-tank weapon. The difference was that Witheridge was also concerned with improving the armour-piercing firepower of British tanks while retaining the ability to fire high explosive rounds. Witheridge tells us that after his stint at Fort Knox, he expected to go back to Egypt. Therefore his posting to Lulworth came as something of a surprise.

In January 1943, while Witheridge was in the United States, the Chief Inspector of Gunnery at Lulworth had many unkind things to say about the A30 Challenger; not specifically on the design, which was poor, but on the concept of a tank that was clearly designed to fight against other tanks to the virtual exclusion of anything else. This was the old British doctrine, and it had clearly been replaced, in many minds, by the American idea of the tank as a multi-purpose weapon. The trouble is, of course, that if anti-tank supremacy had to be sacrificed to achieve this, then there was clearly something wrong.

There are indeed a number of things that did not add up. One practical objection to the A30 Challenger that was raised at Lulworth concerned armour thickness. This had been sacrificed as a concession to weight in order to accommodate the larger gun and turret, even to the point where A30 was less well protected than the Cromwell from which it was derived. The Lulworth view on this was that a tank designed to fight other tanks, which of course A30 was, should also be well armoured so that it might survive a stand-up fight. But if that was to be the doctrine, why was George Brighty permitted to carry on with his work on the Sherman?

ABOVE 8 August 1944: battle debut of the 1st Polish Armoured Division. A long line of Shermans, with a Firefly in the foreground, prepare to play their part in the attack towards Falaise. The Poles were organized and administered as part of the British Army, so the number 51 indicates the senior regiment – 1st Polish Armoured Regiment – in 10th Polish Armoured Brigade.

ABOVE RIGHT 8 August 1944: a VC of 8th Armoured Brigade, probably 24th Lancers, near St Leger on the Bayeux–Caen road. Both turret hatches are open, but the crew are keeping their heads down so they may be anticipating action.

Not that Brighty was having an easy time of it. The 17-pounder would fit into the turret, but it seemed to be impossible, within the confined space available, to contain the recoil. The force was simply too great. There was a solution, but it had probably never been tried in a tank. This was to lock the gun firmly into the turret so that the recoil effect was absorbed by the mass of the tank and the cushioning effect of its suspension. Brighty tried it and it worked, but there was no telling how long a tank would last under such treatment.

This was the state of affairs when George Witheridge arrived. He inspected the A30 Challenger and joined the chorus of complaints about its design. Then he looked at what Brighty was up to and became distinctly nervous. This rigid gun mounting seemed to break all the rules. When he first test-fired it, Witheridge remained outside the turret and tugged on a lanyard. Having fired off three rounds this way, Witheridge saw nothing awful happening and climbed into the turret to fire seven more rounds. Even so, his advice to Brighty, for the benefit of future tank crews, was to continue work on developing a recoil system.

Whether the arrival of Witheridge at Lulworth attracted attention to Brighty's project or whether it was already known we cannot say, but it seems that not long after the former's arrival, a directive came down from the Department of Tank Design (DTD) that work on the up-gunned Sherman must cease. Again, it is difficult to say whether this was decided on technical grounds or because it might threaten the DTD's own project – A30. We may never know; maybe it was a bit of each.

Either way, this was not acceptable to George Witheridge. Possibly, he had been bitten by the bug because he was now clearly a convert to the idea of a 17-pounder Sherman, and unlike Brighty, he had friends in high places. MajGen Raymond Briggs, like George Witheridge and Brighty, was a Royal Tank Regiment officer, which counts for a lot, but he and Witheridge were also old desert hands (Briggs had commanded the 1st Armoured Division). In August 1943, Raymond Briggs was appointed Director Royal Armoured Corps (DRAC), and it seems that he approved of what was going on at Lulworth. Like Witheridge, Briggs was a firm advocate of

August 1944: a Sherman VC (M4A4) Firefly of Guards Armoured Division on the way east. The 'tracks' are taking a cross-country route to leave the roads free for wheeled transport. By this time, a number of regiments seem to have devised simple devices to support the gun in a forward position. This one also retains support brackets for the Houseboat disguise, although it never appears to have been used.

good tank gunnery, and in particular, he was keen to open up fighting ranges, which had been a serious problem for British tanks in the desert, in the face of long-range anti-tank guns.

To be fair, Briggs was not solely concerned with anti-tank fighting. Like Witheridge, he was also keen to develop what are known as indirect fire techniques, where the tanks act more like artillery, firing at targets they cannot actually see. This is normally associated with the use of high-explosive rounds, not armour piercing. On the other hand, work was heading in the right direction, and Briggs may have seen an opportunity to further his cause this way. After all, although it was primarily an anti-tank gun, the 17-pounder could fire a respectable high explosive shell out to a range of 10,000yds, and that must have appealed to Raymond Briggs.

Lacking the authority to set the ball rolling, Briggs put his case to Claude Gibb, the Director General of Weapon and Instrument Production at the Ministry of Supply, and gained his approval. As a result, however, the project was effectively taken out of the hands of the people at Lulworth and placed on an altogether more official footing. The days of the enthusiastic, gifted amateur were over. From now on, the professionals would move in.

DESIGNING THE FIREFLY

In fact, there was just one professional assigned to the project, a Mr W. G. K. Kilbourn, who at the time was assigned to the Department of Tank Design at Chertsey, although in normal times he was a professional engineer employed by Vickers. Not a great deal is known about him, but he must have been a gifted engineer because he tackled and solved the problems that had baffled Brighty; and indeed did it in an ingenious way.

In its regular role as an anti-tank gun, the 17-pounder employed a hydropneumatic recoil system with a travel of 40in., which was far too long for the cramped interior

SHERMAN VC FIREFLY, 2ND BATTALION IRISH GUARDS, GUARDS ARMOURED DIVISION, NETHERLANDS 1944

2nd Irish Guards' VC Firefly, copied from a snapshot taken by a local inhabitant during the liberation of the Netherlands. Many people have chalked slogans or their names onto the hull of the tank but the crew have gone one better and in bold letters written GEEN CIGARETTE on the side to discourage the locals from asking. The tank is entirely standard but there are some interesting details. Brackets holding jerrycans are fitted to each side of the turret radio box, and patches of appliqué armour have been welded to the side of the hull including the so-called 'cheek' pieces on the front quarters of the turret. They added 1in. to the armour in these areas although they did not, on the hull at least, exactly match the ammunition stowage arrangements of the Firefly, having been designed for the regular 75mm gun tank. Notice too that the second and third suspension units on this side feature the earlier, spoked-pattern road wheels. (Art by Tony Bryan, © Osprey Publishing)

of a Sherman turret. Kilbourn therefore decided to replace the existing recoil cylinders with shorter ones. They would be mounted either side of the gun tube, but above and below the centre line of the barrel on opposite sides, all in a special cradle. So far so good, but despite the shorter recoil movement, Kilbourn noticed that the barrel tube was not as well supported as it was on the towed gun because the cradle which he had designed, although totally surrounding the barrel, had inevitably been shortened in order to fit into the turret. The remedy for this was to increase the contact between the barrel and the cradle, and since it was patently impossible to lengthen the cradle, this would mean modifying the barrel tube.

A Firefly prototype or mock-up photographed at Chertsey. The gun may not be real, but a loader's hatch has been installed in the turret roof and the armoured container for the radios fitted at the rear, the lid for which is lying on the engine deck. The tank is an M4A4, or Sherman V, presumably the one that Kilbourn was working on.

1 September 1944: other elements of Guards Armoured Division reach Fouilly on the Somme. Here a standard 75mm Sherman is followed by a Firefly and what appears to be a turretless Stuart. The buildings in the background are French memorials to victims of the Somme fighting of 1916.

Artillerymen and gun makers have a vocabulary all their own, calling that part of a gun barrel that tapers forwards from the breech the 'chase'. Kilbourn reckoned that in order to improve contact with the cradle, it was necessary to extend the gun tube at a constant diameter, and in effect, move the chase further forward. This was a major engineering task: a sleeve had to be added to the barrel and then turned on a large lathe to produce the desired result.

If Kilbourn thought that he had solved the problem with these modifications to the gun he was wrong. The ingenuity he had employed to fit the weapon into the tank was commendable, but there were other matters to consider, in particular the crew and the ammunition. The big gun, with a strong recoil guard behind the breech, virtually divided the turret into two halves. This meant that the loader, on the left side of the gun, would find it very difficult to escape in a hurry if the tank were to be hit and brew up. It would mean wriggling under the gun, climbing onto the commander's seat, and then sliding out through his hatch. The solution was to create a hatch for the loader on the left side, which had another advantage: it made it a lot easier to pass the larger rounds that were required for the big gun into the turret for stowage.

These four gentlemen, we must suppose, are the individuals who produced the redesigned 17-pounder. Features to note are the reshaped rear end of the barrel, the sideways-operating breech block, and the new location of the spring case – low down on the near side of the breech ring.

And that was not all. When the US Army adopted the Sherman tank, following the appearance of the prototype T6 in September 1941, they also adopted the British practice of fitting the radio set in the rear of the turret rather than in the hull. The Americans used their SCR 508 set, which was somewhat larger than its British equivalent, although mounting brackets were provided for both. The British No.19 set, linked with the smaller No.38 set, was perched at the back of the turret where the loader, who doubled as wireless operator, could reach to manipulate the controls. Whether, as some say, a set in this position would actually be destroyed by the recoil movement of the 17-pounder is open to doubt, but it must have come too close for comfort and certainly too close for the loader to operate it properly.

The solution, which may or may not have been devised by Kilbourn, was to cut a hole in the armour at the back of the turret and then weld on an armoured box, large enough to contain the radios that were dropped in from above and then covered with a lid. It has to be said that the opening in the armour was hardly a work of art. In the preserved Firefly at the Tank Museum in Bovington, Dorset, it is a relatively small hole, very roughly cut, through which the loader had to reach in order to manipulate the knobs. That box, such an obvious protrusion on the back of the turret, is probably the best way of identifying a Sherman Firefly if you cannot see the gun.

The ammunition supplied for the 17-pounder was naturally larger and heavier than any previously carried in a British tank. Therefore it was particularly difficult to manage in the confines of a Sherman turret that it had not been designed to fit. An average round was 32.8in long (projectile and case together) and weighed 35.5lb. Even those rounds stowed within easy reach of the loader would have been difficult to load if the gun was mounted in the conventional way – with a vertical-acting breech block – because there was a risk of the cartridge case catching on something at the back of the turret before the pointed end of the projectile was properly lined up with the breech. One only has to imagine how awkward this could be in the middle of a tense action to realize that some improvement would be highly desirable.

The answer, and this is something we must attribute to Kilbourn, was to redesign the breech ring so that the block moved sideways, rather than up and down, which

22 September 1944: a partially camouflaged VC Firefly of the Irish Guards with a column of Shermans crossing the bridge at Nijmegen during the attempt to relieve Arnhem. Netting covers the hull front and turret of the Firefly, which also has vegetation attached to the gun tube, although it looks a bit incongruous here.

18 October 1944: 11th Armoured Division, probably 3rd RTR, east of Venray, with infantry aboard. A Firefly with some additional track across the front at the head of a troop of Shermans on a typically muddy road. The 17-pounder is unmasked, and there is a .30in. Browning machine gun on the commander's cupola.

in turn meant that the loader did not need to raise the round so high and could load it with a turning motion. This brings up another point that might not be obvious at first. In British tanks, at least since the start of World War II, the commander had been located on the left side of the turret, with the gunner in front of him and the loader on the right. These positions were reversed on the Sherman and most American tanks, so it was vital that the open side of the breech ring lay to the left.

That it was not simply a matter of turning the gun on its side may be seen from photographs where, among other things, the breech closing spring case has been relocated to the right side. In this form, the gun was designated 17-pounder, quick-firing Mark IV. Quick-firing indicating that it used one-piece ammunition. The plant selected to manufacture the new gun was the Royal Ordnance Factory, known locally as Barnbow, near Leeds. There had been a shell-filling factory at Barnbow in World War I, but this had been knocked down between the wars, and the site taken over by a coal mine. The new factory – officially Royal Ordnance Factory No.9 – had been built about a mile from the original site in 1939, and it was equipped to produce gun barrels.

This was all fairly conventional work since the guns were established types for which proper working drawings were available. The Mark IV 17-pounder was another matter. It was an urgent requirement, and when work began on the first two guns, the final assembly drawings were still being produced. It is difficult to date the period of Kilbourn's work except to say that it must have been from about August to early November 1943. The design team at Barnbow are a bit more specific in this respect. They tell us that the first drawings for what they called the 'SH-SH' gun were ready on 11 November 1943, and the first weapon was completed and issued to the Chief Inspector of Artillery on the 28th, followed two days later by the second gun. They were so proud of this that they lined up behind what was, presumably, the second gun and had themselves photographed for posterity. The prototype guns were successfully proof tested at Woolwich and Shoeburyness, clearing the way for production to commence.

Returning to ammunition, and by way of comparison, it should be noted that a typical 75mm round for a Sherman tank was about 26in. long, 6in. shorter than a 17-pounder round. Inevitably, it would mean that the ammunition stowage inside

August 1944: tiresome work on a warm summer day. A crew of C Squadron, 1st Northants Yeomanry top up the ammunition in their Firefly. It is going in through the redundant hull machine gunner's hatch and must be handled with the greatest care.

the Firefly would have to be rearranged to accommodate the new rounds. A regular 75mm gun M4A4 (Sherman V) had stowage for 97 main armament rounds, whereas the 17-pounder variant had racks to stow 78 rounds (although for practical reasons only 77 rounds would be carried).

Yet it was not simply a question of opening up the tank and stacking the rounds in wherever they would fit. Regular stowage arrangements had to be worked out that suited the tank and the location of the loader, not to mention the physical difficulties faced by the loader in handling the ammunition and getting it to the gun. The arrangement of stowage within a Sherman VC Firefly was eventually developed – in the turret itself were two small bins containing two and three rounds respectively. These were easy for the loader to access, and a skilled man could load them at the rate of six or seven seconds per round. Once they were used up, the loader turned to another bin, at his feet, which contained a further 18 rounds. In fact, the container had space for 20 rounds but two would be blocked by the gun mounting and could not be used. These rounds were stowed point-downwards at an angle of 40 degrees, pointing forwards. Once the turret floor plates that covered them had been removed, the rounds could be grasped by the base and dragged up onto the loader's lap – he was encouraged to sit when loading from this bin. Here he removed the protective clip from the base of the cartridge case and offered the round up to the breech of the gun. This motion took about nine or ten seconds. The only limitation when drawing rounds from this bin was the position of the turret relative to the ammunition stowage. As the turret turned, the floor panels covered the rounds, limiting those that the loader could reach. However, it was generally assumed that the tank's gun would be aimed across a relatively narrow frontal arc, so this problem was not regarded as serious. The chances of a Firefly in action having to traverse its turret more than a few degrees either side of 12 o'clock, let alone turn even further around – over its shoulder, as it were – did not appear to be very likely and could be discounted. To clarify this, if the main armament was pointing straight ahead in the at 12 o'clock position, then this 18-round bin could be reached with the gun pointing anywhere from 10 o'clock on the left side to 3 o'clock on the right.

Even so, we have not yet accounted for the bulk of the ammunition, all of which was much harder to get at. Forty rounds were stowed in a pair of bins beneath the turret floor on the right side, where the loader was never going to be able to reach them in normal combat conditions. To make matters worse, the rounds were stowed horizontally, in five layers of four rounds, so that they had to be gripped and lifted bodily upwards. As if this were not enough, this ammunition could only be removed from these bins when the turret was in a specific position. In the case of the foremost bin, the turret had to be turned to a point midway between four and five o'clock and then farther round to somewhere near eight o'clock to uncover the rear bin. These bins were therefore regarded as inaccessible in combat and were referred to as replenishment bins. All of which meant that under average circumstances, the gunner of a Firefly had just 23 rounds available to him, after which there would be a pause while the turret crew replenished the ready rounds.

We are left with just 15 more rounds to account for, at least in theory, and these are the cause of the final, rather more drastic, alteration to the basic Sherman. The bin for these 15 rounds was situated to the right of the driver, on the opposite side of the transmission, where the hull machine gunner would normally be situated. Since there was no one to fire it, the machine gun and its mounting were removed and a bevel-edged segment of armour welded over the aperture. This is another very obvious indication, if nothing else can be seen, that the tank in question is, or was, a Firefly.

However, if the two 20-round bins under the turret floor were difficult to access, this one was downright impossible. The rounds were stowed vertically, point upwards, which made them extremely difficult to get a decent grip on. To make matters worse, one location, at the back of the bin, was so difficult to get at, that it was not used, reducing the rounds available to 14. Furthermore, the five rearmost rounds were so difficult to remove and pass back into the turret that the normal drill – done only when the tank was out of action – was to pass them up through the absent hull machine gunner's hatch and then in through the loader's hatch. It was a task that involved at least three of the crew. This could be done with all 14 rounds although it was soon learned that with a bit of effort and contortion, the driver could reach over and pass back the nine rounds at the front of the bin into the turret without having to lift them outside the tank. Of course, this was only possible when the driver had nothing else to do.

If the processes outlined above seem to be organized and thoroughly worked out, it is probably true to say that this was more by accident than design. Although crews were instructed in the use of these new tanks before they went to war, this would have been done on just the barest minimum of experience, and it seems highly likely that the details were worked out by individual regiments in the field. Any effort to

OPPOSITE 19 November 1944: a well-composed photograph showing what is claimed to be C Squadron, Sherwood Rangers Yeomanry, in Geilenkirchen with an American serviceman in the foreground, symbolizing the close Anglo-American cooperation in the taking of this town. This Firefly, a IC Hybrid, is well camouflaged but displays no obvious markings at all.

December 1944: Lieutenant Boscawen's IC Hybrid of the 1st Coldstream Guards on the banks of the Meuse, acting as a backstop in the event of a German breakthrough. Camouflage netting appears to have been used on the rocket launchers on each side of the turret as well as on the turret itself, but it is a bit thin on the hull. Extended end connectors are fitted to the outside edge of each track.

standardize and formalize the practice had to wait until the end of the war. In July 1945, the Army Operational Research Group reported on a trial that it had run at Lulworth on stowage and loading of the 17-pounder gun in the Sherman VC. It seemed a strange time to do it, with the war over and the Sherman Firefly destined, as we know now, never to fire a shot in anger again in British service.

To round off the matter of turret armament, the gun mounting included a separate cradle, attached to the left side of the main cradle, which contained an M1919 Browning .30-in. machine gun, lined up to operate co-axially with the main gun. Both the 17-pounder and the Browning were fired electrically. Two buttons on the turret floor, within easy reach of the gunner's foot, enabled him to fire the machine gun by pressing down on the left button or fire the main armament by putting his boot on the right button. This last, however, was protected by a safety switch so that the mechanism would not operate during the loading process.

To the right of the main gun was another cradle that supported the gunner's sighting telescope, the No.43, x3 L, Mk I, which was calibrated for the 17-pounder and the machine gun. The gunner also had a pivoting periscope in the turret roof that

January 1945: one regiment nominated to take up defensive positions in the Ardennes was 1st Northamptonshire Yeomanry. At least three Fireflies are identifiable in this chilly scene. Despite icy and snowbound roads, the regiment played an active part in Operation *Mullet*, intended to drive the remaining Germans out of the area.

January 1945: Operation *Blackcock* and a snow-camouflaged IC Hybrid of 1st RTR has its gun cleaned in Schilberg. From this angle, the long gun looks very foreshortened. The crewmen are wearing the thick, warm tank suit. A couple of empty shell cases have been thrown down alongside the jerrycans on the right.

was linked to the gun itself so that it moved through the same arc of elevation (plus 25 to minus 5 degrees) as the main weapon. Finally, the turret also contained a 2-in. bomb thrower, as did most British tanks of this period. The weapon was mounted to the left of the gun, firing through a hole in the turret roof and was used to launch smoke grenades. It was controlled, in respect of range, by a valve that provided three options: 20yds, 70yds and 100yds. British stowage diagrams and a few photographs show Fireflies with a pair of the old 4-in. smoke dischargers attached externally to the right side of the turret, although these must have been rare.

THE CONVERSION PROGRAMME

Following inspection of a prototype 17-pounder Sherman, which was available from 6 January 1944, the War Office in London issued a requirement for a total of 2,100 of the up-gunned tanks. Four Royal Ordnance factories are known to have been involved in the work: Woolwich and Hayes in the London area, Radcliffe near Manchester, and Nottingham. The numbers reflected the preponderance of Shermans in British regiments at this time, and of course, Canadian and Polish regiments that were equipped from British stocks. However, the matter became more critical once it was appreciated that the rival A30 Challenger would not be ready in time for D-Day. It had already been agreed that in the interests of commonality, Challengers would only be issued to those regiments that were destined to field the British Cromwell tank. To that end, the total order for Challengers was limited to just 200. Yet despite a head start of at least 12 months, Challenger production was in arrears, and early trials had already revealed the need for modifications. Until such time as the Challenger could be declared fit for service, those regiments slated to receive it would also have to be given Fireflies.

Compared with the Sherman Firefly, the A30 Challenger has always received a bad press. There is no doubt that it inherited most of the frailties of the Cromwell from which it was derived, exacerbated by the nature of the conversion that seriously upset the original balance of the design. However, the most common complaint, that it was taller and therefore a more conspicuous target than the Firefly, can be shown quite simply to be false. The impression is created by the tall, flat-sided turret on a long, low hull, but that is an optical illusion.

Many sources published since the war imply that any type of Sherman could be converted to mount the 17-pounder, but this is entirely erroneous. In fact, there was

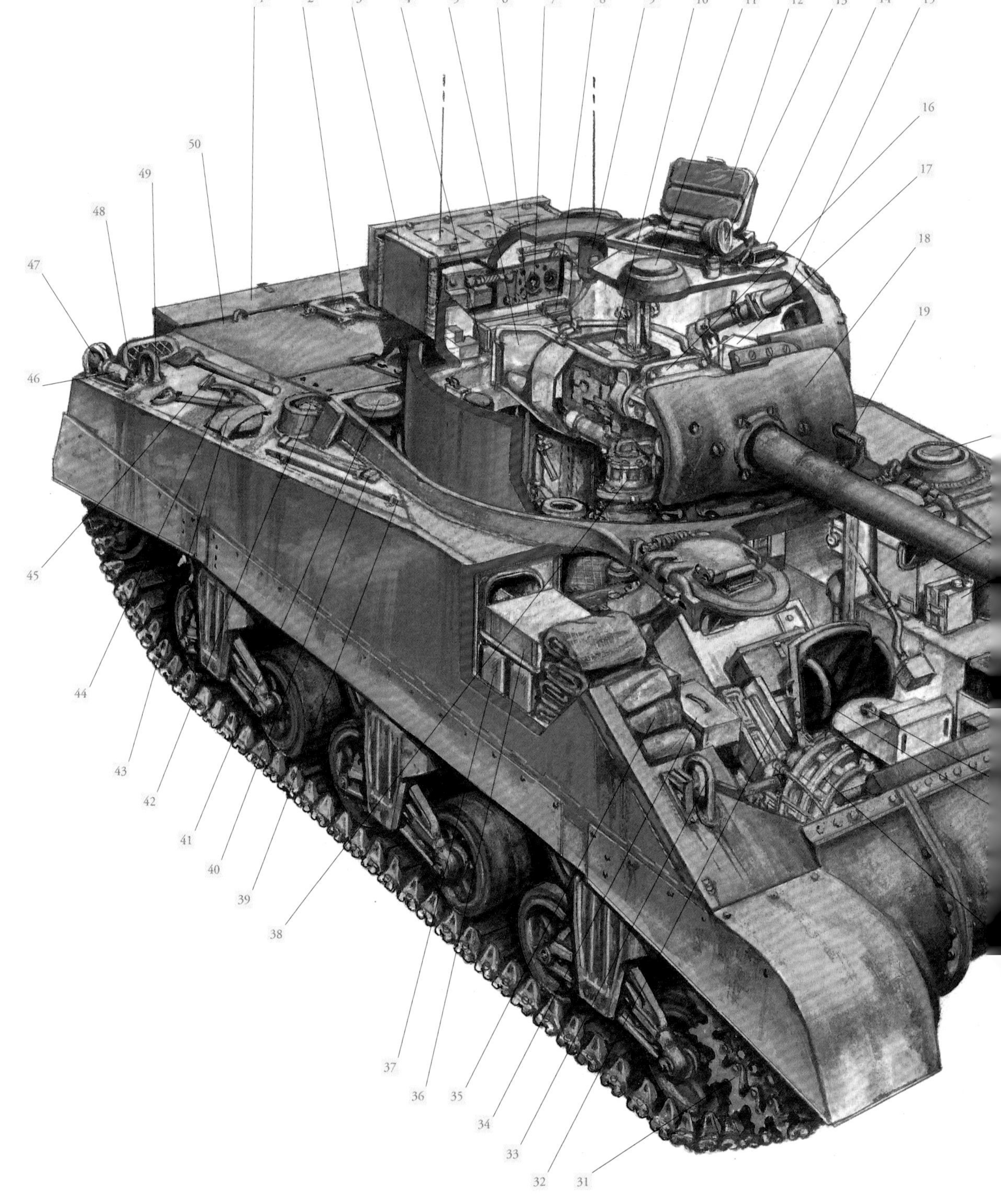
1
2
3
4
5
6
7
8
9
10
11
12
13
14
15
16
17
18
19
31
32
33
34
35
36
37
38
39
40
41
42
43
44
45
46
47
48
49
50

SHERMAN VC FIREFLY

The drawing shows how the gun dominated the tank, leaving very little room for the crew; the driver sat alone at the front, whilst the commander, gunner and loader were crammed into the turret. When it fired the whole tank rocked back on its suspension as the gun recoiled violently within the turret.

Key

1 Rear stowage box
2 Gun support crutch
3 Armoured radio box
4 First aid box
5 Gun recoil guard
6 Sub machine-gun ammunition
7 No.19 Wireless set
8 Hellensen lamp
9 Variometer, 'A' set aerial
10 17-pounder breech ring
11 Turret ventilator
12 Loader's hatch
13 Turret spot lamp
14 Loader's periscope
15 Two-inch bomb thrower
16 Gun mounting cradle
17 Hand grenade stowage
18 Gun mantlet
19 Co-axial Browning .30-cal. machine gun
20 Hull ventilator
21 Vehicle tool stowage
22 Spare periscope heads
23 Fire extinguisher
24 Instrument panel
25 17 Pounder Mark IV QF Gun
26 Muzzle brake
27 Siren
28 Hood for driver's hatch
29 Driver's seat
30 Transmission housing
31 Track drive sprocket
32 .30-cal. machine-gun ammunition
33 Lifting ring
34 .50-cal. machine-gun ammunition
35 Blankets
36 Colman cooker
37 Two 5-gallon water cans
38 Turret traverse controls
39 Crowbar
40 Pickaxe handle
41 Ventilator
42 Fuel filler
43 Shovel
44 Pickaxe head
45 Axe
46 Methyl bromide extinguisher
47 Tail light
48 Ventilator
49 Lifting ring
50 Engine deck

16 January 1945: men of 52nd (Lowland) Division and their Carriers in Tuddern supported by a snow-camouflaged VC of Sherwood Rangers Yeomanry, 8th Armoured Brigade. The Brigade history tells us that on the eve of Operation Blackcock, white bedsheets and whitewash arrived to disguise their dark tanks against the snowy landscape.

a variety of factors, both technical and logistical, that limited the suitability of tanks for conversion. A document dated November 1944 lists features that were essential in a Sherman required for conversion. In the first place, apparently, only petrol-engined Shermans would do, which effectively ruled out the M4A2 (Sherman III). No reason is given, so unless there was some unexplained physical factor, then it can only have been connected with availability. There were similar restrictions in respect of petrol-engined Shermans. Evidence for the existence of a Sherman IIC – that is, a Firefly based upon the cast hull M4A1 – is scarce and difficult to substantiate from official sources, unless the type failed to qualify in some other category. It is unlikely to be due to the hull form alone since the Canadians certainly considered a Firefly conversion to their very similar Grizzly. On the other hand, the M4A3, which in Firefly mode would have been designated IVC, can safely be ruled out since it was almost exclusively a US Army tank of which the British had only a few samples. Thus, in essence, only M4 (Sherman I) and M4A4 (Sherman V) would actually qualify, assuming certain other features were acceptable.

One important feature was that any tank suitable for conversion must have the wide type of gun mantlet that was classified M34A1 in American service. The reason for this becomes clear as soon as one examines the older alternative, the narrow M34 type, which clearly could not be adapted to mount the larger gun. And finally in this list of features, the hydraulic type of turret power traverse was also considered essential.

This raises a number of interesting points. Britain had rejected hydraulic traverse gear quite early in the war in favour of electric on the grounds that if a hydraulic pipe was severed in action it constituted a fire risk. In order not to hold up Sherman production, the Americans had adopted traverse motors by three manufacturers. One, which was electric, came from the Westinghouse Corporation. The other two, by Logansport and Oilgear, were both hydraulic systems, although the latter was far and away the better. Experienced British officers found the Westinghouse electric

25 March 1945 was a Sunday, but it was business as usual on the Rhine, with a Firefly from C Squadron, 4th/7th Dragoon Guards sharing a class 50/60 raft with a D8 bulldozer for the crossing to Rees. An earlier attempt to load two tanks onto one raft ended with it sinking.

traverse difficult to control with sufficient finesse for fast and accurate tank gunnery, while the Logansport hydraulic system was probably too sensitive and could not deal with inconsistencies in the machining of the turret ring, for example. The Oilgear equipment, on the other hand, proved to be smooth, easy to control, and capable of overriding small inconsistencies. Thus, when hydraulic traverse gear is specified for tanks suitable for the Firefly conversion, it is safe to assume that in fact only the Oilgear system would do.

These concerns seem to be simple enough but for the fact that deliveries of Shermans from the United States were inconsistent even in the best of times. Worse still, as one report pointed out, was that even when suitable tanks had been identified from a particular batch, some might still be required to complete deliveries as 75mm gun tanks and could not be made available for conversion to Fireflies.

To return briefly to the topic of turret traverse, is should be noted that according to some experts, the 17-pounder turret, with the counterweight at the back formed by the radio box, was actually better balanced than the standard 75mm version. A trial conducted at Lulworth with a Firefly standing on a 15-degree slope, showed that it was still possible to turn the turret by hand, albeit with a bit more effort and that the power traverse still functioned. On the other hand, traverse speeds on a 17-pounder turret appear to have been slower than the 75mm version, although this was not entirely a bad thing. Creep speed, the ultra-slow traverse required for the fine laying of a gun onto its target, was measured at .125 degrees per second against .20 degrees per second of a regular Sherman with the same equipment. Not a significant difference but clearly a critical advantage for a Firefly gunner.

This raises another significant point because in addition to balancing the turret itself, it was also necessary to balance the gun in the turret. In fact, balance, in this case, was a relative term: ideally the gun should be slightly breech heavy. With the regular canvas holder hanging from the recoil guard behind the breech ring to catch

MINE-DAMAGED SHERMAN VC FIREFLY ON SCAMMELL TRMU/30 TRANSPORTER, NORMANDY, JULY 1944

Despite popular mythology, largely generated by the cinema, tanks were not always totally destroyed if they became casualties. This Sherman Firefly has been mined. The leading suspension unit has been blasted off and the drive sprocket damaged beyond repair, but the tank itself is not a write-off. The tracks have been recovered and stowed on the tank's engine deck and even evidence of fire at the rear is probably no more than superficial. The Scammell TRMU/30 was a classic British design with pre-war origins, designed primarily for tank recovery rather than long-distance transportation. Although officially limited to a payload of 30 tons, it proved quite capable of winching aboard and transporting a 35-ton VC Firefly to an Advanced Base Workshop of the Royal Electrical and Mechanical Engineers. Here the tank would be inspected and, if within the scope of the ABW, returned to serviceable condition. That done, the tank would be sent on to a Forward Delivery Squadron, Royal Armoured Corps and in due course would find its way back to regimental service with a new crew and, if they could be bothered, a new set of markings. (Art by Tony Bryan, © Osprey Publishing)

4 April 1945: a Firefly of the Scots Greys, with extended end connectors on the tracks, crosses the Dortmund–Ems Canal on a Bailey Bridge. Allied armour was now deep inside Germany, and the end more or less in sight, but still the official censor thought it necessary to hide the identity of the regiment by obliterating the insignia.

M4A3 WITH BRITISH FIREFLY TURRET, ARMY GROUND FORCES BOARD, FORT KNOX, KENTUCKY, 1944

At least two complete Firefly turrets were sent to North America, one apparently to Canada where it appears to have been fitted to a Grizzly, Canada's version of the M4A1 Sherman. The other went to the United States, specifically the Army Ground Forces Board at Fort Knox, Kentucky. Here it was mounted on an otherwise unadapted M4A3 hull for trials. American experience of the Firefly in north-west Europe is covered in the main text but we do not know the results of these tests. One assumes that the box on the rear of the turret was the standard British version, designed to accommodate the No.19 set and therefore a bit too small to contain the American radio. At some stage the turret was transferred to an M4A2 hull and in this guise it survives in the collection of the Ordnance Museum, Aberdeen Proving Ground, Maryland. (Art by Tony Bryan, © Osprey Publishing)

ejected shell cases, the 17-pounder mounting was 450lb muzzle heavy. To correct this, it would have been necessary to add 92lb of weight to balance the longer gun. Instead, a perforated metal container was fitted in lieu of canvas and provided most of the necessary weight, although there was provision to add small balance weights to the rear of the recoil guard. Of course, despite the fact that the gun was well balanced in the turret, it proved impossible to fire on the move, so the stabilizing gear fitted to a regular Sherman was removed.

AMMUNITION

For most of their service, Sherman Fireflies were supplied with three types of ammunition: APC (Armour Piercing Capped), APCBC (Armour Piercing Capped Ballistic Capped), and HE (High Explosive). Since they are the subject of much pointless argument, precise performance figures will be avoided as much as possible, but it is safe to say that the APCBC round was a modest improvement in terms of accuracy and penetration on the APC round but that this difference decreased as the range increased. Regular AP (Armour Piercing) shot, which was available for the anti-tank gun, was not, apparently, carried in the tanks. APC was virtually the same round with a hardened cap on the nose to improve penetration, while APCBC had an additional pointed cap to improve aerodynamic performance.

High explosive was the problem. Backed by a conventional charge, the 17-pounder could fire a high explosive round out to a range of 10,000yds, way beyond the normal fighting range of tanks. This was fine if the tanks were to be used in the long-range artillery role that both Briggs and Witheridge had favoured, but that was in the desert. The long view was not available in Europe, where fighting ranges reduced

12 April 1945: C Squadron, Coldstream Guards wait on the road to Bremen while a spot of bother is cleared up in the woods on the right. The nearest tank is a Firefly equipped with Typhoon rockets that were unique to this squadron. On the right side of the turret the launch rail is empty but the tail of a rocket can be seen on the left.

dramatically, yet there was still a need for high explosive. Indeed, figures published at the end of the war showed that Allied tanks used far more high explosive ammunition than armour piercing in the course of the campaign. The solution seemed to be to reduce the charge in the high explosive cartridge so that the projectile would not fly so far. However, the result of this was that a shell impacting on soft ground did not have enough force behind it to set off the nose fuse, and so the shell failed to detonate. The problem was resolved in due course, although the Firefly was primarily a tank-fighting tank and stood or fell by the armour-piercing performance of its gun.

In August 1944, a new round appeared: APDS (Armour Piercing Discarding Sabot), a solid tungsten core surrounded by a light casing that filled the bore of the gun. As it left the muzzle, this casing, with the full charge of the cartridge behind it, broke away from the core (at some risk to anyone in the immediate vicinity), enabling the core to proceed on its way with less air resistance due to its smaller size. The results could be impressive. In theory, even the thick, sloped frontal armour of the massive Tiger II could be penetrated at ranges up to 1,500yds – if one could hit it. The trouble was that, certainly in the early days, APDS became chronically inaccurate at anything above about 500yds, which was a suicidal range for any Sherman to fight from. Accuracy improved in due course, but that was not the only problem.

For one thing, due to its shape, the APDS round was liable to foul the baffles in the 17-pounder's muzzle brake. These had to be altered. It also tended to clog up the rifling with tiny shards of metal, and this could ruin the accuracy of subsequent APCBC rounds that might be fired. This was duly reported and the Americans notified, but there was no easy answer. One theory considered having dedicated APDS tanks, but that always raised the problem of ensuring that the right tank was in the right place at the right time – and there are special laws that govern that sort of thing.

CONCRETE BUSTERS

Back in May 1943, while George Brighty was still struggling to get a 17-pounder gun to fit inside a Sherman turret, a trial took place at Shoeburyness, the artillery testing ground on the north shore of the Thames Estuary. The trial involved six of the 17-pounder anti-tank guns, all firing armour-piercing rounds at a reinforced concrete wall about 7ft 6in. (2.3m) thick. Among the observers was LtCol O'Rorke, commander of the Gunnery School at Lulworth, who was clearly there to represent Royal Armoured Corps interest.

Apparently, there was not much to see while the guns were firing, just a huge cloud of dust. But when the test was over, the result seems to have disappointed many of the observers. Rounds had certainly penetrated the concrete, indeed there was a great gap in the wall like an inverted triangle, but the steel reinforcing bars were

28 April 1945: C Squadron, Coldstream Guards sporting their famous Tulip rockets halted near Westerimke prisoner of war camp. In the foreground a Sherman IC Firefly displays a camouflaged gun barrel, a disguise of dubious value in most situations.

still in place, and there was a ramp of rubble at the base. Since the object of breaking down the wall was to enable a tank to get through, it is odd that no tank was present to try its luck, but the watchers had their doubts. It may have been difficult for a tank to climb over the rubble because the gap at the base of the wall was much too narrow, and no one could be sure whether the reinforcing bars would stop the tank or not. A request was made for a Churchill tank to be available next time, but it is not clear whether there was a next time or not.

It is surprising, therefore, to discover that the very first action involving Sherman Fireflies was in a concrete busting role on the early morning of D-Day itself. How it came about is unclear, and all we know for sure is that on the morning of 6 June 1944, among the Tank Landing Craft heading for the Normandy beaches were three of the short but beamy Landing Craft Tank Mark 5 (LCT[5]). They are believed to have been fitted with a raised section of deck at the forward end of the tank deck so that the Fireflies could fire over the lip of the bow ramp. A similar arrangement was made for the Centaur tanks of the Royal Marine Armoured Support Group.

A private snapshot of an M4A4 VC Firefly of 5th Royal Tank Regiment at rest in an orchard with suitable foliage attached to the turret. The domestic arrangements suggest that the crew are experienced at making themselves comfortable. This crew likes its beverages: there is a coffee pot on the ground and a kettle dangling from the back of the tank.

SHERMAN IC FIREFLY, HEADQUARTERS SQUADRON, PRETORIA REGIMENT, 6TH SOUTH AFRICAN ARMOURED DIVISION, ITALY, MAY 1945

South African 6th Armoured Division was formed in 1942 but, due largely to manpower problems, was not ready to move to Italy until April 1944. By the end of the war the regiment, indeed probably all three regiments of 11th South African Armoured Brigade, had been issued with the Firefly's American equivalent, the M4A1 with 76mm gun in the T23 turret, the Sherman IIA in British service. The Fireflies may have been concentrated in HQ Squadron in order to rationalize the distribution of ammunition. With their reduced crews they would hardly be ideal for any sort of command function but they would probably still represent the most potent firepower in the regiment. The South African Shermans in Italy appear to have been painted a dark green towards the end of the war and as second in the brigade the Pretoria Regiment would bear the number 52 in conjunction with the divisional sign, a green and yellow triangle (the national colours) and display squadron signs in yellow. (Art by Tony Bryan, © Osprey Publishing)

LANDING CRAFT TANK (5) CB NO.2337, 330TH SUPPORT FLOTILLA CARRYING TWO SHERMAN VC FIREFLIES OF 259 DELIVERY SQUADRON, OFF SWORD BEACH, NORMANDY, 6 JUNE 1944

As explained in the text this curious business has only recently enjoyed any serious publicity and a lot of questions remain to be answered. Contemporary records from the D-Day period indicate just three of these craft: two with the Canadians on Juno and one with the 13th/18th Hussars on Sword, the two tanks manned by crews from that regiment. None are associated with Gold sector but the Americans seem to have had a similar arrangement, with 75mm gun Shermans, on Omaha. The American-built LCT(5) was a good deal smaller than other classes of LCT and its capacity was limited to four or five tanks at most, depending on weight. In this role the raised deck section must have added to the weight and, as far as one can tell, this example, destined for Sword, only carried the two Fireflies. However they would be something like one metre higher than normal, which must have upset the vessel's stability. The tanks would have been waterproofed in order to wade ashore, yet one assumes that this did not include the turret ring or mantlet area since the gun would need to traverse and elevate during the run in. It is understood that in this case the tanks did not engage any targets on the way in, although this has not been explained. They were under orders to join up with the two DD squadrons of their regiment once ashore but they are not mentioned in the regimental history and nothing more is known of them from this point. (Art by Tony Bryan, © Osprey Publishing)

Surviving evidence suggests that one LCT carrying a pair of Fireflies was part of the assault force that approached Sword Beach, while two more were allotted to the Canadian regiments that were heading for Juno. No evidence can be found for their use on Gold Beach. On paper, the six tanks were on the establishment of 259 Tank Delivery Squadron, although in fact each pair was allocated to a Sherman DD regiment. These were the British 13th/18th Hussars and two Canadian regiments, the 1st Hussars (6th Canadian Armoured Regiment) and Fort Garry Horse (10th Canadian Armoured Regiment). Each tank was crewed by a reserve crew from the relevant regiment.

The intention was clearly to engage specific concrete defences on the beach during the run in. Shooting accurately from tanks on the moving decks of relatively small craft might be regarded as impossible, but it appears to have worked, at least in the case of the 1st Hussars. Each tank stood on the raised deck with a good stock of spare ammunition alongside and extra men to pass it up to the loader as required, presumably in order that when the tanks landed they would still be fully stowed. One assumes that the tanks would be equipped with deep wading gear because once the landing craft touched down, the Firefly crews were instructed to go ashore, finish off the obstacles they had been shooting at, and then join up with their parent regiments. Thus, for example, the two Fireflies of 13th/18th Hussars (which according to reports did not fire

OPPOSITE The visual evidence suggests that this Hybrid IC Firefly belonged to B Squadron, Vth Inniskilling Dragoon Guards. The square on the turret tells us the squadron; the red jerboa of 7th Armoured Division shows up on the front stowage box, nearside. On the other side, one can just make out the stag's head of 22nd Armoured Brigade facing upwards, and beneath it what could be '52' or '53'. The name *St Michael* sounds appropriate for the Skins.

Another fascinating snapshot showing two Fireflies, both with camouflaged guns but different hull forms. Inevitably, these private photographs were taken when the tanks and their crews were at rest, revealing the domestic arrangements. Brackets like the one across the front of the nearest tank seem to have been favoured by 5th RTR.

OPPOSITE This unusual photograph shows tanks of C Squadron, 2nd RTR, in Italy. It is remarkable because the squadron is operating a mixture of Fireflies, notably the second tank in line, and Shermans equipped with the American 76mm gun in the enlarged turret, such as Cameron, in the foreground. Naturally, there will be 75mm gun tanks in the line as well so that the quartermaster is faced with handling at least three different types of ammunition.

at all on the way in) joined up respectively with A and B, the DD Squadrons, to stiffen up their firepower in the event that any heavy German tanks were encountered.

To round off the story of the DD regiments on D-Day: they were followed ashore some 45 minutes later by the tanks of their regimental headquarters and their third, non-swimming, squadron. This last would be equipped with Fireflies on the scale of one per troop, but once they were all ashore and out of action, Fireflies would be delivered for the DD squadrons on the same scale. From now on, they would be organized and would fight like regular Sherman regiments.

There was, of course, one non-DD regiment equipped with Shermans that landed on D-Day. This was the Staffordshire Yeomanry, otherwise the Queen's Own Royal Regiment, which formed part of 27th Armoured Brigade. One looks to them as, hopefully, a fruitful source of early use of the Firefly. But one looks in vain. The regimental war diary tells us that in June 1944, they were equipped with 48 M4A2 (Sherman III) and 12 M4A4 (Sherman V), which must have been their Fireflies because the diesel-powered M4A2 was considered unsuitable for conversion. Since the Staffordshire Yeomanry played a significant part in frustrating the advance of the 21st Panzer Division against the beachhead, it is a pity that more particular information on the use of their Fireflies is not available. At least we can rely on one good photograph to prove that the regiment did have Fireflies.

THE FIREFLY IN ACTION

Even if we cannot confirm that the Staffordshire Yeomanry was probably the first regiment to employ Fireflies in combat, it seems a reasonable bet. On the other hand, it appears that impressions gleaned at the time were not always reliable. For example, the Sherwood Rangers came to the conclusion within a few days of landing that the Germans were singling out their Fireflies for priority destruction, presumably on account of their longer guns. This is not an unreasonable assumption, but it is not borne out by the evidence. According to a British report dated 23 June 1944, the total 'wastage', as they put it, of Fireflies in one Canadian and three British armoured brigades ashore, was 19 per cent of the total available compared with 29 per cent of their regular tanks – and that includes 22nd Armoured Brigade in 7th Armoured Division, which had lost 101 Cromwells against just six Fireflies by that date. Surely, if there was anywhere that the Fireflies would stick out, it was while mixing with flocks of the comparatively diminutive Cromwells. On the other hand, as far as regular tanks were concerned, much of this wastage had already been made good: of 264 tanks knocked out 188 had already been replaced. Where Fireflies were concerned, 22 had been lost, but as of 23 June, only six had arrived at replacements.

Crossing a Bailey Bridge in Italy, this Firefly belongs to 18th New Zealand Armoured Regiment. The turret is reversed, the gun barrel supported in its crutch, and with plenty of stowage attached. Notice too that there is a substantial towing attachment at the rear.

Such statistics are always cold-blooded. They mask a great deal of pain. It is more heartening to read of some complimentary user opinion. Colonel Readman, commanding the Royal Scots Greys in 4th Armoured Brigade – which was not included in the statistics above – reported his initial reaction to the Firefly on 24 July 1944. He says that based on experience in Italy, where heavy German tanks such as the PzKpfw V Panther and PzKpfw VI Tiger were rare, the regiment had been minded to organize its Fireflies into separate troops, each troop to provide long-range cover to three troops of 75mm Shermans in each squadron. Experience in Normandy, where one seemed to find a Panther or Tiger waiting around every corner, resulted in a rapid reorganization, so that each tank troop had a Firefly of its own. While they

SHERMAN VC FIREFLY, 19TH ARMOURED REGIMENT, 4TH NEW ZEALAND ARMOURED BRIGADE, ITALY APRIL 1945

Having experienced the muddy conditions of an Italian winter, 2nd New Zealand Armoured Brigade applied locally made Platypus grousers made from lengths of angle iron fixed to the tracks and extended outwards for quite a long way; even after the weather improved, the New Zealanders seem to have retained them on their tanks. They were certainly seen on 17-pounder Shermans operated by the Brigade as late as April 1945. This impressive front view shows a Sherman VC, so equipped, thundering along an Italian highway. The 17-pounder gun has been camouflage painted to try to disguise its length and this tank has patches of appliqué armour fitted ahead of the driver's and redundant co-driver's positions. There is also a .30-cal. M1919 Browning machine gun mounted on the commander's cupola. New Zealand Shermans are reported to have been painted in a shade similar to US olive drab although this would soon acquire a patina of local dust. (Art by Tony Bryan, © Osprey Publishing)

SHERMAN IC HYBRID FIREFLY *ZEMSTA II* (REVENGE) OF C SQUADRON, 1ST KRECHOWIECKI LANCERS, 2ND POLISH ARMOURED BRIGADE, ITALY 1944

From this angle the bulbous front end of a Hybrid Sherman IC (M4) shows up clearly as it eases its way across a Churchill ARK. Like most tanks in the Polish 2nd Armoured Division, this one has a name painted boldly in yellow on the side of the hull and yet employs the approved method of camouflage on the gun barrel. The hull also features patches of appliqué armour covering the regular areas but not on the turret. The ARK is simply a redundant Churchill tank hull with hinged ramps at each end that would be driven into a gap to provide a causeway for other tanks to cross. They appear to have been popular in Italy, yet there is no evidence for their use in north-west Europe. Those used in Italy had exposed tracks that service tanks would normally drive over but in this case planks have been laid to provide a smooth surface. A small fascine in the form of a tightly bound bundle of sticks is seen on the nose of the tank to be used for crossing a muddy ditch or similar obstacle, but otherwise the front end of this tank is remarkably free of clutter. (Art by Tony Bryan, © Osprey Publishing)

were in short supply, this seems to have been common practice, but Col Readman looked forward to a time when each troop in his regiment would have three Fireflies to one 75mm Sherman, which would be there to provide high explosive or smoke. Indeed, Readman said, if sufficient Fireflies were not available, he would be prepared to take M10 self-propelled guns armed with the 17-pounder instead.

Individual crew experiences are rarely reliable, no matter how interesting they might be, for the simple reason that one individual in a tank has little idea of what is going on around him, never mind farther away. As a result, where we are obliged to be concise, a more general source is better. One of the best was compiled by Col W. E. H. Grylls in 1945 for Brigadier Charles Dunphie, Deputy Commander of the Royal Armoured Corps. Grylls clearly had a lot of experience of tank combat in north-west Europe and had sounded many crews for their views. This experience enabled him to place things in perspective and give a reasonably dispassionate appraisal.

For example, he estimated that despite the many unkind things said about it, the Chrysler multi-bank engine was a lot more reliable than it was ever given credit for, particularly by those who had to service it. He reveals that on early Fireflies the muzzle brake had a tendency to work loose because the locking device was not

OPPOSITE This M4A4 VC appears to be receiving some attention. It seems totally devoid of markings, not even a WD number, which suggests that it is a replacement tank. The identity of the individual posing alongside is not recorded, but the tank is believed to belong to 22nd Armoured Brigade.

15 August 1945: a troop of Fireflies from B Squadron of one of the regiments of Polish 2nd Warszawska Armoured Division spruced up for a parade at the end of the war in Italy. Rycerz 1 is a IC, the other three IC Hybrids providing an interesting comparison. The parade was in honour of a visit by Field Marshal Sir Harold Alexander.

satisfactory. He also says that in Normandy, Fireflies suffered a number of traverse gear failures because the gear was not capable of handling the greater weight. However, he claims that the Department of Tank Design had already appreciated this and soon had an improved type ready. Another interesting conclusion concerns the risk of fire in Fireflies. Despite an enduring belief that this was due in the main to petrol fuel, trials had clearly shown that in fact the most important factor was the way that ammunition was stowed. Until the Americans introduced wet stowage, the Shermans were particularly vulnerable in this respect since ammunition was stowed all around the fighting compartment, easy to reach in a hurry but just as easily hit if the tank's armour was penetrated. In the Firefly, where much of the ammunition was located below the turret floor, it was a lot less exposed, so that fires in Fireflies were uncommon, relatively speaking.

13 June 1944: this Firefly, apparently in an ambush position, belongs to the Staffordshire Yeomanry. The regiment, part of 27th Armoured Brigade, landed on D-Day and played a key part in preventing 21st Panzer Division from reaching the beachhead. Its Fireflies were VC (M4A4), while the rest of its Shermans were the diesel M4A2 variant.

There are other things that Grylls does not mention. For example, many crews reported that the flash at the muzzle when the gun fired obscured the view of the target and made it difficult to ensure that they had hit it. Grylls says that it was normal practice to fire at an enemy tank until it caught fire, thus making sure that it was destroyed, so perhaps that was not quite such a problem. From the crews' point of view, it was a flash at the breech end that bothered them, despite being informed loftily by the Medical Research Council that it would not do them any harm. Even so, a canvas curtain was installed to shield the loader, and it was suggested that the turret crew might be issued with hoods to protect them, such as those worn by naval turret personnel. However, common sense and ingenuity prevailed when George Witheridge modified the electrics to create a delayed action breech that was introduced as the Mark VII gun. Another small but irritating fault reported by some crews was that rain leaked into the radio box on the back of the turret, presumably around the lid on top. None of this did anything to diminish the popularity of the Firefly, and the demand for more continued. Indeed, from statements he made at the time, it appears that Field Marshal Montgomery believed that ultimately Fireflies would replace 75mm gun tanks in all British regiments. In practice, the best that any regiment achieved, and probably as many as they required, was two per troop because the greater versatility of the 75mm gun continued to be appreciated.

A pristine IC M4 Firefly undergoing trials at the Mechanization Experimental Establishment at Ottariano in Italy. Every hatch is open, including that of the absent hull machine gunner and it is clear that this tank, perhaps the first Firefly to arrive in Italy, is fitted with rubber block tracks.

Italy was another theatre where the firepower of the Firefly would be welcome, but its demands could not be met until those of 21st Army Group had been satisfied. The demands became more urgent and the calls for them more strident as time went on. As the Allied armies moved north, encounters with heavier German tanks became more common, but it was October 1944 before Fireflies could be spared for that theatre. By the time these had been shared out between British, Canadian, New Zealand, Polish and South African regiments, one per troop was the best that could be hoped for and the most they ever managed.

Perhaps for this reason, regiments in the Italian theatre treasured their Fireflies all the more. They certainly went to far greater lengths to camouflage them than did their counterparts in northern Europe who relied on disruptive painting and a trick of the light to confuse the enemy. It was the gun, of course, that was the problem. Some senior officers had already criticized it for the way it stuck out in front of the tank, entirely missing the point that it was the length of the barrel, more than anything else, that ensured the high velocity and hitting power of the weapon.

Trying to disguise the gun was not easy. Camouflage experts in Italy accepted the concept of paint and even embellished it by fitting a device midway along the barrel that looked like a muzzle brake. Whether it would have fooled anyone, any of the time, is open to question, but at least it was not as drastic as the alternative. This was for the tank to operate as much as possible with the turret traversed aft and the barrel camouflaged with suitable vegetation on the engine deck. Meanwhile, a dummy

A very odd arrangement indeed: an M4A4 Sherman V that is pretending to be a Firefly, with a long dummy gun paralleling the real one and a box on the rear of the turret. Unfortunately, we cannot see whether a loader's hatch has been added or the hull machine gun blanked off. Why on Earth should anyone do this?

75mm gun, fitted to the rear of the turret was supposed to fool the Germans into thinking that this was an ordinary Sherman they were dealing with. The trouble was that one could only maintain this deception for so long: at some point the big gun had to be traversed forwards in order to do its business, and then the cat was out of the bag. Logic seems to suggest that if the tank was close enough to the enemy for the dummy gun to be seen, then it was time to have the real gun facing forwards, loaded and ready for action.

Perhaps because they were farther from the seat of power, troops in Italy displayed a degree of independence that was not so evident in north-west Europe. One example will suffice. The 2nd Lothian and Border Horse, in 26th Armoured Brigade, did not take kindly to the idea of dumping a crew member, and so they went into action with the fifth man stuffed into the front with the extra ammunition. Obviously, he had nothing to do because the machine gun had been removed. The practice was portrayed as an example of team spirit, which it undoubtedly was, but there may have been a secondary agenda: work shared between five men was easier than between four.

The presence of a Comet in the background suggests 29th Armoured Brigade towards the end of the war in Germany. However, the cap badges, along with the visible markings of this crew and their Firefly, seem to indicate 5th RTR in 22nd Armoured Brigade.

THE AMERICAN RESPONSE

Raymond Briggs, in a report compiled on his return from the United States, reckoned that the Firefly had to some extent re-established British credibility in American eyes. There had been a lot of criticism before this time because the Americans believed that the British were wasting good tanks by adapting them to other roles and then demanding more. Now at last the Americans saw an adaptation that they could approve of. Not that they had any more direct interest in the tank: they had something similar of their own.

The American 76mm, in contrast to its British counterpart, had been developed as a tank gun and only later adapted to a towed mounting. Like the British weapon, it was in fact 76.2mm-calibre, or 3in. It was part of a programme launched in summer 1943 to develop the 'ultimate' Sherman, although the Americans could afford a more wholehearted approach than the British and created what was, in effect, a new tank with a new and bigger turret to take the longer gun.

The adoption of the new gun seems to be a tacit admission on the Americans' part that defeating enemy armour was an important function of a tank after all, but that did not impress everyone. Indeed, in the lead up to D-Day there was a marked reluctance on the part of some US Army units to part with their 75mm gun tanks because they valued the dual role of the older gun. Experience of the heavier German tanks, notably the Panther, soon changed that. One can imagine the disappointment when it was discovered that the armour-piercing performance did not come up to expectations. The reverberations reached the top. General Eisenhower is recorded as saying, 'Ordnance told me this 76 would take care of anything the Germans had. Now I find you can't knock out a damn thing with it.' An exaggeration of course, but it is indicative of the frustration felt among American tank men that individually, their tanks were no match for the Germans' best.

As a result, the Americans developed what they called a High Velocity Armour Piercing (HVAP) round – what the British would call APCR, or Armour Piercing Composite Rigid – that relied on a core of tungsten to do the damage. Even this had a poor record when tested on a captured Panther, and it was always in short supply. General Omar Bradley decided that what the Americans needed was the Sherman Firefly.

We know this is 5th RTR, probably in Hamburg at the end of the war, where the crew appear to have appropriated a German Army raid car. Retaining camouflage on the turret seems rather pointless in this situation.

This VC Firefly was one of three or four that fell into German hands at various times. What appears to be a number 6 is in fact 'G' for Guss, meaning cast armour, while 'W' is Walzstahl, which indicates areas of rolled (or flat) plate; presumably for instructional purposes. Apart from an A Squadron triangle on the turret and a bold War Department number on the side of the hull, there are no other indications of the previous owners.

A letter from US 12th Army dated 13 August 1944 requests that sufficient Fireflies be made available until such time as the new American 90mm gun was ready or improved ammunition for the 76mm gun was issued. In all respects, it was a forlorn hope. The British were struggling to produce enough Fireflies for themselves, the Canadians and the Poles in France, and the Italian theatre was also demanding them. The Americans were a long way down the list. In the United States, British liaison officer Brig G. McLeod Ross suggested that the 17-pounder gun should be mounted in the larger T23 turret, designed for the 76mm Sherman, but mounted on the new American T26 chassis. This was turned down on the grounds that the T23 turret was inadequate in terms of armour, and the alternative – to fit the 17-pounder

May 1945: it is quite surprising to discover that immediately after the war ended in Europe, the British Army arranged a major display in Paris. This M4 (IC) Firefly, presumably from a Canadian regiment, stands polished to a high standard with the muzzle brake burnished and gleaming. Field Marshal Montgomery strolls by with a bevy of Allied officers.

into the T26 turret in place of the designed weapon, the 90mm – was regarded as a waste of effort; all this despite the fact that it was believed that the British gun would outperform the larger American gun. One report said, 'It will doubtless take a lot of pressure to make the USA adopt the 17-pr, but it would be well worth while.'

Evidence for the existence of the American Firefly is by no means comprehensive, but there is sufficient documentation in print to provide a reasonable picture. Naturally, due to the supply situation, it was 1945 before anything concrete was done. However, an initial requirement is specified for 100 Fireflies based on M4, M4A1 and M4A3, all of course, with the M34A1 gun mount and Oilgear power traverse. At some point, undated, two M4A3 tanks were taken from US Army stocks at Tidworth on Salisbury Plain for conversion to mount the British 17-pounder. One of these is recorded as having armoured ammunition stowage and one with 'wet', that is to say, Glycol stowage. Whether these can be regarded as prototypes for the American Firefly is not clear, but there are a number of interesting specifications. For example, a larger armoured box is required on the back of the turret because the American SCR 508 radio is bigger than the British No.19 set, and the Americans also require stowage clips for a Browning M2 heavy machine gun on the back of this box. Furthermore, they specify their M9 elevating quadrant to replace the British Clinometer.

It was one thing to issue a requirement for tanks but quite another to find them. On 9 March 1945, 22 Shermans arrived at Southampton, presumably from stocks in France. A convoy of 26 tank transporters awaited them at the docks, and they were soon on their way to Woolwich for conversion. Whether this was the first batch is not clear, but further records, often detailed down to individual tank numbers, are for similar quantities. On 11 March, the full requirement was specified as 160 Fireflies. About a month later, on 8 April, this was halved to 80, and it was suggested that the balance could be converted to flails. The last word is a document issued on 26 May 1945, and it states that 86 tanks, M4 and M4A3, equipped with the 17-pounder gun, were in theatre. It recommended that due to a shortage of ammunition, they should be issued to occupation troops in Germany or 'offered elsewhere', whatever that might have meant.

SUPPLY AND DEMAND

The American plan to upgrade the Sherman also affected Firefly production for the British Army. Since it was not considered suitable for combat by the Americans, the M4A4 (Sherman V) was not included in their 76mm gun programme, and production of the 75mm version was due to cease. This alarmed the British, who had grown to like it and even regarded it as one of their most reliable tanks – which under the circumstances might not be saying very much. As a consequence, a good deal of pressure was put on the Americans to keep the tank in production. All the same, 75mm Shermans of any type were in short supply, and Firefly conversions dropped off dramatically in the third quarter of 1944. They only got going again when a new supply of suitable tanks was tapped. This was a curious version of the basic M4 (Sherman I) built by the Detroit Arsenal, featuring a combination cast and welded hull that looked a bit like an M4A1 from the front and a regular M4 from the back. The British called it the Sherman I Hybrid.

This problem had started to raise its head as early as August 1944. The workforce at Woolwich had already experienced two breaks in the production of Fireflies due to a shortage of suitable tanks. The result had a negative psychological effect: when people went to work and found nothing to do, they tended to drift away and take

jobs elsewhere. In the face of a third break, the authorities decided to close down the Firefly production line at Hayes and divert the work to Woolwich. The theory was that with a reliable flow of tanks for conversion, the pace and quality of work would be maximized. Clearly, the matter was resolved because in returns from 21st Army Group early in 1945, Sherman IC tanks, most likely Hybrids, outnumbered the VC.

OPPOSITE TOP 9 June 1945: Montgomery again, in a smartly turned out half-track, passes a long row of Fireflies when he inspects Guards Armoured Division at Rottenburg as they prepare to disband. Many criticized the idea of putting Guardsmen in tanks, arguing that they were too rigid in their training. The Division proved them wrong.

WHAT'S IN A NAME?

The origin of the name Firefly and its use to describe the 17-pounder-armed Sherman seems to engender a lot more interest than is perhaps justified. The name was previously coined for the ridiculous installation of a 6-pounder gun in a Morris Light Reconnaissance Car, and it seems impossible to deduce any connection with the tank. Even so, the name appears to have been in fairly common usage from about March 1944 to describe the 17-pounder Sherman irrespective of mark. It will not be found on any official publications, although it appears in some war diaries, which suggests that the name was used among the troops.

The true firefly is an insect with a type of phosphorus appendage, and so there is no obvious connection there – except maybe an unconscious one. Presumably, like most insects, the firefly enjoys a short but brilliant life, and the same may be said of the tank. The Sherman Firefly fired its first shot in anger on 6 June 1944, and its last, as a frontline tank, probably in May 1945, being in the spotlight for about 11 months. True, some were passed on to other armies, and they may well have seen some action, but that is not the same thing.

The British Army shed its stock of Shermans very quickly after the war, although the 17-pounder gun remained in service with the first Centurions for a while. Yet there is no denying that the Firefly made its mark in the brief time of its service. It is easily recognizable (from the right angle), and it was the instrument of some remarkable and heroic deeds. However, if one is looking for a meaningful explanation of the tank's importance, it is probably because, at last, British troops could go out looking for Panthers and Tigers with every hope of killing them. When the Germans dominated the battlefield, with exotically named tanks of fearsome power, the Firefly, albeit a late arrival, was regarded as the antidote. It may be worth adding that in 1953 a report was issued by the Fighting Vehicle Research and Development Establishment at Chertsey with the title 'Tests of a Rigidly Mounted 17 PR. Gun'. Two of the signatures on the cover were G. H. Brighty and W. G. K. Kilbourn. Perhaps the last word can be left to MajGen Sir Campbell Clarke, the Director General of Artillery from 1942 to 1945. Writing in the Daily Telegraph after the war he said, 'The 17 pdr Shermans were under-armoured, but were very reliable mechanically, unlike the Tigers which they could outpace, out-manoeuvre and also outshoot.'

OPPOSITE BOTTOM 8 June 1946: two immaculate Fireflies devoid of any unit markings roll by the saluting base during the huge London Victory Parade. Compare the front plates of the two tanks: closest to the camera, the original model with the bolted final drive cover, while the other features the single-piece cast type. A board on the side of the nearest tank only tells us that it is a Sherman.

CHAPTER 5

DUPLEX DRIVE

Most tank-producing nations had toyed with the concept of amphibious tanks in the years between the wars, and these appeared in two distinct forms. Either you had the conventional tank, made to float by the addition of buoyant attachments, or you had a tank designed from the drawing board to swim, which could simply drive into the water and sail away.

PROBLEMS AND SOLUTIONS

The former had the advantage that once the tank emerged from the water it could shed its flotation gear and roll into action like any other tank, with the same degree of firepower, protection and mobility. There were two serious drawbacks, however. In the first place the buoyancy aids were so bulky that they had to be carried around by transport and fitted, not without considerable effort, to the tank just before it took on its amphibious role. The location for this work had to be secure from enemy interference, but not so far from the water that the tank would need to travel any distance since it was quite likely to damage itself in the process. Inevitably these fixtures made the tank a lot wider, so the risk of damage against trees, buildings and other obstacles was very real and, if seaborne operations were contemplated, it would be too wide to pass through the bow section of a landing craft. In addition some other temporary modification was required to enable the tank to propel itself in the

Another Covenanter, here fitted with a pair of floats, prepares to take the plunge into Fareham Harbour. Notice how the long-range fuel tank, normally carried at the back of the Covenanter, has been transferred to the port-side float.

water; this could be anything from paddles bolted to the tracks. The drawback in this case was that thick armour was incompatible with an outboard motor or some alteration to the transmission that provided conventional propeller drive. The purpose-built amphibious tank was not so wide, since the hull itself was a significant part of the buoyancy factor and the drivetrain had been adapted at the design stage to incorporate a propeller and rudder.

The drawback in this case was that thick armour was incompatible with buoyancy. Consequently, such tanks were vulnerable out of the water and, since they were invariably small vehicles, they could not carry much in the way of firepower and so their role on land was limited. Not only that, but, being small, they lacked freeboard and could only function safely on calm, inland waters.

Although one true amphibious tank was being tested in Britain shortly before World War II, much of the effort was concentrated upon making regular tanks float. This was done primarily at the Experimental Bridging Establishment at Christchurch in Hampshire and concerned Light Tanks Mark V and VI along with the two new cruiser tanks Covenanter and Crusader. In all cases making the vehicles amphibious involved fitting pontoons, as floats, to each side of the tank, with all the problems already mentioned. The only alternative was a small vessel known as the 17-ton Lighter.

The curious Lighter, looking like an enlarged shoebox fitted with an outboard motor, had been designed for use with a type of vessel known as a Landing Ship Stern Chute that was, in fact, a modified train ferry. The idea was to carry as many of the little Lighters as possible so that, on arrival off an invasion beach, one tank would be lifted into each Lighter and the combination launched down the vessel's stern chute to chug ashore.

Thus each tank had its own means of amphibious transport but, once ashore, was ready to fight as a conventional tank. Trials were carried out in Portsmouth Harbour in the summer of 1941 but, according to a report published after the war, went no further due to the development of larger, tank-carrying landing craft. However, it is worth noting that work on the prototype Duplex Drive tank was going forward at the same time and this may also have had a bearing on the decision to drop the Lighter.

OPPOSITE With the turret of a Covenanter tank just visible above the bulwarks, a prototype of the 17-ton Lighter makes its way carefully from ship to shore in Portsmouth Harbour. The helmsman is in the housing at the back with the outboard drive in an extension at the rear.

DESIGN AND DEVELOPMENT

NICHOLAS STRAUSSLER

Born in 1891, Nicholas Straussler settled in Britain shortly before World War II. He already enjoyed a reputation as an innovative automotive engineer in his native Hungary, but by forming links with firms such as Alvis Ltd in Coventry and the armaments manufacturer Vickers he found more potential business in Britain. For the former he designed a range of armoured cars and for the latter, in the main, various attachments and accessories for tanks. Straussler's innovative streak could get out of hand, particularly with automotive projects that were not always practical. When it came to amphibious tanks, however, he could at least see the wood for the trees.

In a note written in 1945 Straussler claims that after examining various types of buoyant tanks he reached the conclusion that it made more sense to apply flotation equipment to standard designs. Thus, in cooperation with Vickers-Armstrong he developed a range of collapsible floats that could be used to create pontoon bridges and rafts or, attached to each side of a light tank, keep it afloat. The War Office was sufficiently interested to test this equipment and various light tanks were modified for trials, sometimes with the addition of an outboard motor. They appear to have worked well enough, but Straussler had visions of invasion beaches cluttered up with discarded floats after a landing, and duly turned his attention elsewhere.

One has to be cautious when dealing with recollections, particularly when the subject was amassing evidence for a Royal Commission that might result in a substantial reward, and Straussler's suggestion that he realized the limitations of his floats and cast about for an alternative as early as 1934 does seem a bit surprising. If true he was way ahead of the War Office, who persisted with the float idea well into World War II.

THE PROTOTYPE

Whenever it did occur to him, Straussler's idea was a stroke of genius. It was simple enough in theory since it relied upon displacement; the clever bit was Straussler's method of achieving it. In order to avoid the bulk normally associated with displacement he surrounded the tank with a collapsible, waterproof screen. This in turn was attached to the tank's hull, just above track level and the joint securely sealed, with the result that the upper half of the tank and its turret, although essentially below water level, remained dry while the lower half, including the tracks and running gear, was immersed.

For trial purposes Straussler was given a redundant Tetrarch, or Light Tank Mark VII, from the 1st Armoured Division, which thus became the first Duplex Drive (DD) tank, and this is the odd thing. Anyone looking at the tank, in its amphibious guise, would be struck immediately by the canvas screen that effectively enclosed the upper part of it. This screen, with a slightly pointed bow and rounded stern end, was kept in shape at the top by a tubular rail but was raised and held upright by a

The prototype Tetrarch DD prior to its first swim in Langstone Harbour. The marine drive equipment can be seen at the back; notice how the propeller, which is controlled by the line that vanishes over the screen on the right, faces forwards.

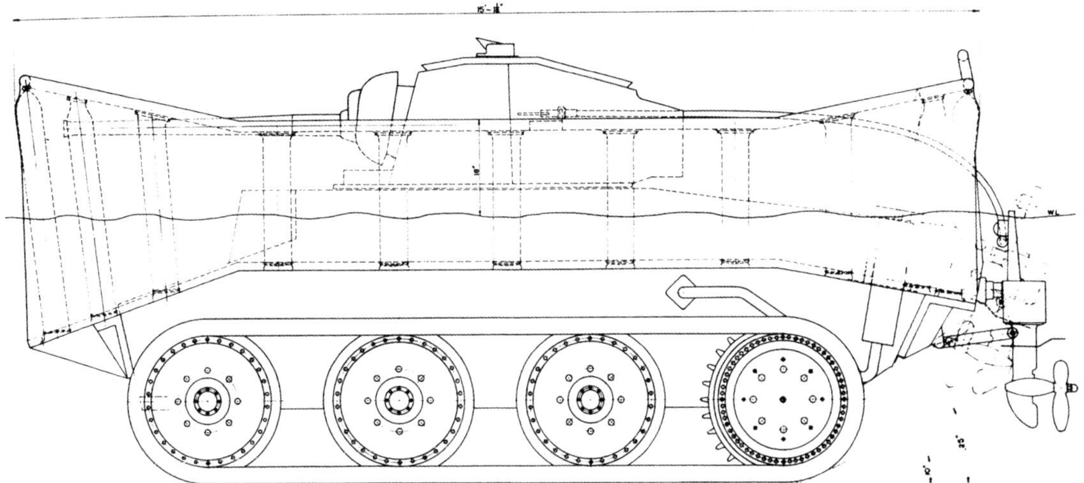

Nicholas Straussler's drawing of the Tetrarch DD with its screen raised. Notice how the exhaust pipes would be extended to clear the screen and that, on this drawing at least, the propeller faces in the conventional way.

series of rubber tubes, inflated with compressed air and held that way while the tank was afloat. Yet this strange screen and its amphibious capability formed no part of the tank's title. Duplex Drive simply indicated that it had two methods of propulsion: tracks on land of course but in the water a marine propeller.

A casual glance suggests that some sort of outboard motor was fitted to the Tetrarch, but upon closer inspection it is more like a marine inboard/outboard, probably designed especially for the tank. The three-blade propeller, which faces forwards, is suspended below a gearbox arrangement from which a splined shaft extends into a tube at the rear of the tank that is driven from the tank's gearbox. When the Tetrarch is on dry land this drive is disengaged and the outboard part held at an angle, but for entering the water it is swung into an upright position, when the two drive components meet. A flexible shaft, running from the top of the outboard to a position on the right side of the turret, controls steering, pivoting the outboard's lower section with a screw handle.

The little tank took its first official dip in Hendon Reservoir in London in June 1941. General Sir Alan Brooke witnessed the display, and soon gave the go-ahead for further development. Later the tank went to Portsmouth and did some saltwater flotation trials from the beach at Hayling Island, but it can only have been suitable for calm sea conditions. The screen itself was waterproof enough, being made from a rubberized canvas fabric produced by the P.B. Cow company, makers of the Lilo inflatable air bed. Even so it did not offer very much freeboard and was probably not sufficiently rigid to hold up in rough conditions.

THE VALENTINE

At the Fourth Meeting of the reconstituted Tank Board, at Shell Mex House in London on 19 September 1941, it was agreed that following the successful application of Straussler's principle to the Tetrarch it should now be tried on the Infantry Tank Mark III, or Vickers-Armstrong Valentine to give its popular name. It was a sensible choice; in many respects Valentine was the coming tank. It was already proving to be far more reliable than many of its counterparts, it was due to be produced in considerable numbers and, on account of its unusual lower hull shape, angled not unlike the bottom of a boat in order to deflect mine blast, it had a slight tendency to float already.

A very early Valentine DD, quite probably the prototype, with its screen partially raised and attended by people who could well be members of Straussler's staff. The tank itself is an early example running on the lubricated, double-pin tracks.

However, a Valentine, fully laden, weighed more than twice as much as a Tetrarch. In terms of displacement this was no problem – one simply enlarged the flotation screen – but trials with the prototype (Valentine II T16518) revealed that the air-filled tubes alone were not adequate to support the screen. To give the tank sufficient buoyancy Straussler doubled the height of the screen and introduced another tubular strengthener midway up. From the point where it was attached to the tank, up to this intermediate point, the waterproofed canvas was double thickness and single above that. The additional weight on land or pressure from water when afloat required more support so the designer introduced four collapsible struts, two each side, which locked both of the framing tubes into place.

Now that production had been agreed, a more practical means of operating the propeller from inside the tank was introduced. Drive still involved a rearward extension shaft from the back of the transmission, passing through the rear of the hull and ending in a ratchet clutch that engaged another shaft to which a three-bladed propeller was attached. The difference was that on the Valentine the propeller was simply pivoted on a bracket and raised or lowered as required. The cumbersome semi-outboard arrangement on Tetrarch was eliminated. The Valentine was a simple and reliable tank, but the additional equipment needed to make it swim required more careful maintenance because once it was afloat there was a lot more at stake. The Mark II converted by Straussler was powered by an AEC diesel engine, carried a crew of three and was armed with a 2-pounder gun and co-axial Besa machine gun.

Preliminary trials of this first Valentine DD were conducted on 21 May 1942, but under whose auspices and where are not clear. It was reported that the tank's hull, an old one, leaked but that it floated well enough on calm water and remained on an even keel. It appears that on this tank the controls were shared by the driver and the loader; the latter was either in the turret or 'on deck' since there is room for just one in the cab. The loader was, in effect, the helmsman, while the driver, besides controlling the engine and gearbox, could engage or disengage the propeller. Four days later Headquarters Combined Operations was pressing for the tank to go to Portsmouth for landing craft trials, but it seems that somewhere over that period the tank had sunk, because a report states that it

An early Valentine DD afloat. These first examples have a characteristic dip in the middle of the screen, and on this one the driver appears to have an extended periscope to view over the screen. The studied nonchalance of the rest of the crew suggests very calm water.

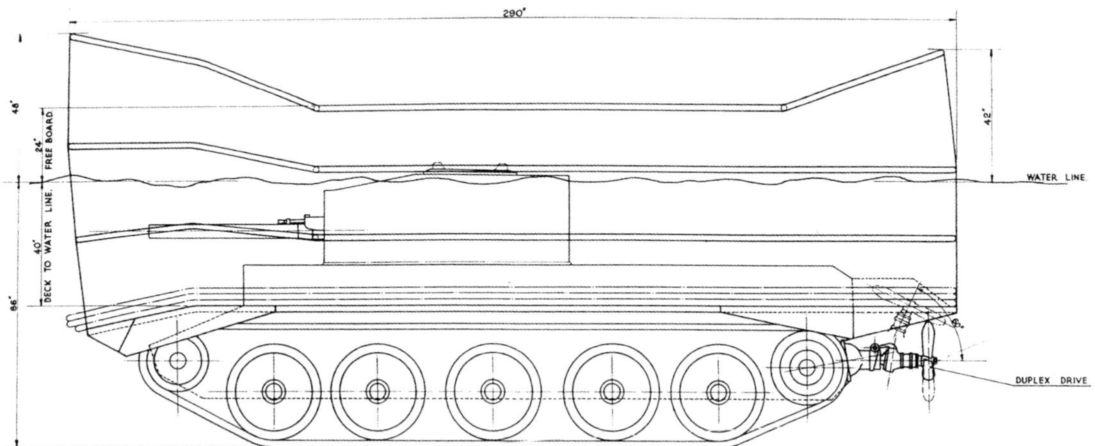

Straussler's patent drawing for a proposed Cromwell DD, which would have had twin propellers driven off the transmission.

had been partially stripped and that the non-standard controls would be installed in a second vehicle. In the meantime a decision to order production was put on hold. In fact the sinking may have been deliberate, since the subsequent report refers to a trial 'recently undertaken' in which two Bren guns were fired at a DD tank at ranges between 800 and 1,500 yards (731 and 1,371m) and resulted in the tank sinking.

The second prototype, as it is described in this report, was T27661, another Valentine II. However on 16 June 1942 it is stated that a Valentine V (GMC diesel) was earmarked to go to Straussler's Royal Park works, which suggests that this was a replacement for the first prototype, and that the second was an entirely different vehicle. Whatever the case, things must have looked promising because on 3 July 1942 it was announced that the Ministry of Supply had given financial approval for the manufacture of 450 Valentine DD tanks, all with the GMC engine; 214 with the 2-pounder gun in a three-man turret and 236 with the 6-pounder in a two-man turret; 200 to be ready by the final quarter of 1942, the other 250 by the end of the first quarter of 1943. These details are confirmed by the Royal Armoured Corps' (RAC) six-monthly report for the first half of 1942, which adds that sea-going trials were being undertaken 'at the present moment'. It is probably worth pointing out that at this time the idea of a major invasion of the Continent was by no means popular with the authorities, and in the second half of 1942 the General Staff issued a policy statement on amphibious tanks that quite simply said that they had no requirement for such a thing. The idea of using such tanks as the first wave in a large-scale invasion was not on the cards.

The contractor for all Valentine DD tanks was Metropolitan Cammell Carriage and Wagon Company of Birmingham, a firm partly owned by Vickers and popularly known as Metro-Cammell. Yet it is interesting to note that special contracts do not appear to have been issued. To judge from known War Department (WD) numbers, the Valentine DDs were simply selected from two large contracts for conventional tanks. The only other thing the two contracts had in common is that they were all for tanks fitted with the General Motors (GMC) diesel engine imported from the United States. DD production was scheduled to begin in March 1943 at the rate of 35 per month.

It is around this time that mention is made of a Cromwell DD and later still a Churchill. Drawings for both survive and show twin prop arrangements at the rear. In the event neither was adopted, almost certainly because the authorities could see that both tanks had a long period of development ahead of them before either could be regarded as reliable. Early in 1943 the Department of Tank Design had carried out

VALENTINE V DD, A INSTRUCTIONAL WING, 79TH ARMOURED DIVISION, FRITTON DECOY, 1942

This was one of the main production versions of the Valentine, powered by a General Motors diesel engine and armed with a 2-pounder gun and co-axial Besa machine gun. It was fitted with an enlarged turret to take three men and, as shown, this was traversed aft when the flotation screen was raised. The colour of the screen is described in official documents as 'Mountbatten Pink', whatever that was, but to the average viewer had the creamy look of canvas with a greyish tint probably caused by the impregnated rubber that kept it waterproof. It all became somewhat darker when wet.

Although they had been trained in the use of special underwater escape apparatus, most crews during training relied on conventional lifejackets and a standard lifebelt, carried on top of the turret for emergencies. The insignia of the 79th Armoured Division reflects the fact that the first three regiments to be trained for DD work, on tanks such as this, all came from that division's 27th Armoured Brigade. (Illustration by Tony Bryan, © Osprey Publishing)

further firing trials against a floating DD tank that had been strengthened by fitting extra support struts. Apparently it survived, even with the range down to 700 yards (646m), although it was still regarded as vulnerable. By the summer of 1943 it seems that quantities had been adjusted: down in the case of 2-pounder tanks to 135 and up in respect of 6-pounder tanks to 430. The RAC also reported a requirement for a DD version of the Sherman, a prototype of which would be ready shortly.

Meanwhile production of the Valentine DD was proceeding and it was time to consider what to do with them. In April 1943 the 79th Armoured Division and its abrasive commander, Major-General Sir Percy Hobart, learned that in future they would take over responsibility for the development and employment of most types of specialized armour – the so-called 'Funnies'. In the main this simply meant taking existing organizations under one command, but the DD tanks were something new so it was agreed to convert the division's 27th Armoured Brigade to the role. Thus 4th/7th Dragoon Guards, 13th/18th Hussars and the East Riding Yeomanry handed over their existing tanks and moved to East Anglia to commence DD training. At this stage, it seems, the plan was to make every regiment fully amphibious but this would change, as would many other things, before they joined battle. From May 1943 they commenced training on Valentine tanks and began to receive DD variants the following month. Initial amphibious training was conducted on freshwater lakes at Narford and Fritton in Suffolk. The latter was the main DD training school, run by Canadian Army staff under the 79th Armoured Division.

VALENTINE XI DD, 3RD KING'S OWN HUSSARS, ITALY, 1944

This was the last mark of Valentine tank to be built and the only Valentine DD to see active service. Powered by a more powerful version of the GMC diesel it was armed with a 75mm dual-purpose gun and a Besa machine gun in a cramped turret that could just about accommodate two men. This drawing has been contrived to show how the tank sat in relation to the flotation screen. These later-production Valentines were somewhat longer than the early versions, but even so the longer gun still required the turret to be traversed aft before the screen could be raised. The air pillars that raised the screen and the tubular bars that held it in place are shown on the far side and the single propeller is in the lowered position ready for swimming.

Some of these tanks were sent out to Italy where they were issued to the 3rd Hussars (whose badge is shown) and 7th Hussars. This last regiment used some of them on active service, albeit in a support role, but there is no recorded evidence of their seeing combat action. (Illustration by Tony Bryan, © Osprey Publishing)

All this while the Valentine tank itself was evolving. Two-pounder (Valentine V) and 6-pounder (Valentine IX) versions have already been noted, but in 1943 a new 75mm gun was introduced that provided tanks with the ability to fire respectable high-explosive rounds in addition to armour-piercing. In truth the gun was not really new; it was the 57mm 6-pounder reamed out to 75mm and modified to chamber American 75mm ammunition as used in the Sherman. Since it hardly affected the tanks at all it was easy enough to convert them but even so the Valentine, approaching

The proposed Churchill DD reveals a much-enlarged screen to cope with the additional weight and a far more complex method of powering the propellers, seemingly from the final drive.

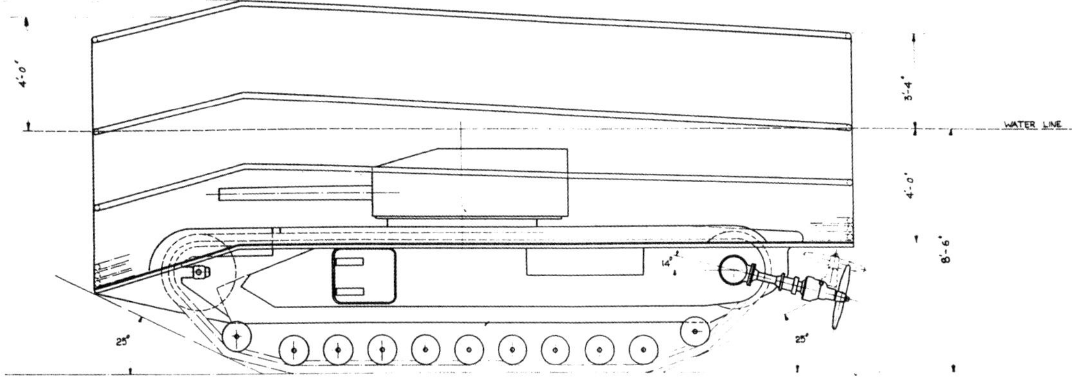

obsolescence by this time, was the lowest priority. However, as it happened it affected DD production. An RAC report from the summer of 1944, looking back over the previous six months, stated that total production of 2- and 6-pounder DDs would run to 365 tanks while the 75mm Mark XI DD would be produced to the number of 260. The report went on to state that those tanks with the smaller guns would be used for training purposes, that 75 operational and 30 training Mark XIs would be delivered to the Italian theatre and the rest apparently to South East Asia Command for use in the Far East. Figures released in December 1944, when production was complete, show 137 Mark V, 198 Mark IX and 260 Mark XI in all.

Ultimately Fritton became the nursery of all American, British and Canadian DD regiments that took part in the North-West Europe campaign. To increase realism a section of Bailey Bridge was erected, jutting out over the water, with a landing craft ramp at the end by means of which tanks were launched upon the lake. Crews learned the basics of boat handling and the tricky ritual of escape should their tank sink at sea. This was probably the most difficult operation of all. Close by the lake at Fritton was a deep concrete reservoir, at the bottom of which, according to some veterans, was a complete tank. Surviving photos only show the upper hull of a Sherman surmounted by a turret without a gun, but this could have been another location. Either way the purpose was the same. A trainee crew would get inside the tank, take up their approximate stations and then wait while the entire structure filled up with water. Then, on an order, they would activate the life-saving apparatus, wriggle out through the appropriate hatch and rise gently to the surface.

The risk of drowning while going down with your tank was very real, not just for those inside but even those 'on deck' who were liable to get caught if the screen collapsed inwards. Thus it was vital that crews had the proper equipment and were adequately trained, which was the purpose of the sink-training structure. At first it was assumed that escape would be no more difficult than from a sunken submarine so tests were carried out with Davis Submarine Escape Apparatus (DSEA), which comprised an inflatable pack worn across the chest and a little reservoir of oxygen. In practice the DSEA proved too bulky, so a more compact device known as the Amphibious Tank Escape Apparatus (ATEA) was developed by the Siebe Gorman Company and proved far more suitable. Even so, many survivors still believe that what they were issued with was the Davis gear.

SWIMMING THE VALENTINE

In preparing their tank for a swim, the crew first had to check all joints below screen level and ensure that they were sealed. Next the turret was turned through 180 degrees and trained aft and the gun brought to full elevation, otherwise the gun was liable to foul the screen.

This done the driver now opened a valve, and air from a bottle stowed at the rear inflated the side tubes, which in turn steadily raised the screen. Next the supporting struts were locked in place with a good, hard kick and the bilge pump engaged. The pump was mounted on a bracket low down at the rear, and it worked by the simple expedient of a small, rubber-tyred wheel that was brought into contact with the drum of the left-hand steering clutch and worked by friction once it was primed, shifting up to 24 gallons (109 litres) a minute.

The driver now grasped a special lever and inserted it into a socket that enabled him to lower the propeller until the ratchet clutch engaged with the driveshaft extension. The driver selected first gear and, under orders from his commander, drove

OPPOSITE Viewed from aboard an LCT, a Valentine DD enters the water. The propeller is visible, ready to engage, but the commander is more interested in the safety of his screen. The stripes painted beneath the propeller at the back are a night driving aid.

carefully down the ramp until the tank was afloat. Now he selected neutral and, while the tank drifted, moved the prop-elevating lever to another socket, which was the steering control. The reason for using the one lever for both operations was to avoid the risk of elevating the prop at any position other than dead centre, since it could be damaged. This procedure was adopted even if, as often happened, the commander took charge of steering from outside, using a temporary tiller bar that was stowed at the back.

An early Valentine DD with the raised front screen launching from an LST(2) in the Kyles of Bute. This was no easy task, only possible in deeper water and therefore improbable in practice. The tank is obviously carrying more than its normal complement of crew; notice the soldier watching from half way up the port side door.

Once in the water the driver shifted into third gear and, holding the revolutions steady so that the speedometer showed 5mph (8km/h) (the tracks, of course, were still going round), proceeded to follow a course on his binnacle compass relayed by the commander. Among other things the instruction book for the Valentine DD speaks of a pressure-operated depth gauge near the front of the tank that was visible through the driver's periscope. Once it inflated the driver knew he was in water over 3ft (1m) deep and therefore effectively afloat. Some sources suggest that the 'inflatable bulb' was in fact a condom.

Once the commander had selected a suitable landing spot the driver manoeuvred the tank until it was square on and then brought the revs up to full speed, still in third gear. As soon as it was established that the depth of water was less than 3ft (1m) the driver slowed to disengage the clutch and raise the propeller. Then the air was released from the tubes and the screen collapsed. That done the turret was returned to the forward position and the tank was ready for action.

DOWN TO THE SEA

From the calm, fresh waters of Fritton Lake crews now had to be trained at sea. A number of locations were developed, commencing with Inverary on Loch Fyne. This site on the west coast of Scotland had been selected as the Combined Operations Training Centre and the tanks set up their headquarters nearby at Castle Toward. From here they carried out training in the Kyles of Bute, a sheltered stretch of water near the island of that name. Another site was Fort George on Scotland's east coast where a number of exercises were held on the waters of the Moray

Valentine DD tanks manoeuvring off the Kyles of Bute on the west coast of Scotland. Notice how some of these examples have a prominent raised bow section of the screen. They have less freeboard elsewhere than the main production variant.

Firth. Barafundle Bay, on the coast of South Wales, was also chosen because it was adjacent to an army firing range. It was here that various 'firing against' trials were carried out against unmanned DD tanks. On one glorious occasion a DD regiment, having swum their tanks ashore, were invited to line up along the water's edge and blaze away at the cliffs.

There were two important sites in the south of England. The sheltered waters of the Solent, separating the Isle of Wight from the mainland, proved to be an ideal training ground but for one thing. Tanks loaded on landing craft at Stokes Bay near Gosport and were launched to swim ashore in Osborne Bay on the island. One veteran recalls that if, during the passage, an Isle of Wight ferry got too close the crew had to stop the tank and drape a large canvas over the turret until it had gone by. The other location was Studland Bay, just outside Poole Harbour in Dorset. Here, among other things, was one of the special installations established to set the sea on fire in the event of invasion, which played a part in the trials, as we shall see. But Studland Bay was also the site of a very unfortunate accident involving the 4th/7th Dragoon Guards on 4 April 1944.

It is worth noting that the 4th/7th was still in Valentines at this time, although Shermans were also being used for training. Exercise Smash was a two-squadron landing in Studland Bay that began soon after dawn. No sooner were the tanks afloat

Stokes Bay, on the mainland side of the Solent, was the principal centre for training DD crews to work in conjunction with the Royal Navy. Here Mark V (foreground) and Mark XI Valentines DD wait, with turrets traversed, to back onto landing craft. Crews wear conventional life preservers while the tank carries one lifebelt. Note the air cylinders on the engine decks of the nearest tanks.

than the wind got up, the sea turned rough and tanks began shipping water. Before long it was more than the bilge pumps could cope with and six tanks sank, taking six men with them. Others remained afloat but drivers were sometimes up to their waists in water before they reached the shore. Operational use of the Valentine DD was minimal and so closely linked to activities of Shermans that it can be covered later.

TOP LEFT Screens raised and engines fired up, Valentine DDs prepare to launch from an LCT(2) in the Solent. Packed aboard like this it is difficult to move off, line up and launch without damaging the screen. These tanks feature a new type of driver's and commander's periscope.

TOP A frontal view of a Valentine XI DD with the screen folded down and turret swung round to face forwards. The arrangement of the decking, beneath the screen, is well shown in this view, as is the location of the WD number, painted where it can be seen even when the screen is raised.

ABOVE LEFT 'Firing against' trials were conducted off the rugged coast of South Wales. The screen is damaged and torn, exposing part of the frame, but in calm conditions such as this the tank is still afloat.

THE SHERMAN DD

The decision to adapt the DD programme to the Sherman tank was taken in 1943, and was a perfectly natural one given that the Valentine was past its prime by then and the Sherman was effectively the main battle tank of all the western Allies from this time. The programme remained essentially a British project, although the Americans had expressed an interest and would soon be gearing up to produce a version of the British design. In fact there remains a certain amount of confusion, even in original sources, about the types of tanks and quantities involved. For example the first mention of the Sherman DD in the RAC six-monthly reports – in this case for the second half of 1943 – states that there was a requirement for 100 Sherman V (M4A4) DDs and 593 Sherman III (M4A2) DDs.

Clearly at least one working prototype existed by then, since it was described as having been used in launching trials from the LST (Landing Ship Tank) 2 and the LCT (Landing Craft Tank) 2 with the result that both vessels were deemed unsuitable because their ramps were too short to ensure a safe launch. All of which seems to have been a bit of a waste of time, since neither type of vessel was destined to become operational in the future, and the RAC knew that.

Six months later, but probably compiled well before D-Day, the report states that development of the Sherman IV (M4A3) DD and Sherman V DD were finalized and the tanks were now in service. Yet there is no evidence of a Sherman IV DD, and the M4A3 itself was rare in British service. It may well have been a prototype built for the Americans but this cannot be confirmed. Meanwhile, development of the M4A2-based

The chalk stack known as 'Old Harry' near Studland Bay in Dorset watches over the progress of a Sherman DD in quite heavy sea conditions. Why it should be heading out to sea is not so easy to understand. It was in these waters that the 4th/7th Dragoon Guards suffered their losses in April 1944.

In the calmer waters of the Solent a Sherman DD I, probably an M4A4 given the extra freeboard, approaches the Isle of Wight with Norris Castle visible in the trees. This version featured a stiffened upper rail and raised screen at the rear.

Sherman III DD, the diesel version, was continuing. The results of flotation and cooling trials are described as satisfactory and it seems that on this version the propellers could swing upwards by 72 degrees, which was an improvement on the M4A4. Orders had been placed (with Metro-Cammell again) for just 293 Sherman III DDs while the requirement for the Sherman V DD had risen correspondingly to 400. A further statement reveals that the tanks would be issued to 'DD Brigades' on a scale of 15 tanks per squadron, but there is no explanation of what a DD brigade consisted of. The change in respective quantities appears to reflect problems in developing the M4A2 DD, but it is worth noting that production of the M4A4 had already ceased in the USA so the extra tanks would have to be drawn from British holdings.

The average weight of a basic Sherman tank was around 30 tons (30.4 tonnes) fully stowed, a substantial increase on the Valentine. To accommodate this weight the screen was enlarged yet again. It now stretched 7ft (2.1m) from deck to rim and was divided into three bands. The lowest part was three layers thick, the middle part two layers and the top just one layer. It is worth noting that in the case of the Sherman V DD, which had a longer hull and was the heaviest type, the additional canvas required to surround it provided additional buoyancy, causing the tank to ride about 1ft (30cm) higher in calm water.

Of course the Sherman, like all contemporary American tanks, differed from British types in the layout of its transmission. Gearbox and final drive and driving sprockets were located at the front, which posed a problem for Straussler and his design team. It was impossible to take the propeller drive straight from the gearbox, although the alternative adopted was quite ingenious. Two propellers were located at the back, beneath the rear overhang of the hull. They were driven from the tracks, via additional sprocket rings bolted to the idlers, which, in turning, rotated shafts through bevel boxes to the props. Ratchet clutches enabled the propellers to be raised clear when the tank was driven over land.

Steering the tank in the water was achieved by swivelling both propellers, either through a hydraulic system from the driver's seat or manually by a large tiller bar, operated by the tank commander, for whom a special platform was fitted to the rear of the turret, raising him high enough to see over the rim of the screen. Hydraulics were also employed to raise the propellers upwards and clear of the ground which, of course, also detached them from the drivetrain. Note that in the Sherman the driver was not expected to use the same lever to steer the craft and lower the propellers. One other difference from the Valentine was the provision of an electrically driven bilge pump that ejected surplus water through a pipe situated close to what would be the starboard bow of the swimming tank.

A Sherman III (M4A2) DD on the beach at Studland Bay. Notice that the propellers are still folded up and that the idler does not have an extra sprocket ring to facilitate drive. By this time it had been discovered that friction between the tracks and conventional idler was quite sufficient.

Performance in the water was slightly better than that of the Valentine with a top speed of around 6mph (10km/h) but the greater weight, particularly suspended below the surface, tended to make the Sherman DD more sluggish in choppy weather so it did not rise to the waves quite so easily and therefore tended to ship more water. Even so, many writers remark on the fact that, once they became accustomed to it, the Sherman was easier to steer when afloat than one might expect from its shape.

CHANGES IN ORGANIZATION

There appears to have been a diminution of interest in DD tanks late in 1943, but it is not clear what was driving it. At the outset it seems, or so the regiments believed, each regiment was to convert almost entirely to the amphibious role – three squadrons and regimental headquarters, only excluding reconnaissance troops and other ancillaries. Under the new system each regiment would nominate two squadrons for conversion to Duplex Drive, the remainder retaining conventional tanks. Whether this was due to a change in policy or a shortage of DD tanks is not clear, but the East Riding Yeomanry (ERY) thought they knew.

In February 1944 the ERY was told that it would hand over its DD tanks and revert to the normal role and it was claimed that this was due 'to a shortage of equipment', but this was belied by the fact that at the same time, the Nottinghamshire (Sherwood Rangers) Yeomanry took over its DD role. During the same period there was one of those curious organizational changes within the British Army that tended to baffle people at the time and have confused historians ever after. From February 1944 it was announced that the 8th Armoured Brigade would now comprise 4th/7th Dragoon Guards, 24th Lancers and Sherwood Rangers Yeomanry – the first and last being DD regiments. Meanwhile, the 27th Armoured Brigade, which would retain 13th/18th Hussars as its sole DD regiment, added the Staffordshire Yeomanry and retained the East Riding Yeomanry as conventional armoured regiments.

So was there a shortage of DD tanks? The answer seems to be yes, probably due to the delay in finalizing the design of the M4A2-based Sherman III DD and the requirement to supply DDs to the Canadians as well. It was solved when the Americans agreed to transfer 80 of their M4A1 DDs, which became the Sherman II DD in British service. Even so there are some curious inconsistencies. A 21st Army

SHERMAN DD TANK SWIMMING, VIEWED FROM ABOVE

The crew have been omitted from this unusual view in order to show as much detail of the tank as possible. In fact, during the run-in to the beach all but the driver would probably be 'on deck'. The commander, as helmsman on the platform at the rear of the turret, and the other three crew members are doing their best to prevent the sides of the screen from being forced inwards due to the pressures of wind and tide.

Most accounts imply that once the skill of handling the tank afloat had been mastered it was not difficult to manoeuvre, although with a top speed in the water of no more than 6mph (10km/h) it was very much at the mercy of the effects of wind and tide. As mentioned elsewhere, for seaborne operations each tank was issued with a small dinghy of the Royal Air Force pattern, which self-inflated for use in an emergency. Unfortunately it has not been possible to establish just where on the tank it was stowed, so it has not been included. (Illustration by Tony Bryan, © Osprey Publishing)

Group report allegedly showing holdings as of 30 June 1944 gives the following figures:

> Sherman II DD 76 issued to 8th Armoured Brigade plus a reserve of four
> Sherman V DD 76 issued to 2nd Canadian Armoured Brigade
> 38 issued to 27th Armoured Brigade
> 75 issued to 15th/19th Hussars
> 57 reserves

The Sherman III DD does not appear anywhere in this table.

Ignoring 15th/19th Hussars for the present, what was the establishment of a DD-equipped regiment under the British system in 1944? According to a table published by the 13th/18th Hussars a DD squadron comprised a squadron headquarters of four DD tanks plus four troops, each of four DD tanks – that is 20 DD tanks in all per squadron, 40 per regiment. And just to complete the picture regimental headquarters had four Shermans described as wading, to distinguish them from DD, and a wading squadron with four tanks in squadron HQ and four troops each of three 75mm and one 17-pounder (Firefly) Sherman tanks.

The picture this table paints is of all five regiments short of establishment by two DD tanks at this time. Photographic evidence, for what that is worth, seems to bear out the distribution as listed above, so that any image of a Sherman II DD in British service should show a tank of 8th Armoured Brigade. If the tank is a Sherman V DD

SHERMAN V DD, A SQUADRON, 13TH/18TH ROYAL HUSSARS, NORMANDY, 6 JUNE 1944

One peculiarity is the screen, seen in many photographs draped over the rear of some DD tanks of the 13th/18th Hussars. Each screen was divided into a chequerboard pattern of blue/green and white squares. They were visible when the tanks were swimming and can also be seen hanging down the back of tanks operating ashore. Whether they were unique to this regiment, or even to one squadron of the regiment, cannot be established but an example is shown here as a tank, in the shallows, drops the front of its screen and engages enemy targets on Sword Beach. The 13th/18th had another practice that appears to be unique. Bearing in mind that the brigade sign and arm of service marking would normally be invisible below the surface they are seen, on some tanks, painted on the gun mantlet. The seahorse is, of course, the insignia of 27th Armoured Brigade while 51, in white on a red square, indicates the senior regiment in that brigade – 13th/18th Royal Hussars. The larger turret number 43, in red outlined in white, indicates an A Squadron tank. (Illustration by Tony Bryan, © Osprey Publishing)

then it should be 13th/18th Hussars if it sports a large, two-digit number on the turret; if not, then it is Canadian: 6th Canadian Armoured Regiment (1st Canadian Hussars) or 10th Canadian Armoured Regiment (Fort Garry Horse). The three American DD battalions, the 70th, 741st and 743d, would all have M4A1 DD tanks, many of which would have an improved hull casting with larger overhead hatches for the driver and radio operator. These were assembled at the Lima Locomotive Works in Ohio from DD kits supplied by the Firestone Tire Company.

LANDING CRAFT

Two classes of amphibious warship are linked with the use of DD tanks when operating from the sea. These were the LCT, or Landing Craft Tank, and larger LST, the Landing Ship Tank. Of the latter, as we have seen, the LST(2) proved difficult to launch from, but in any case there was a different problem affecting the Sherman DD. It was simply too tall to pass through the bow door section when fully inflated and the alternative, of driving onto the outer ramp with the screen half raised, and then inflating at the next stage, seems fraught with difficulty.

This failing was remedied with the subsequent LST(3), but it came too late to participate in the Normandy landings. Meanwhile, in conjunction with the Royal Navy experiments were conducted off the Kyles of Bute to examine the possibility of transferring tanks from LST to LCT at sea. This procedure involved having the

FAR RIGHT Since Landing Craft Tank (LCT) would be preferred for DD launching, trials were conducted with extended ramps, seen here on an LCT(2). They not only guided the tank through the narrow gap at the bow, but also launched it well clear of the leading edge of the ramp, which was always a dangerous moment.

TOP In the United States production of 76mm gun DD Shermans was undertaken to fulfil British requirements. Meanwhile in Britain a similar tank is fitted out with a replica of the tubular framework to show how it will accommodate the longer gun.

two vessels come together bow to bow with their ramps down and then driving the tanks, with their screens folded, from the larger to the smaller ship. Presumably the idea was to take advantage of the greater carrying capacity of the larger ship and its better seaworthiness to undertake voyages, while the LCTs acted as ferries off the invasion beaches. However, there would appear to be a problem in that once aboard the LCT the DD tanks would all be facing the wrong way and neither the Valentine nor the Sherman had the facility of a neutral turn; they certainly could not launch backwards. It goes without saying that this operation could only be conducted in a flat, calm sea.

As mentioned earlier, of the smaller craft the LCT(2) had already been rejected as unsuitable for DD tank work so the longer LCT(3) was selected instead. In its normal role the LCT(3) was capable of carrying nine Sherman tanks and in the early days of training Valentine DD tanks were packed aboard like the proverbial sardines. However, the importance of getting DD tanks into the water without damage to the screens led to the practice of carrying just five DD tanks on British and Canadian craft. These would be arranged herringbone fashion on deck. The Americans used the shorter and wider LCT(5). Incidentally, note that the Americans carried just four DD tanks on each LCT and it is assumed that the five per craft practice adopted by British and Canadian regiments included one DD tank from squadron headquarters with each troop.

COMBAT HISTORY

SWORD BEACH

The wind was blowing steadily, Force 5 from the west. All night long the LCT(3)s pushed on in line ahead, their square bows slapping into a succession of choppy waves. Tank crews, those not prostrate with seasickness, worked on their tanks. At some time, while it was still dark, each crew activated compressed-air bottles on their tank that inflated the black rubber tubes and up went the canvas screens to surround

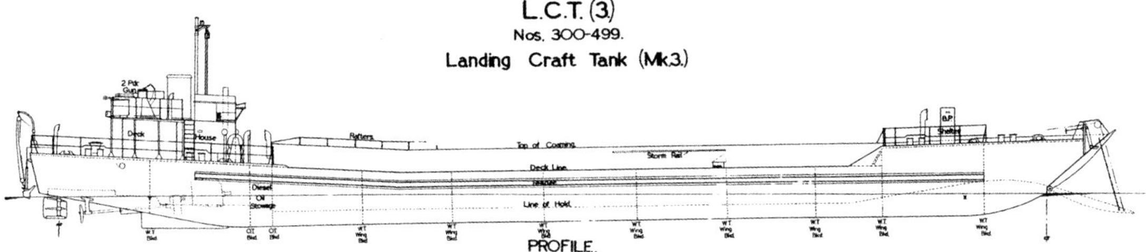

Side elevation on an LCT(3), the type that carried British and Canadian DD tanks on D-Day. This represents the first series of these craft, which were powered by twin Paxman diesel engines.

the upper hull and turret. Then the crews went around inside the screens and carefully locked the various supporting struts in place before settling down to await the dawn.

Each LCT, which was designed to carry nine ordinary tanks, tightly packed, had five of the Duplex Drive Shermans on board, since the DD tanks were bulkier than a conventional Sherman and needed more space to manoeuvre. Ten thousand yards (9,144m) from shore, the point marked by a midget submarine, the LCTs carrying the DD tanks of the 13th/18th Queen Mary's Own Hussars fanned out until they were in line abreast. At H-Hour minus 110 minutes Major Wormald commanding A Squadron received the order 'FLOATER' on LCT number 101. His second-in-command on 102, Captain Lyon, went around his crews and dished out a tot of rum. More air was blown into the support tubes and at 5,000 yards (4,572m), some 2,000 yards (1,828m) further in than the original plan called for, the LCTs rang down to stop engines and each craft dropped a stern anchor while the crew prepared to lower the ramp. The sea was a bit calmer here, but not much.

Ten minutes was allowed for the launch and one by one the tanks manoeuvred onto the centre line of the tank deck and eased forwards. This was the tricky bit: first each tank had to make its way carefully through the narrow bow – touch either side and you would rip the canvas screen. Then you had to negotiate the ramp and slip into the water. According to the drill this was to be done in second gear so that the tank had enough velocity to drift clear of the ramp, but Wormald and Lyon had already agreed that their tanks would move off and stay in first, edging down the ramp with careful use of the clutch before taking the plunge. As each tank settled in the water and ensured it was clear of the ramp the driver lowered the two propellers and the unwieldy little craft started to get under way.

As his tank slipped down the ramp Major Wormald glanced at the shore; there, ahead of him he could make out the church tower at Lion-sur-Mer and calculated that his landing beach was 45 degrees off his port bow. At this time the shoreline was clear, but in a very short while it was obscured by shells from the warships behind him, by bombs from above and by more shells fired from self-propelled artillery on other landing craft. Very soon rockets from modified landing craft would also come roaring over to add to the noise and smoke. The major had absorbed a fair amount of nautical lore during training, and so had Captain Lyon, who was worried about the state of the sea: it had never been as rough as this during training. Lyon was most concerned about the effect of a beam sea – waves striking the sides of his tanks and swamping them – so he adopted a zigzag course to counter this. He remarked afterwards how well the tanks stood up to the conditions and was particularly pleased that a modification to the rear struts prevented them from collapsing under pressure. Struggling against the waves the flotilla of tanks formed straggling columns behind their pilot boats and headed for the shore.

ABOVE Two abandoned DD tanks share Sword Beach at Lion-sur-Mer with other debris from the great storm. These tanks are from the 13th/18th Hussars and feature the brigade insignia and arm of service markings on the mantlet, a practice that appears to be unique to this regiment.

RIGHT A classic view of a Sherman DD launching from an LCT(3). This was the dangerous time: one could easily rip the screen on projecting parts of the landing craft or crash back into the ramp after launching, due to the action of the sea.

Not that it went smoothly for everyone. The first tank to try and launch from LCT 467 tore its screen and since the others could not get past there were two options – either dump the afflicted tank in the sea or take the whole troop ashore and land dry, which is what they did. As the last tank but one plunged off LCT 465 the ramp broke and the landing craft was obliged to sail home with the fifth tank still on board.

This Sherman DD of the 4th/7th Dragoon Guards made it ashore on Gold Beach, only to become trapped in a soft patch on the beach. Although it is not recorded elsewhere, this regiment appears to have used turret numbers for identification purposes, although a contemporary colour photograph suggests that these were just white outlines with no colour infill.

SHERMAN V DD, 2ND CANADIAN ARMOURED BRIGADE, NORMANDY, 6 JUNE 1944

The tank is preparing to launch from the deck of an LCT(3). The screen is fully raised and the propellers deployed in readiness for the swim ashore to Juno Beach. Tarry sealant compounds such as Bostick were used to cover all those parts of the screen where metal and canvas met, and most particularly where bolts passed through the fabric. However, photographic evidence from D-Day suggests that some Canadian crews went mad with the stuff and plastered it everywhere to improve their chances of staying afloat.

At least one of the Canadian regiments, the 1st Hussars or Fort Garry Horse (or maybe both), seems to have used two- or three-digit numbers in varied colours painted high up on the back of the screen for identification purposes, although no explanation of the system can be found. The insignia is that of the 2nd Canadian Armoured Brigade. (Illustration by Tony Bryan, © Osprey Publishing)

Meanwhile, the remaining tanks of A and B Squadrons were ploughing on through the waves. Glancing round Captain Lyon counted 19 tanks, all keeping good station, but progress was slower than the timetable called for due to the rough weather, and that was not all. Some 1,200 yards (1,097m) from shore, Lyon said, they were overtaken by other LCTs 'apparently steered by maniacs' that threatened to run them down. His squadron altered course to avoid them but Captain Denny's tank, from LCT 103, was hit and rolled over in the water. Denny was the only survivor.

Minutes later the LCT(R) rocket craft opened up. Major Wormald estimated that 10 per cent of the projectiles fell short, in amongst the swimming tanks. Now the LCTs that had driven through them went astern, but the DD tanks were unable to stop and overtook the landing craft. At this point the DD tanks were supposed to spread out in line abreast but this did not prove so easy; at about 300 yards (274m) from shore the drivers felt their tracks bite on the sand – they had made it.

OPERATIONS *NEPTUNE* AND *OVERLORD*

The preceding passage describes the landing on D-Day from the point of view of the 13th/18th Hussars, but since D-Day was the action debut of the DD tank it seems reasonable to follow the fortunes of all eight regiments/battalions on this significant day. We shall begin at the opposite end of the invasion zone, off Utah Beach. The pattern of tidal movement in the English Channel means that the tide begins its rise from the west, so H-Hour here was 0630 hours. Even so the DD tanks of 70th Battalion were running some 15 minutes late due to the loss of a control vessel, and four tanks were lost prior to launching when their LCT was hit by enemy artillery fire. Although sea conditions were not too bad in the lee of the Cherbourg Peninsula, the DD tanks were carried in to within 1,000 yards (914m) of the beach; 28 tanks from the two DD companies launched and 27 swam ashore to a very mild reception. Confused by a massive smoke screen the leading infantry landed about 2,000 yards (1,828m) away from their objective and encountered relatively little opposition, so the tanks did not find a lot to do.

Further east, off Omaha Beach, sea conditions were much worse. Local fishermen claim that west of the Calvados Reef waves are shorter and steeper in certain conditions of wind and tide, and this was the situation on 6 June 1944. Indeed it looked so bad that it was agreed that landing craft carrying two companies of the 743d Battalion towards Dog Sector should finally sail all the way in and land them more or less dry. Just east, in the unfortunately named Easy Sector, DDs of the 741st Battalion launched at about 5,000 yards (4,572m) and created a legend that endures to this day. Twenty-nine tanks launched and were soon swept off course by the wind and tide. Struggling to regain their position, one after another they were swamped and plunged to the bottom until just two made it to the beach, joined later by three more that never launched. Men of the 116th Infantry, heading for Omaha in their landing craft, noticed dozens of men in the water, mostly in little orange dinghies, and assumed they were all downed aircrew. Only later was it realized that these were the survivors of the 743d.

It has to be said that many American officers were very sceptical about the safety and effectiveness of DD tanks, and there is some justification for this. On the other hand where they did make it ashore the DD tanks did very good work, and those that reached Omaha gave an extremely good account of themselves while they survived.

Off Gold Beach, where H-Hour was 0725 hours, it was now the turn of B and C Squadrons of the Nottinghamshire Sherwood Rangers Yeomanry (SRY) to land on Jig Sector. Sea conditions were not good here so they launched at 700 yards (646m), but even so the two squadrons lost eight tanks between them. They were late in landing and in the interim Sherman Crab flail tanks of the Westminster Dragoons had been doing their work for them, taking out gun positions and machine-gun nests.

However, it is interesting to note that in this case the SRY records that A Squadron and Regimental Headquarters (both waders) arrived about 90 minutes later. Immediately to their east the 4th/7th Dragoon Guards encountered similar conditions, so its senior naval officer decided to run them all the way in. The water was deep enough to justify raising the screens, but in essence the DD tanks of B and C Squadrons simply drove ashore through the breakers. Unfortunately, having made it to the beach a number of 4th/7th Dragoon Guards tanks were then trapped in patches of soft sand and were subsequently swamped by the incoming tide.

Next along the coast was Juno Beach where the 3rd Canadian Division was due to land, supported by two Canadian DD regiments. Here H-Hour was 0735 hours on Mike and 0745 hours on Nan Sectors and the former was to be assaulted by the DD tanks of A and B Squadrons, 1st Hussars (6th Armoured Regiment). On account of the sea conditions the A Squadron tanks were carried to within 1,500 yards (1,371m) of the shore where ten launched, of which seven actually made it while the remainder landed dry. B Squadron, on the other hand, launched at about 4,000 yards (3,657m), deployed at 2,000 yards (1,828m) and put 14 out of 19 tanks ashore.

ABOVE Sherman V (M4A4) DD tanks, probably from one of the Canadian regiments, photographed well inland. The nearest tank still retains stumps of some rubber pillars; the next tank still has the special turret fittings while the one in front of that seems to have been more thoroughly stripped.

LEFT Moving inland with infantry in support, this 13th/18th Hussars Sherman shows another unique feature, the chequered panel of white and blue/green squares draped over the back of the flotation screen, presumably with some special 'follow me' purpose.

The Fort Garry Horse (10th Armoured Regiment) launched its A and B Squadrons much closer in, and although some claim to have used their propellers the majority simply had what they describe as a wet wade before deflating on the shoreline. Apparently the code word indicating that DD tanks had made it ashore was POPCORN.

Of the 13th/18th Hussars on Sword Beach we already have an account. A and B Squadrons were in DD tanks and of their combined total of 40 tanks 34 took the plunge and 31 made it ashore. Casualties were few although once on the shoreline, and this seems to have been a common failing, the tanks were so absorbed in the business of picking and destroying targets that many failed to notice the encroaching tide and were swamped, although they kept firing until rising water made the turrets untenable.

There is one very curious feature of the 13th/18th, a practice that none of the other DD regiments appear to have adopted. Draped over the rear of the screen of each tank was a large fabric panel divided into a chequerboard pattern of eight squares, alternatively green and white, which showed above the surface when the tank was afloat. Once ashore, if the crew remembered to arrange it, the panel hung from the collapsed screen like an apron. Logically it was some sort of 'follow me' indicator for accompanying infantry, but no mention of it has yet been found and it is not even clear if it was specific to one or both DD squadrons.

Depending on the situation ashore many tanks went quite a long way inland still sporting their folded screens. The SRY were certainly photographed passing through Bayeux in this state. However, as soon as there was time available most tanks had their screens removed, there being a fear that once the screen dried out it could be very vulnerable to flamethrowers. So off came the screens, air pillars, struts and

SHERMAN II DD, C SQUADRON NOTTINGHAMSHIRE (SHERWOOD RANGERS) YEOMANRY, NORMANDY, 6 JUNE 1944

The launching process was probably the trickiest operation for DD crews. They had to avoid catching the screen on any part of the ship and ensure that as soon as they were afloat the tank moved clear of the submerged ramp. Here the commander/helmsman watches anxiously as *Lily* of the Sherwood Rangers takes the plunge for the run-in to Gold Beach.

Lily was later photographed in Bayeaux with her screen down. The tank was a Sherman II (M4A1) DD supplied directly from the USA as a DD tank. In addition to the name it carried the turret number and C Squadron circle as shown. (Illustration by Tony Bryan, © Osprey Publishing)

propellers. Even so most crews tried to retain the lower decking, particularly at the front where it formed a useful tray for carrying extra stores.

And there we must leave them. Once ashore they fought as regular tank units and, when the DD machines had shed their amphibious apparatus, there was little to distinguish them from those that landed dry.

Topee was a system of metal panels that enclosed a DD tank's screen while it was folded down, but which dropped away when it was raised. As the name implies it was intended for use in the Far East where, it was feared, dense undergrowth might otherwise tear the screen.

IMPROVEMENTS AND FUNNIES

A protective spray with the uncompromising name of Belch was developed for the DD tanks that, with the aid of a pump, sucked up sea water and squirted it over the vulnerable screen as the tank sailed through a formidable flame barrage of oil, burning on the sea, at Studland Bay. The flame barrage had been established as an anti-invasion measure in Britain and there was a fear that the Germans might have something similar.

Perhaps it is not surprising that when DD tanks were discussed in the immediate aftermath of D-Day, it was their sea-keeping qualities that dominated. After the war, when gathering evidence for his claim to a Royal Commission, Straussler solicited the opinion of various senior officers who had commanded in Normandy and they concentrated on the value of the DD as a gun tank. But in the face of losses such as those off Omaha the more immediate concern is understandable. There is some evidence to suggest that before D-Day the vulnerable top rail of the DD screen, where it runs down each side, was stiffened by an additional strip of metal but afterwards more extensive steps were taken.

These included adding extra struts from the sides of the turret to the upper rail and making all the struts self-locking, so it was no longer necessary to kick them. At the same time what is described as a flap was added to the rear of the screen that provided 12in (30cm) more freeboard, presumably to counter the effects of a following sea. Rough sea trials proved that these measures were effective, and they were applied retrospectively to all surviving DD tanks, which were now being referred to as the Mark I type.

The report that carried this information, which covers the second half of 1944, also refers to the Sherman III (M4A2) DD, the diesel version, development of which, it says, 'continued and proved satisfactory'. This long period seems to suggest problems that took a lot of sorting out, but what these may have been is not clear. Meanwhile, work was going forward to develop an improved model that became known as the Mark II DD. This not only had the improvements already recorded but a strengthened top rail of 3in (75mm) diameter, greater depth of freeboard fore and aft by extending the bow and stern canvas, and stronger, self-locking struts. A new design of bilge pump was installed and hydraulic steering was extended to the commander's position on the turret. The old tiller bar seems to have been retained for

A Valentine DD with a carpetlaying device was tested at Burton-on-Stather as another antidote to soft and slippery riverbanks. It was known by the codename Holy Roller, but does not appear to have been developed.

This is Hopper, in effect a Valentine DD ARK that carried ramps over which other tanks climbed when leaving the water. In this view, for some reason, it is deployed the wrong way round: the large, fan-shaped ramp on the left should be in the water. Naturally the Hopper tank would not be afloat at this stage.

emergencies, but the commander now had a pillar on his platform, with a handle on the top that duplicated the hydraulic steering system used by the driver. It was hoped to convert 691 DD tanks to this standard by the summer of 1945.

At least one tank had been lost on D-Day when, after launching, the propellers failed to engage and after wallowing for a while it was swamped and sank. The Mark II had improved propeller-locking gear to remedy this and a portable compressor was carried in place of the compressed air cylinders. Trials at sea in a Force 7 gale and a sea state of 5 to 6 proved that these modifications would make the tanks far more seaworthy. Meanwhile the Sherman itself had been improved. A new turret with a longer 76mm gun on a reshaped hull with a new type of suspension and wider tracks was steadily replacing the old 75mm gun models. A DD variant was clearly desirable and Britain expressed a requirement for 300, based on the M4A2 diesel version that would be designated Sherman III AY DD III where A indicates the 76mm gun and Y the modernized suspension. Firestone Tire Company in the United States (who made the original DD conversion kits in the USA) carried out the design work, but when the war in Europe ended the order was reduced to 200 for use in the Far East. In the event, very few appear to have been made and only two reached Britain.

The coastal flame barrage in Studland Bay has already been mentioned. It was feared that if the Germans were using something similar it could have a serious effect on DD tanks, so a device known as Belch was introduced to deal with it. This involved mounting a suction pump on the deck of the tank that drew seawater from below and then squirted it through holes in the topmost tubular frame of the screen so that it soaked the canvas. Trials at Studland soon showed that this worked remarkably well; Belch entered production but was never required on active service.

Landing DD tanks on a gently shelving beach was not a serious problem but 79th Armoured Division, with an eye to the future, put its collective ingenuity towards solving problems of high or muddy riverbanks. For the latter they devised Holy Roller, a Valentine DD with a roll of coir matting sticking out in front that could be laid, like a carpet, over soft ground as the tank emerged from the water. Another Valentine DD, stripped of its turret, was fitted with folding ramps to become an amphibious version of the Churchill ARK device used on dry land. Hopper, as it came to be called, carried a set of folding ramps above the screen so that when it grounded against a high river bank one dropped into the water while the other rested on the bank. DD tanks would follow, scrambling up the submerged ramp, over the other and onto dry land. It was certainly tested at Fritton but whether it ever actually worked is not recorded. Both Hopper and Holy Roller expired at the prototype stage. Another less dramatic solution to the mud problem was Moses, a sort of floating raft, towed by a Landing Vehicle Tracked (LVT) and deployed over the questionable surface. Trials on the River Trent revealed that it was impossible to control in high winds.

There followed the Porpoise, a small, flat raft designed to carry extra supplies of ammunition. Towed behind a conventional Armoured Fighting Vehicle (AFV), as they were on D-Day, they were dragged ashore fully laden, but for DD tanks they floated when half full. Although tested on DD tanks they seem to have hampered performance afloat and were soon dropped.

NEW SCHEMES

Despite the unmitigated horror of Omaha the Americans were not yet ready to give up on the DD. With landings in the South of France planned for August 1944, an Amphibious Training Center was established in the Bay of Naples and three Battalions, the 191st, 753d and 756th, were trained there. In the event sea conditions were much calmer and resistance much less intense when Operation *Dragoon* was launched and 20 DD tanks swam safely ashore followed by 16 more that landed dry.

In Britain, meanwhile, it was time for another round of military musical chairs. Early in July 1944 the 15th/19th King's Royal Hussars were notified that they were to convert to a Water Assault Regiment and moved down to Fritton to start training. The entire regiment went through the process, that is to say headquarters squadron and the three sabre squadrons, which would require a total of 64 DD tanks and may explain why, as seen earlier, the regiment had 75 DD tanks allotted to it. Training was complete by the end of the month, at which time the regiment was informed that it would not go into battle as a DD regiment after all.

Nobody ever explained to the men what they were supposed to do when the DD training was complete. The most popular theory was a diversionary landing, perhaps in the Calais area, but although they did sea training from the beach at Lee-over-Sands in Essex they never practised launching from landing craft, and that may be indicative. What they did not know was that a change was taking place in France. At that same time, late July 1944, the 27th Armoured Brigade was broken up. Of its three regiments the 13th/18th Hussars, which had used DDs in action, and East Riding Yeomanry, which had trained on them in Britain, were re-allocated while its third armoured regiment, the Staffordshire Yeomanry, which had no DD experience at all, was shipped back to Britain to acquire some. They, presumably, took over the DD tanks now being handed in by the 15th/19th Hussars.

NORTH-WEST EUROPE

The Staffordshire Yeomanry, just like the 15th/19th, had all three squadrons and RHQ trained on DD tanks, first at Fritton and then at Burton-on-Stather on the River Trent near Scunthorpe. This location may have given it a clue as to its future since the land is flat and low-lying, the rivers broad and very muddy. Early in September there was a hurried move to Belgium where, following further training on the Lac d'Hofstade, B Squadron was ordered to Terneuzen. From here, early on the morning of 26 October, 18 DD tanks launched and undertook a 7-mile (11km) voyage across the West Scheldt estuary to land on South Beveland. This journey must qualify as the longest operational cruise ever undertaken by DD tanks, but it is rarely noted by published histories and it came to a sticky end. The original landing place proved too steep for the tanks to climb so they launched again and sought better places along the shore. The result was 14 tanks stuck in thick mud with just four

TOP DD tanks of the Staffordshire Yeomanry, already veterans of the Scheldt battles, prepare for the Rhine crossing in March 1945. The nearest tank shows well how neatly the screen could fold down if done with care. In the background another DD waits, with its screen raised.

ABOVE An American Sherman DD in trouble during training for the Rhine crossing. Owing to shortages both American battalions involved in this operation were brought up to strength with British-built M4A2 and M4A4 types; however this would appear to be a regular American M4A1 type.

ready for action, and it was three days before the rest were freed.

There were important lessons to be learned, driven home by an attempt in November by C Squadron to swim the Mark Canal near Breda, which proved impossible again due to the steep banks. Ahead lay something even more formidable: the mighty River Rhine. In preparation for what would prove to be a major undertaking, the 79th Armoured Division created a series of training camps in the area, which they called Wings. G Wing, on the River Maas, was responsible for DD tank and Buffalo amphibian training while J Wing, on the Waal, taught navigation. Among other things G Wing undertook the challenging task of training the 44th Royal Tank Regiment (RTR) on DD tanks in just three weeks, in addition to a company from the American 736th Tank Battalion, which was mostly equipped from British stocks.

Two major problems faced the DD regiments on the Rhine: one was a fast-running current, the other steep and muddy banks. For the first a technique was developed that enabled tanks to enter the river upstream from the landing point so that, as they crossed the effect of the current brought them to the far bank in just the right place. For the second the regiments employed reconnaissance parties equipped with LVTs (Buffalos) fitted with special mats that they laid at the exit points as they climbed out, over which the DD tanks would follow. As far as the DD tanks were concerned, Operation *Plunder* commenced late on 23 March when, among others, the Staffordshire Yeomanry made a successful night crossing, losing just two tanks in the process. Since 44th RTR had not had enough time to do the navigation course they crossed in daylight, early the following morning. One or two tanks were lost but again, apart from a struggle to get out of the river, the crossing was considered a success. Another American battalion, the 748th, which was to cross further up river with General Patton's forces at Oppenheim, was obliged to make a long road march up to the river that rendered many of their DD tanks unfit for the operation.

The swansong of the DD in north-west Europe fell to an enlarged squadron of the Staffordshire Yeomanry that swam the Elbe at Artlenburg on 29 April 1945 and, rather fittingly, they were temporarily attached to 33rd Armoured Brigade of 79th Armoured Division. The village in which they assembled and inflated their tanks, preparatory to launching, was entirely cleared of its residents. This could hardly have been in the interests of secrecy – presumably there was some fear of sabotage to the vulnerable screens.

There remains one intriguing DD operation that might have been. Very late in the war plans were drawn up to liberate Amsterdam by sailing an amphibious force across the Zuider Zee. For no obvious reason the Westminster Dragoons, who since D-Day had been operating Sherman Crab mine-clearing flail tanks in 30th Armoured Brigade, were ordered to commence DD training and, while waiting for the tanks to arrive, were given some Valentine Archer self-propelled guns to train on. This led them to believe that they would be issued with Valentine DD tanks, rather than Shermans but, of course, the attack was never launched.

Another Staffordshire Yeomanry picture showing crew members struggling with a heavy canvas cover in ghastly winter conditions. The tank, an M4A4, seems to have been pulled out of some very wet ground to judge from the ropes at the front, although these may simply be ready to throw over the front of the screen once it is raised.

ITALY AND BEYOND

There was always a sense that things were done slightly differently in the Italian campaign, and this was equally true where DD tanks were concerned. In 1944 the 3rd Hussars began training with DD tanks but then handed them over to the 7th Hussars who, after an initial training period, were ordered to cease. Late in February 1945 the 7th Hussars once again took over DD tanks, both Valentines and Shermans, and started re-training. All three squadrons were involved.

On 24 April 1945 the regiment, split into squadrons that each supported a different division, was sent to cross the River Po on a broad front. From now on each squadron was on its own, and it would take too long to recount all their activities. Suffice it to say that, following a successful crossing of the Po those DD tanks still fit enough to swim took part in an assault crossing of the river Adige on the 28th where two Valentine DDs of A Squadron were used to bring up 400 gallons (1,818 litres) of diesel fuel for the Shermans, which must have been M4A2s. This is the only recorded use of Valentine DD tanks on active service. On the final advance to Venice, which did not require more swimming, the 7th Hussars' DDs carried infantry and discovered that with the screens folded down it was possible to get an entire infantry platoon onto each tank. Finally in the war period, it remains to record that the 25th Dragoons, then fighting in Burma, were recalled to India in July 1944 to convert to the DD role for operations in Malaya that, in the event, came to naught when the

B Squadron, 7th Hussars gives a lift to troops of the 8th Indian Division during the advance on Venice. Whether all those boots and weapons are good for delicate DD equipment is another matter. Notice the heavy-duty track extenders, which were locally made and essential in this low-lying country.

Sherman III DD II *Gosport* sporting 79th Armoured Division insignia, now inherited by the Specialized Armour Development Establishment, which had an amphibious wing based at Gosport in Hampshire. The mayor of Gosport stands alongside the tank with General Jean de Lattre de Tassigny on an official visit from France. Notice how the towrope is rigged for emergency use at sea.

war ended. The regiment was based at Cocanada in Andhra Pradesh where it did extended sea trials, but after all this effort it rushed back to Burma in April 1945 in conventional tanks. At the end of the war an experimental squadron was formed, operating a variety of specialized tanks, including DD tanks, and for a while the squadron appears to have been under the control of the 3rd Dragoon Guards (Carabiniers). A surviving DD at the Indian Cavalry Museum at Ahmednagar suggests that most of these tanks were handed over to the Indian Army when the British finally pulled out.

POST-WAR DEVELOPMENTS

Writing at the end of World War II Field Marshal Montgomery noted, 'The smaller our Army in peace-time the greater the need for a strong and robust organization devoted to research and experiment; in the British Army the nucleus of this organization may well be the 79th Armoured Division.' And so it was – for a while. The Specialized Armour Development Establishment (SADE) was formed by amalgamating what remained of 79th Armoured Division with the Assault Training and Development Centre plus the Canal Defence Light School. What concerns us here is C Wing, the AFV Flotation Centre based at Gosport in Hampshire, although it continued to carry out experiments at other sites, particularly where these were already functioning.

Interest in specialized armour expanded rapidly after D-Day, and the number of experiments snowballed to such an extent that even those relating to DD tanks will get no more than a few words here. Two were concerned with assisting a DD tank out of a river where it must first cross an area of soft mud, following the wartime trials of Hopper and Holy Roller.

Nicholas Straussler himself was behind the design of Gin-and-It, which consisted of a large mat, already deployed on the right, and a set of panels folded concertina fashion that stretched out beyond the mat as a tank climbed up the bank.

Gin-and-It was one of Nicholas Straussler's inevitably complicated efforts. An Sherman III (M4A2) DD was fitted with a three-piece shield in front of the screen and a folded mat on the end of a flimsy jib structure that stuck up above the screen. In theory, as the tank came ashore a spade at the front dug into the mud and triggered the shield, which fell forward and opened out to provide a firm surface for the tank to stand upon. At the same time the jib, activated by compressed air, would start to unfold the five-section mat ahead of the tank and, when it was laid, gave the tank a 40ft (12.2m) path onto dry land. In practice it never seems to have worked properly.

Rockets were another source of amusement for the staff at SADE. At one time it seemed there was nothing they could not do. In terms of DD operations rockets were seen as an alternate method of extricating tanks from mud or assisting them over riverbanks that they could not climb unaided. Once again the trials tank was a Sherman III (M4A2) DD and the trials locations were Tidworth on Salisbury Plain, Stokes Bay on the Solent and Hawley Lake in Kent. The rocket employed was the 5in (127mm) ATOG No.5 Mark I, which had been designed originally to provide assisted take-off for aircraft. It developed 1,410lb (640kg) of thrust for 3.5 seconds and the trick was getting the number of rockets right for a 35-ton (35.5-tonne) tank. The rockets were mounted on each side of the tank, on brackets at suspension level and angled back at 30 degrees. They were fired electrically. Various combinations were tried, sometimes too few to have any effect, sometimes too many and the tank virtually took off, but always with spectacular results. Generally it appeared to work quite well and drivers soon got used to it, but there were occasions when the screen buckled under the pressure or even caught fire, which was not at all what was required.

TOP Another method of overcoming a difficult landing was by rockets. A bank of ATOG aircraft rockets are attached to the suspension of this Sherman DD to be fired as it comes ashore. Success tended to depend on how evenly the rockets burned and how much soft ground had to be covered.

ABOVE Trials of the rocket egress system carried out at Gosport sometimes achieved interesting, if unpopular, results if the tank's screen was set on fire. Here observers on an LVT(4) Buffalo watch as the flames take hold. The tank is certainly not afloat and further shots in the series show the rear end of the screen burned down to the waterline.

The fact that a DD tank could not shoot while it was swimming exercised some minds. Wise men might feel that swimming was quite enough, but others are never satisfied and at least three experiments were conducted. In one a pair of .30-calibre Browning machine guns were mounted on the screen and fired by cable. In theory they were linked so that both would fire in the same direction, at the same elevation, but this was never achieved during trials and the project was dropped.

Working on the principle that a recoilless gun might be fired from the top of the screen without bending it, trials were conducted with a 3.7in (94mm) weapon – fortunately never actually on a DD tank. These weapons rely, of course, upon blast to counter the effect of recoil and the trials team found that there was no way of firing the gun or deflecting the blast that did not involve totally wrecking the screen, so they gave up.

British trials of the American M12 flotation device that employed two inflatable engineer pontoons, powered by twin outboard motors. Despite having to fit deep wading gear as well, the Americans preferred this system since the tank could shoot while afloat. However, it was much too wide to operate from landing craft.

Altogether more promising was a scheme to fire a 3in (75mm) mortar attached to the turret of a Sherman DD, in order to bring down fire on the hostile beach. With the mortar loader working from the commander's hatch and the helmsman aiming the tank this seemed to work reasonably well, but only in a flat calm with no effect from wind or tide. Accuracy fell off rapidly as conditions deteriorated, so this scheme was also abandoned.

SADE was also involved in trialling different types of inflatable dinghy for DD tanks. Their favourite was the five-man D Type Mark 2 as used aboard Air-Sea Rescue launches. Unlike the round type normally issued, this model had a distinct bow shape at the front and could be paddled in a given direction rather than round and round.

Mention should be made of other SADE trials that were DD related, including one to fit twin rudders for steering, which certainly showed an improvement, and experiments with various types of extended periscopes that were intended to give the driver of a DD tank something to look at rather than just the interior of the screen. They even went so far as to evaluate a new type of grease gun that, it was hoped, would make the task of packing the bearings of a DD tank easier, which it did.

Knowing, as we now do, that the whole concept of the DD tank, at least as it was at the time, was already doomed it is interesting to see to what lengths SADE was prepared to go in order to expand it. For example, in October 1946 it began tests of what they called an APCDD, or Armoured Personnel Carrier Duplex Drive, using a turretless Sherman tank just like the wartime Kangaroo. A prototype was created on a Sherman III (M4A2) but then had to be switched quickly to an Sherman V (M4A4) when the former were withdrawn. It was simple enough: the tank's turret was lifted off and the space used to carry infantry, presumably a section, say ten men. A mushroom-shaped overhead cover provided protection, but the report does not reveal whether or not it was easy for the men to scramble out once ashore. Indeed the trial seems to have been simply to see if the Sherman V could be converted to this role, not whether it worked.

The unique Sherman Kangaroo DD, here in the M4A4 form, showing the protective cover over the turret ring from which infantry peer out. A regular DD gun tank named Galashiels follows the Kangaroo.

It may seem to be tempting providence to launch a DD tank with a trailer, especially after the experience with the Porpoise. Yet it was done, apparently as part of an attempt to create a DD version of the Sherman Crocodile flame-thrower. The Sherman Crocodile had been developed for the Americans and used on a limited scale during the war. These post-war trials probably involved an ordinary Sherman DD to which the standard Crocodile trailer was attached. Three methods of providing buoyancy were tested: by attaching an inflatable boat or a steel flotation chamber to the trailer or by simply towing it and relying on the wash from the

End of the line: a Sherman III (M4A2) DD in the process of being stripped of its flotation equipment. Severed air pillars hang limply at the sides and some of the folding screen support struts remain, but this shot affords a very good view of the commander's platform on the back of the turret. Notice too the practice of repeating the War Department number on the lower hull side.

tank and the trailer's tyres to keep it afloat. All three worked after a fashion, although it proved too difficult to secure the rubber dinghy to the trailer firmly enough, and with no buoyancy aids at all the trailer floated very low in the water and affected the tank's steering. The steel box worked best, particularly when trials were conducted in launching both tank and trailer from a landing craft, but the trailer was never entirely stable in the water. As it was, following attempts to apply the DD principle to more modern types of tanks, it was dropped entirely (at least using Straussler's system). For a generation the British Army restricted its amphibious role to lighter AFVs, in fact to virtually anything except tanks, using a concertina screen that just about worked in calm conditions but relying on the vehicle's tracks or wheels to move it through the water.

CONCLUSION

While making a case for an award for his invention after the war, Nicholas Straussler solicited opinions from a number of senior officers, and their replies were preserved. Writing of D-Day they all agreed that without the DD tanks things might have been a lot tougher, at least on the British beaches, but D-Day was a one-off event and always will be. One could debate the value of subsequent DD operations.

Yet, as we have seen, DD development continued for some years after the war and was succeeded by other amphibious creations that did more or less the same thing. Thus it is probably safe to say that Straussler's DD system had its day on 6 June 1944 and was a wasting asset thereafter. Never mind, it was a brilliant innovation employed with remarkable courage that still generates an amazing amount of interest.

CHAPTER 6

SHERMAN CRAB FLAIL TANK

Most readers will know that the Western Desert is meant to be a 'tactician's paradise', an open expanse in which the gifted commander can exercise his skills to outmanoeuvre his opponent. Even so, this is only true in a limited sense. There are all manner of natural features in the desert that inhibit what a commander can do, and the sensible soldier improves upon these with man-made ones, among which the minefield is the most effective. Well sited, the minefield can turn vast swathes of desert into no-go areas for mobile forces and channel them elsewhere at the dictates of the defender. For the Allied armies operating in the theatre during World War II, some system or machine had to be created to counter the threat of mines.

BORN IN THE DESERT

When Rommel took Tobruk in June 1942, the British and Allied forces began a massive retreat back over the Egyptian frontier, hoping to reach Cairo and Alexandria before the Germans did. Among them was a British workshop unit (No.4 Ordnance Workshop) that had been based, until this time, at Buq-Buq near the coast, and which had with it a very strange vehicle. Carried in the back of a Canadian Ford lorry was another Ford chassis, shortened somewhat although still retaining the engine, transmission and rear axle. At each end of the axle, where the wheels might have been, were drums, from which hung lengths of wire rope and chain – it was, in effect, the original anti-mine flail. In action the shortened chassis would be suspended from the front of the regular lorry like a jib, but facing back to front so that the flail drums were at the forward end where they beat the ground to explode mines in the path of the vehicle.

The officer responsible for this piece of work was Major Norman Berry, then Assistant Director of Ordnance Stores (ADOS) at HQ XIII Corps. A year earlier, in September 1941, Berry had been ordered to Pretoria to examine a South African proposal for a mine-sweeping flail device described as a threshing machine. He was introduced to a Captain Abraham du Toit and shown a short colour film of the contraption in action. It appealed to Berry and he suggested that work should begin

A Crab going all-out. This photograph is presumably a training picture since there are no markings on the tank and no photographer with any sense would stand just here if there was any risk of a mine going off.

at once, preferably at a desert workshop where secrecy could be maintained, but this was overruled. Instead du Toit, as the inventor, was to go to Great Britain and pursue his work there. Berry went back to the desert; du Toit departed for London on 14 October 1941 with details of what General Claude Auchinleck described as an Anti-Tank Mine Springing Device.

Berry found this all very frustrating. He was sure the concept could be made to work, but he heard nothing more. He pestered everyone he could find. Visiting officers from Britain, particularly those with a technical background, were his favourite targets, but nobody had so much as heard of du Toit, never mind a threshing machine that would destroy mines. Berry's decision to continue the experimental work unofficially was interrupted by Rommel's latest attack, and when No.4 Workshop arrived in the Alamein area they were simply too busy patching up damaged tanks to do any more with the threshing machine. Rather than write the project off, Berry found a South African unit (21st Field Company, South African Construction Company) with manpower to spare and handed it over to them.

Although the lorry chassis had worked up to a point, Berry believed that a full-width rotating drum would prove a better proposition than narrower ones on each side, and with the injunction that they must use only standard vehicle components, he set a mixed Royal Engineers (RE) and Royal Electrical and Mechanical Engineers (REME) team on the project, for which an A12 Matilda Infantry Tank was delivered early in August 1942.

Little is known of the problems that the engineers faced, but something over a month later the tank flail was completed and, on 13 September, it was recorded as having passed its final test. One trial involved comparison with a Matilda equipped with Fowler Rollers (see New Vanguard 8, Matilda Infantry Tank 1938–45) and the

A useful view of a Matilda Scorpion I preparing for action. The commander is in his cupola, one crew member is checking the joints on the wire and chain flails, while the flail operator is in his engine box on the side.

flail proved to be so much better that, in Berry's words, the rollers were 'dropped as being useless in comparison with the Threshing Machine'. It must have impressed others besides Berry, because in mid-September the Eighth Army commander (by now General Montgomery) announced that he required 24 of them in four weeks' time.

The work was to be done by No.7 Base Ordnance Workshops in Alexandria and they would require proper drawings, not the back-of-an-envelope plans that Berry and his men had been working on hitherto. Berry was also on the lookout for a more powerful engine. The original Ford V8 was underpowered, but attempts to find Berry's preferred choice, a V-12 Lincoln Zephyr, were not successful. The code name 'Scorpion' was adopted when the original choice of 'Durban' was rejected.

If the task of getting the work done on the 24 Matilda tanks was difficult in the time allowed, it was no easier finding crews for them. Two battle-worn regiments, 42nd and 44th Royal Tank Regiments, were combed for crews with Matilda experience, while the RE was to supply the flail operators. This latter position was no sinecure. It meant occupying a cramped position within a box on the right side of the tank, which also contained the flail engine, radiator and drive system. Despite the fact that at least one Sapper NCO described it as preferable to finding and lifting mines by hand under fire, that is not saying very much. Not only was there more noise and heat than the average man could bear, it was also found necessary to wear a gas mask during flailing operations in order to filter out the dust.

Having acquired the tanks, or at least most of them, just in time, and General Montgomery's enthusiasm notwithstanding, it was still not easy to sell the concept to some corps and divisional commanders. Many feared that as experimental devices on old and unreliable vehicles, the flail tanks were likely to break down and block such routes as they had cleared. It was not an unqualified judgement; pre-battle demonstrations had been blighted by failures. However, to the south 7th Armoured Division welcomed them. Perhaps it was due to the fact that they were eager to pass through a minefield in order to get at their old adversaries, 21st Panzer Division.

ALAMEIN DEBUT

It is an unfortunate fact that the two regiments earmarked to take these new devices into action for the very first time make little of it in their histories. As a result, most contemporary comments come from other sources, the majority of whom were not aware of the difficulties these crews were facing and were only too ready to write them off as failures.

There was no previous experience to go on, so the plan, thrashed out on the eve of the battle of El Alamein in October 1942, was probably not as effective as it might have been. One idea, to send all the available flails across in one area to sweep a wide route, was rejected at the outset due, presumably, to its practical limitations. In most areas the Scorpions were simply ordered to flail a route through the minefield and then turn round to widen it on a return run. Only in the 7th Armoured Division's area was a more structured plan produced, which saw the Scorpions operating in company with Sappers on foot and other vehicles. Available figures indicate that between 12 and 15 Scorpions were in a fit state to take part, of which six would be allocated to 7th Armoured Division.

According to the British official history, the sight of a Scorpion flailing through soft sand 'had to be seen to be believed' and there were those on the opposite side who wondered what on earth was coming. Huge clouds of dust, giving off loud mechanical noises and the occasional explosion, were all that could be seen. Not that it was a continuous threat. Even the best of the Scorpions could not keep up flailing

A Matilda Scorpion II heading west on a transporter. The flail apparatus is camouflaged, but the nearside arm can be seen, along with the engine box on the far side.

for very long. Dust choked the air intake of the flail engine and it soon got so hot that petrol was vaporizing before it even reached the carburettor; at which point the engine stopped. Then there was nothing to do but sit and wait while it cooled down, to see if it might start again. Many tanks also suffered mechanical breakdown from other causes and, although no figures can be traced, it seems that a high percentage only ever managed a one-way crossing of the minefield, if that. A mere handful were fit enough to tackle the return run.

Discussion after the battle revealed a number of shortcomings with these pioneering Scorpions. The lattice girder arms that supported the rotor were not strong enough, air cleaning for the flail engine had to be improved and the wretched Sapper needed to be located somewhere else to save him from the purgatory of the engine housing. All of these matters were resolved, up to a point. The lattice girder arms were improved; better air filters were installed; the Sapper, with his controls, was moved into the tank's turret. Experience had shown that among the Scorpion crews the most under-employed individual was the gunner, who could not see to shoot at anything. He was therefore removed, along with the ammunition and the gun itself. The commander was retained, obviously, while the loader was still able to act as wireless operator and fire the co-axial machine gun.

In this form came the Scorpion II – the simplest way to identify it from the original model is to see whether it has a gun or not. Another clue is to look at the set of the turret. If it is traversed somewhat to the left of the centre line, say at 11 o'clock in gunnery terms, then the chances are it is a Mark II because this position was best for the flail operator. But to be absolutely sure, look at the boom support arm on the left side of the vehicle: if it looks like two triangles, tapering off fore and aft from the centre it is a Mark II. If it is square at the rear end then it is a Scorpion Mark I.

DEVELOPMENTS IN BRITAIN

Abraham du Toit arrived at the War Office in London with General Auchinleck's endorsement in his pocket. Although effectively now working with the Department of Tank Design (Special Devices) section he was based, for most of the time, at the Southall Works of the Associated Equipment Company Ltd (AEC), the 'Builders of London's Buses' as they liked to style themselves. In fact, the company's customer base was far broader than that title suggested, embracing an extensive range of commercial and military vehicles as well as buses, coaches and railcars. It was a thriving organization with progressive attitudes and a very talented design team headed by one of the most brilliant mechanical engineers of the day, George J. Rackham. Rackham had so many strings to his bow that they cannot all be covered here, but it should be noted that he had been a Tank Corps officer on the design side in World War I and, in addition to his later work on flails, was also heavily involved in the design of armoured flamethrowers (see *British Battle Tanks: British-Made Tanks of World War II*). It is in the matter of flail design that he was destined to make what was probably his most significant contribution to the British war effort, although he would still be involved with matters of tank design after the war.

While it is entirely fair to say that du Toit was the inspiration for flail development in both the Middle East and United Kingdom as it ultimately appeared, he was by no means alone. The earliest design of which we have details was drawn by a Captain O'Shaughnessy in November 1939 and shown to Major S. G. Galpin at Bovington,

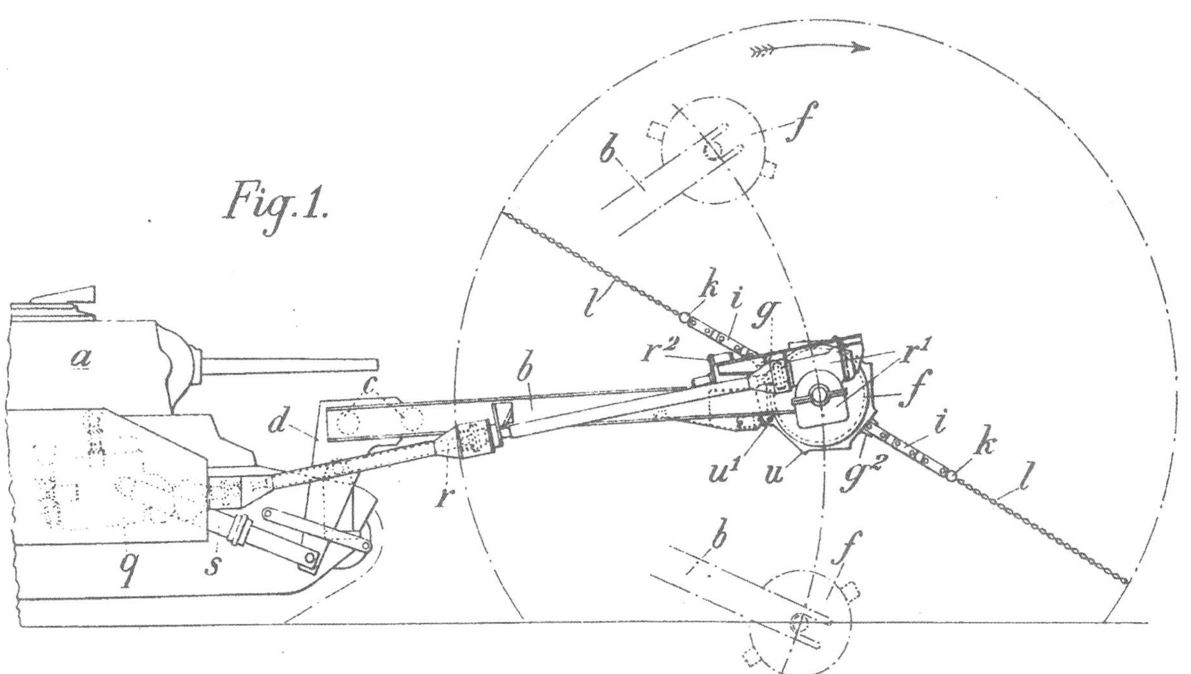

Patent diagram for the second Matilda Baron prototype showing the drive arrangement, arc of movement of the rotor and rotational direction and diameter of the two sets of flails.

the centre of tank activity in Great Britain, in May 1940. In fact it was one of two, the first being a relatively conventional motor-driven flail, the other a system of rollers, pushed ahead of the tank, with sprung beaters that thrashed the ground. In a covering note Galpin says that O'Shaughnessy's device is 'similar to those which have been put forward in the past'. At about the same time Galpin was shown another design by a Mr G. J. Sutton, a civilian member of the War Office Anti-Tank Mine Committee. Later, in September 1942, a Major Paterson submitted a flail device for attachment to British Cruiser Tanks, notably the Covenanter and Crusader, which was driven by a pulley arrangement from the front idler wheels. Paterson claims that Galpin himself had come up with a workable flail design but made no effort to claim any reward for it, since he regarded it as his duty. No doubt there were many more that failed to leave even this modest evidence.

ENTER THE BARON

Known, initially, as the 'du Toit Winch', the Matilda-based flail tanks developed in Britain were rechristened 'Barons' in February 1942. Like its Middle Eastern counterpart, the British prototype retained its turret and mounted a separate engine compartment, in this instance containing a Chrysler unit, on the right side of the hull. The engine was housed in an armoured box, situated in line with the turret, from which a driveshaft extended forward into a small gearbox. Here motion was translated to a sprocket which, by means of a long loop of chain, activated another sprocket on the end of the rotating flail drum. The big difference from Scorpion was that the arms supporting the rotor drum could be raised hydraulically, using the turret traverse mechanism, to keep the chains clear of the ground when they were not needed.

It is worth recording that the prototype Baron was first demonstrated on 6 June 1942, not only two years to the day before D-Day but a good two months ahead of the prototype Scorpion in the Middle East. It was viewed by the General Staff and

VALENTINE SCORPION III, 22ND DRAGOONS, 79TH ARMOURED DIVISION, SUFFOLK, JANUARY 1944

Events moved so fast once the mine-clearing flail tank was accepted that by the time the Valentine Scorpion was entering regimental service it was already being replaced by the Sherman Crab. The 22nd Dragoons was one of six cavalry regiments revived early in the war and at this stage was senior regiment in 30th Armoured Brigade, which joined 79th Armoured Division as a flail brigade in November 1943. Inset: This is a typical set of markings painted on the rear of the counterweight box of a Scorpion III. The well-known device of 79th Armoured Division is balanced by the unit code 51 on a red square, indicating the senior regiment in the brigade, the red/white/red recognition mark that preceded the adoption of the Allied white star, and the War Department serial number T18072, which reveals that this tank began life as a Valentine I, built by Metro-Cammell in 1939. (Art by Tony Bryan, © Osprey Publishing)

their impressions reported to the Commander-in-Chief Middle East, General Auchinleck, who was at least aware of it, even if Norman Berry was not. The difference was that with a major battle pending those in the Middle East were happy to go with what they had got and improve upon it afterwards, whereas in the UK they wanted something better before committing it to battle.

The immediate result of the prototype Baron demonstration, issued four days later, was a complaint that the Matilda seemed to be overloaded and that the flail drive engine was not powerful enough. Thus the tank was rebuilt, with a 73hp (54kW) Bedford MW engine instead of the Chrysler, and Cardan shafts replacing the chain. The hydraulic system (turret traverse) was retained and one source claimed that this enabled the operator to adjust the rotor height to suit different types of ground. However, another commentator was at pains to explain that this should not be seen as an early example of contouring. On both prototype Barons the complicated arrangement of bars and chains that made up the flails were limited to two sets, so that with every rotation the ground was only struck twice. The need for more flails was fully understood, but a good deal more power would have to be applied before this could be done.

Between June and November 1942 du Toit came up with the idea of a self-contained flail device, on rollers, that could be pushed across a minefield by any tank. A crude sketch is all that survives, but the official description claims that a form of box on wheels, propelled by the tank, contained two engines with an operator sandwiched between them. Some sort of boom extended forward from this box to a rotor, but the precise arrangement is not clear. Often referred to as a Perambulator

Matilda Baron Mark IIIA viewed from the front to emphasize the width. Seen like this, one can examine the complicated rotor and flail arrangement, the serrated teeth of the wire cutters and the drive at each end of the rotor.

Device it was, briefly, everyone's favourite and on a much higher priority than the conventional flail. It vanished just as swiftly at the design stage, as did a wheeled version of the Baron, presumably for armoured cars; it was noted at an Armoured Fighting Vehicles (AFV) Liaison Meeting of 9 November 1942 that: 'Baron on wheeled vehicle not to be proceeded with'.

Reading between the lines, it appears that Rackham and du Toit differed on future flail development. Rackham, at least at this stage, probably favoured a dedicated mine-clearing vehicle, while du Toit seems to have preferred the perambulator system that could be applied to any tank. At least, in a statement released at the end of the war, the South African engineer implies that while he saw a future for the 'pram' he magnanimously put it aside in order to co-operate with Rackham.

The result was the Baron Mark III, about which we have very little information. All we are told is that in its production form, as the Baron Mark IIIA, it incorporated a number of improvements, particularly in respect of the hydraulic arrangements. Thus it seems safe to assume that in general appearance the two were much the same. It is fascinating to observe how certain trends appeared at the same time in both Britain and the Middle East and this one, of a dedicated mine-clearing device with no other offensive capabilities, is a case in point.

On the production version of the Baron IIIA the entire turret assembly of the Matilda was removed and replaced by a fixed superstructure, stepped upwards from the front, which housed the flail operator with the vehicle commander above and behind him. The flail operator had one forward-facing periscope, the vehicle commander had two, looking each way, but all three periscopes could be rotated and withdrawn into the vehicle for cleaning. Access for both operator and commander was via a two-flap hatch in the roof, but ahead of them in the usual place, sat the driver with his own hatch. The official handbook uses the term 'Pannier Fashion' to

Viewed from the rear this Valentine Scorpion displays the markings of the 22nd Dragoons, 79th Armoured Division, and is towing a set of Centipede rollers. The markings are painted on the counterweight box, and one can also see the exhaust pipes from the auxiliary engines.

describe how the two Bedford engines, each with its clutch and modified gearbox, were mounted on either side of the tank, but it is worth remarking that although these units were contained within armoured covers, they were open to the air at the bottom to improve cooling and, presumably, to reduce weight.

The driver's main job during a flailing operation was to keep the tank on a dead straight course, creeping forwards at just 0.5mph (0.8km/h) and, through the muck thrown up by the flails and intermittent explosions, attempting to keep station on the other flail tanks of his troop. The commander's role was clearly one of overall supervision, but it was the flail operator who really had his work cut out. He probably had more controls to juggle with than the driver, in addition to operating the No.19 wireless set installed on his left. Even so, as the handbook points out, a close understanding between the three crew members was essential if the job was to be done properly.

Without getting too bogged down in technical matters, it is important to explain that although two engines were used to power the flail, each with its own starting and cooling system as well as its own clutch and gearbox, the two engines were, in effect, operated as one. The flail gearboxes had been modified to run on first, second and reverse gears only but, from the operator's point of view, this involved just one gear lever, one clutch pedal and one throttle each for the hand and foot. A series of four jointed Cardan shafts from each engine powered the rotor by means of a worm drive at each end of the shaft. Nothing is said, either in the handbook or elsewhere, about any discrepancy of power between the flail drive engines (presumably this was negligible if the two units were tuned precisely), nor what happened if one engine failed.

The rotor itself was the typical Baron type with a central tube of 6in. (15.2cm) diameter surrounded by a framework to which three banks of chains were attached. The ideal flailing rate was around 80rpm, indicated by an engine speed of 1,200rpm. However, by this time two other roles had been envisaged for the Baron. One was wire-cutting, for which purpose a mechanical cross-cutting device, acting more or less on the same principle as hair trimmers, could be activated from the operator's cab. Used in conjunction with rotary side cutters, this operated at first-gear speed, catching and chopping up the barbed wire as it went. There were limitations; too much wire could choke it and if mines were also present, the handbook noted that the tank should only advance into the wire as far as the rotor extended from the front of the tank, about 10ft (3m), then withdraw and flail over the same ground. It was also possible to use the rotor as a crude device for breaking up ground. With the rotor lowered to ground level and rotated slowly until the flail chains were wrapped around it the rotor then proceeded to chew up the ground and wear away obstacles such as anti-tank defences. The driver was supposed to move the vehicle gently to and fro a short distance while this was going on. The process was described by one witness as 'somewhat akin to the scratching of a dog'.

The failure of the first hydraulic system, run from the tank's original turret traverse gear, encouraged Rackham and his team to develop something stronger, with a separate hydraulic pump driven off each flail engine. Operating via a common reserve oil tank and a control unit in the operator's compartment, the pumps were used to activate big hydraulic jacks that raised and lowered the rotor booms as required. Some reasons for raising and lowering the rotor have already been described. Another would be in order that the tank could drive in the normal way without the flail chains touching the ground and it would also cut down storage space if the Barons could be parked with the boom from one overhanging the engine deck of the vehicle in front.

Illustrations in the handbook suggest that a good deal of the hydraulic plumbing around the control cab was woefully exposed to potential damage when the vehicle was clearing mines or under fire, but these may show a pre-production machine. It does, however, seem clear that on the Baron IIIA the operator was expected to exploit the easy movement of the booms by following contours in the ground so that deep hollows might not be missed and bumps not struck by the rotor. Operators were informed that a height of about 4ft 6in. (1.4m) was best for the rotor (given that the flail chains were not damaged) in order that each chain would strike the ground at around 60mph (96.5km/h), which was sufficient to detonate a German anti-tank mine buried up to 4in. (10.2cm) in the ground.

The greatest drawback to the Baron was, with an engine at each side, its overall width of 13ft (4m). This prevented it from crossing a normal Bailey Bridge or from passing through the bow section of a contemporary landing craft, both serious operational limitations. In addition, as the handbook explains, it was a logistics nightmare since for transportation, presumably by rail, both flail engines had to be removed, as did the rotor, rotor arms (in four pieces), along with the Cardan shafts and gears.

One experiment, which theoretically would have applied to all flails, was the idea of rotating the chain drum in the opposite direction, that is to say anti-clockwise if one were watching the tank from the right. Trials suggested that reverse flailing gave a higher percentage of detonations but, since these now happened a lot closer to the tank than with conventional rotation, the practice was abandoned. It is also worth remarking that with the flail going round in the regular way there were instances of live mines being thrown up by the chains and landing on top of the tank. Generally this was not a problem even if the mine detonated, so long as the crew were totally closed down.

Production of the Baron IIIA was placed in the hands of Curran Brothers of Cardiff in 1942. They were given an initial contract for 60 conversion kits with a promise of 60 more to follow. The idea was that the kits would be delivered to

Matilda battalions earmarked for conversion. These would then be visited by travelling teams of trained fitters working in conjunction with local REME workshops. Space had been arranged to ship a dozen Baron IIIAs to the Middle East, but they could not be completed in time and, as far as is known, none ever went abroad. Some were issued to No.1 Assault Squadron Royal Armoured Corps (RAC) which, on 29 July 1943, was placed under command of General Hobart's 79th Armoured Division where it was ultimately absorbed into 43rd Royal Tank Regiment, which became the division's experimental trials unit.

THE BRITISH SCORPION

At least two quite separate factors influenced subsequent developments both in Britain and the Middle East. First was agreement that by 1943 the Matilda was too slow for the work; not for flailing itself, which was a slow process at the best of times, but in the ability of the device to move into action at the pace of other vehicles. Second was a growing appreciation in both theatres that, sooner or later, the Allies would become involved in amphibious operations for which existing types of flail were unsuitable on account of width.

Also, by this time there had been some exchange of information between flail tank users in Britain and the Middle East, as a result of which AEC was tasked with investigating a new design to incorporate the best of both systems, mounted on a more up-to-date tank hull. The type selected was the Infantry Tank Mark III, or Valentine, and the Director RAC had 120 of the diesel-powered Mark II types set aside for conversion.

Following two prototypes, a contract was issued to AEC for a production order that appeared to grow steadily as the requirement for the type was re-evaluated. Even so, the design was not without its limitations. The Service Instruction Book for the Scorpion indicates that hulls of both the Valentine II and III could be employed, although in practice these were the same – the difference lay in the type of turret fitted but, since that was removed as part of the conversion process, this was academic. Both versions were powered by the AEC 131hp (96kW) diesel engine.

Since vehicle width was now a significant factor, the two auxiliary engines, Canadian Ford V8 petrol units rated at 82bhp (61kW), were housed in a curious, six-sided structure that replaced the turret. The exact shape is difficult to judge, even from

A rainy day at Westward Ho! and a Valentine Scorpion III reverses up the ramp of a dried-out Landing Craft, Tank (4). Deep wading gear has been erected behind the superstructure, so a wet landing is contemplated.

Views of the Grant Scorpion III, turreted or otherwise, are hard to find. Here we see one in Tunisia, taken from an angle that emphasizes the great width and cumbersome nature of the device. It must have been a nightmare to manoeuvre in any kind of restricted space.

photographs, but in essence it consisted of a central box of welded construction and armoured to a maximum of 0.5in. (14mm). It contained two members of the crew, the vehicle commander and the flail operator. In action they stood upright, side by side with the commander on the left, viewing the world through a pair of standard tank periscopes. They shared this cramped compartment with a fuel tank for the two flail engines and a No.19 wireless set, which rested on top of the fuel tank. On the front wall, ahead of the flail operator, were the controls for the two Ford engines: separate starter buttons, a single tachometer for both engines and a single throttle control operated by Bowden cable. Lower down was a single clutch pedal and a lever to engage the gearbox. There were access hatches in the roof of this box, although the commander and operator had the option of crawling through to or from the driver's exit hatches.

The engines were housed in lockers on either side of the central box, the lockers being triangular in shape and fitted with overhead hatches so that the engines could be serviced. They were not mounted in line with the vehicle but set at odd angles so that universal joints on the Cardan shafts were vital. Each engine was attached to a single-speed gearbox and, as with the Baron, the controls were unified and under the control of one operator. Placing the engines either side of the central superstructure must have made it uncomfortably noisy for the two men inside, but of course it reduced the overall width of the vehicle and eliminated the need for external plumbing.

In a sense, the only true Scorpion feature of this design was the lattice arrangement of the rotor arms and the cross-member that braced them. The drive system was based upon the later Baron and the rotor itself was also of the Baron type, although the flail chains were Scorpion style with 32 sets of independent links with no secondary connections. Unlike the Baron there was no hydraulic equipment to elevate or depress the rotor arms, so that earth moving – and wire cutting to begin with – were not options. The lattice arms were pivoted to the superstructure, but vertical movement was limited to four positions marked by bolt holes in two upright

CRAB STAGES IN FLAIL DEVELOPMENT

girders, known as 'goal-posts', attached to the front of the tank. Since all of these flail devices created a lot of additional pressure on leading suspension units, an attempt was made to even this out, in the case of the Valentine Scorpions, by fitting a large open tray at the back which, of itself, acted as a counterbalance weight to the booms and rotor. It was also used to hold spare flail chains.

The Valentine Scorpion was, by any standards, an ungainly looking machine and to make matters worse it was attended with tragedy. Unlike the final Baron design it does not appear that the flail engines were equipped with reverse gears. Even so, in one live trial at the Obstacle Assault Centre in May 1943, it seems that the tank reversed over two live German mines, one of which was detonated by the flail while the other went off in sympathy directly under the hull of the tank, causing the deaths of all three members of the crew. This event led to a demand for more protection beneath the tank, but the amount of armour required also created a weight penalty that was unacceptable.

News from the Middle East now drew attention to the fact that the enemy had started sowing mixed minefields of Teller anti-tank mines and the anti-personnel S-mine, but that, for some reason, flails had no effect upon the latter. Since this could prove disastrous for human mine clearers and following infantry, the Scorpion was also tested towing a device called Centipede, which consisted of multiple, tiny rollers and this is said to have worked reasonably well in detonating the anti-personnel mines.

A firm named T. C. Jones & Co., in the unlikely surroundings of Shepherds Bush in London, became the design parents for Scorpion III and the plan was to send them the conversion kits, which they assembled to be mounted on Valentine hulls at the Chilwell Ordnance Depot. Various figures have been bandied about as to numbers, anything from 125 to 300, but it seems that production was painfully slow. As far as 30th Armoured Brigade was concerned, they had a requirement for 90, yet they were receiving Sherman Crab flails long before the last Scorpion was delivered. By this time the Scorpion was only regarded as a training machine since its limitations had become obvious.

First among these was the rigid mounting of the jib, adopted in the first place only because the hydraulic arrangements on the Baron had proved unreliable. Experience soon showed that on a cross-country course, unless the driver was very careful, the jib was in constant danger of damage from striking the ground when a ditch or bank was encountered. Cooling was not all it might be, but that was par for the course, and now everyone wanted to know why the Valentine Scorpion could not deal with barbed wire.

Late in 1943 and early in 1944 trials were conducted by the Fighting Vehicle Proving Establishment (FVPE) on a Scorpion fitted with wire cutters. These were simply the serrated discs on each end of the rotor, and a new shield device developed by AEC, but not the horizontal cutting bar employed on Baron since everyone now agreed that this did not work. Faced with typical combinations of wire the Scorpion did very well, but when FVPE constructed huge entanglements, the tank was invariably defeated. In the end it was noticed that the lattice girder arms had been twisted out of shape, so the tests were abandoned. Nobody seemed able to agree whether this damage was as a result of the wire trials, or whether the booms had been weakened at some earlier stage, but by now this hardly seems to have mattered since Scorpion III was due to be replaced by an improved version that became known as the Sherman Marquis.

OPPOSITE Crab flail development. Most of these are heavy-duty shackles rather than conventional chain, mixed with manufactured links. The ends consist of bob-weights or manufactured links.

SHERMAN MARQUIS FLAIL TANK, AEC LTD, SOUTHALL, OCTOBER 1943

Perhaps because it was so heavily overshadowed by the Crab, a good deal of detailed information on the Marquis flail has not survived. We know that the superstructure housed a crew of two, situated side by side, with a rooftop hatch to enter and exit by and standard tank periscopes to view through. What we cannot say for sure, for example, is whether a fourth crew member sat alongside the driver. Since the hull machine-gun position was masked, he may not have had a lot to do, but in any case, since the tank was never accepted for service, it is probably irrelevant. The vehicle is shown here in the final stage of production, before final painting.

It seems reasonable to assume that the turret layout was very similar to the Valentine Scorpion and we know that the flail engines drove through single-speed gearboxes but that, unlike the Valentine, hydraulic pumps were used to raise or lower the rotor arms. The distinctive badge is that of AEC – the Associated Equipment Company of London – which built the prototype. (Art by Tony Bryan, © Osprey Publishing)

PROTOTYPES PROLIFERATE

The summer of 1943 was a busy time for flail development in Britain. The matter had become urgent but nobody seemed entirely sure which was the correct system, so many different ones started to appear, some incorporating very outdated ideas. In fact one man was sure. George Rackham, in the midst of all his other work, had concluded, as early as June 1943, that a flail driven directly off a tank's main engine, assuming that engine was powerful enough, was the way to proceed.

About a month later a high-powered meeting was held at the War Office to review the situation with regard to the assault on obstacles. Not everyone was in favour of flails. A representative from the RE said that flails were not the final answer and could never be 100 per cent successful. A staff officer from 21st Army Group did not think that they should be included in the first stages of an amphibious assault, since there would never be sufficient room for everything on the available landing craft. General Hobart took a stronger and characteristically more positive view. He was all in favour of flails, and thought they should 'go the whole hog' and include contouring flail rotors and wire cutters in the package as a matter of course. The meeting agreed, adopted all of Hobart's specifications and went further in stating that, in their collective view, the most suitable tank for flail work had to be the Sherman.

By 1943 the Sherman was the most significant tank in the Western alliance, so in the interest of standardization alone its adaptation to the flail role made sense. Whether the Americans would agree was another matter. They became very sensitive to what they considered British misuse of the tanks that they were stretching every sinew to

ABOVE The Sherman Pram Scorpion, showing the cumbersome flail arrangement and the vulnerable system of chains and sprockets required to transfer drive from the tank to the rotor.

LEFT The turret on the Sherman Marquis flail looks enormous in this picture. Notice how much the drive shafts have to move when the rotor is raised, and the hydraulic system used to effect this.

produce in suitable numbers. On the other hand, the British were slowly learning that it was no use trying to modify old, out-of-date tanks to these support roles. Invariably they were unreliable, too slow and difficult to maintain as spares stocks dwindled. By using the current service tank most of these problems would be eliminated.

Viewing events with hindsight can be frustrating. To see a gifted character, whom history has judged to be a genius in his field, ignored and overlooked by his contemporaries is very hard to understand. For example, at the meeting held in July 1943 to discuss adapting Scorpion to the Sherman, Rackham rocked the boat by saying that auxiliary engines posed too many problems; he continued to advocate a flail driven off the tank's own engine, a configuration that not only simplified the mechanical arrangements but enabled the tank to retain its firepower.

Rackham's suggestion was brushed aside by the engineer-in-chief who told him that the Scorpion project would be continued, but he was thanked for his endeavours in what read like somewhat patronizing terms. Rackham's response was typical – he would continue with his own project anyway and expected to have a prototype ready by August. One thing that contrasts sharply with this attitude is the story of the Sherman Pram Scorpion, which began in March 1943. As we have seen, Captain du Toit continued to favour the perambulator concept even after it was first rejected, but whether he had any influence on subsequent events is not clear; he is understood to have returned to South Africa in June 1943.

The Sherman Pram originated from the Leeds-based engineering company Samuel Butler Ltd, one of a number of firms then engaged on flail projects. Quite why they should be permitted to pursue this as far as the prototype stage is not clear, since it must have looked complicated enough on paper, never mind as hardware. There were advantages: the flail device required very little modification to the tank itself and, of course, the Sherman retained its turret and armament. But these were outweighed by the disadvantages on a grand scale.

One document, printed at the end of the war, refers to it as Crown's Pram, and may well be the only surviving record of the member of the firm's staff who designed it. Drive was taken by a loop of chain, from an extension of each drive sprocket, through a series of secondary sprockets and chains to the drum at the front. The sprockets varied in size since they were required to increase the rotation speed of the drum in relation to the speed that the tank was making over the ground. Although it was attached to the nose of the tank, most of the weight – something over four tons – was supported on two pairs of fairly small rollers that pivoted beneath the arms. These performed reasonably well on a firm surface, allowing fora fair amount of rolling resistance, but they became absolutely hopeless on soft ground so that the entire contraption was immobilized. In order to engage the flail, the tank was obliged to stop and one or more crew members dismount. The task then was to insert pins through the primary sprocket of the flail drive on each side into the drive sprockets of the tank, and the chances are this would not be as simple as its sounds.

Because the rotor was driven from the tracks, and because tracks will move at different speeds when a tank is turning, the actual rotor on the Pram Scorpion was split in the centre. Obviously, steering while flailing was a very dangerous practice but since it might be necessary for the tank to turn before it reached the edge of the minefield, but after the flail drive had been connected, this at least solved that problem so that, while turning, the separate halves of the rotor were flailing at different speeds. Like everything else about this design this all seems to have been more trouble than it was worth.

The Sherman Marquis, or Octopus as it was originally called, was the official rival to Rackham's Crab. Design work began in July 1943 following comparative trials between the Matilda Baron and Valentine Scorpion, with a view to incorporating the better features of both. It is ironic that even as Rackham was working on his own design, in the shape of the Crab, he was also, as Chief Engineer at AEC, responsible for building both a prototype Octopus/Marquis and a full size wooden mock-up for inspection purposes.

Like most experimental Sherman flails, the Marquis was based upon a Chrysler-powered M4A4 tank, or Sherman V as the British would call it. Like the Scorpion it had a superstructure replacing the turret that housed a crew of two along with a pair of Ford V8 engines, but it had solid flail booms like the Baron yet with the larger-diameter, tubular rotor as seen on the Middle East Scorpions. It also introduced, or rather re-introduced, a hydraulic system to raise or lower the booms.

It is worth recording that this system was one of the most heavily criticized features of the Matilda Baron because it was always going wrong. At the same time, however, the fixed lattice arms of the Valentine Scorpion were not popular because they could not be raised and consequently suffered damage on uneven ground. Yet like the Valentine the Marquis had a pair of driveshafts, one from each engine, running more or less parallel to each arm and driving the rotor from both ends. And again it should be emphasized that the facility to raise and lower the boom was not to permit contour following by the flail operator, but in order to keep the boom up high while driving and to reduce storage space, particularly on landing craft. Reports say that using hydraulics alone the boom would hold up for about 15 minutes, but for longer periods a locking device was incorporated.

Viewed after an encounter with a wire entanglement, the Sherman Lobster does not look promising, but it can all be straightened out and, in any case, it was the purpose of the flail to sustain damage if it saved men's lives.

Another failed development was the Sherman Lobster, although it came after the successful development and use of the Crab. Early trials of the Crab were disappointing, as we shall see, largely due to damage inflicted on the rotor and chains by exploding mines. Since, at that stage, the true reasons for this effect were not properly understood, it was hoped that a skeletal rotor would be better and that, in effect, is what the Lobster was: a Crab with a Baron-type rotor. AEC assembled it, using the original Crab prototype T150483 as the basis, in February 1944. Had it been successful, the scheme was to introduce it once the Crabs already ordered had been completed. As it was, there was no need. In terms of mines detonated it was slightly inferior to the Crab, but when it came to dealing with barbed-wire entanglements it was a lot worse. The stuff wound itself around the rotor and brought the entire thing to a halt. It was also somewhat heavier than the Crab and not so easy to stow. Even so, the prototype was retained and used for various experiments, among them a method to make the rotor follow the contours of the ground.

THE SCORPIONS SPREAD

Following their limited success at Alamein, the surviving Scorpions, plus those that had missed the battle, were passed on to 41st RTR, which was destined to become the one and only flail regiment in North Africa through to the end of the campaign on 13 May 1943. The existing tanks were steadily returned to workshops and a few new ones added until the regiment had 24 of the improved Scorpion Mark IIs, sufficient to equip A and B Squadrons.

Meanwhile, in recognition of 41st RTR's singular role, application was made to the War Office for the regiment to be renamed 1st Scorpion Regiment Royal Armoured Corps. This took time, so for a while it was known as T (for Temporary?) Scorpion Regiment RAC. In fact, it was May before the change became official and the regiment was issued with a cloth shoulder badge showing a red Scorpion, which looked more like a lobster, on a yellow rectangle which was worn on the left shoulder.

An official organization chart was also delineated in which each of the three squadrons had the following equipment: a Squadron HQ consisting of one armoured

GRANT SCORPION III, C SQUADRON, 1ST SCORPION REGIMENT, ROYAL ARMOURED CORPS, TUNISIA, APRIL 1943

The turret gun having proved useless on the Matilda Scorpion, the first Grant Scorpions were issued without turrets. At the same time the 75mm hull gun was removed because it interfered with the flail attachment and the resulting aperture appears to have been blanked off by a curved shield of armour plate. Naturally, without a turret the Grant hull was open at the top and somewhat vulnerable. The unit Light Aid Detachment fabricated a temporary overhead cover from old petrol cans and sandbags, for want of anything better, which gives the tank this rather untidy appearance. In a short time the turrets were replaced. The men, coming from the 41st RTR, still wore the RTR badge on their berets, but to display their special role they adopted the special scorpion shoulder flash in May, which was worn on the left sleeve. (Art by Tony Bryan, © Osprey Publishing)

car or scout car and two Valentine pilot tanks with four troops, each of three Scorpions. The pilot tanks were fitted with anti-mine rollers and used to locate rather than clear minefields. Later on they were also equipped with the Centipede towed roller device.

There is no space here to cover the various actions that the Scorpion Regiment engaged in with both Eighth and First Armies in the weeks leading up to the German capitulation in North Africa, but one aspect cannot be ignored, as it was typical of the British Army. Here we had a new device, probably as valuable in its own right as any weapon. Yet it had been created on a shoe-string budget with little official encouragement and kept going by the enthusiasm and dedication of its personnel for the benefit of all. It had started off with lame tanks that nobody else needed and these were now almost completely worn out. The War Diary records more mechanical failures than successes in most of the later battles, particularly as more barbed wire was encountered, which wrapped itself around the flail rotor and effectively choked the tank's flail engine. Help was on the way, but it was still of the 'make do and mend' variety.

Efforts to find a suitable replacement began early in 1943 and eventually settled upon the American M3 medium tank in its British guise as the Grant. Back in Alexandria, No.7 Base Ordnance Workshops began a programme which, it was hoped, would provide sufficient Scorpions to equip all three squadrons of the regiment, plus 100 per cent replacement, or near enough. The total order was for 70.

The Grant was a wise choice, given that there was not a lot to choose from anyway. It was reliable and fast enough to move from place to place a lot quicker than a

GRANT SCORPION IV, NO.1 TROOP, 400 INDEPENDENT SCORPION SQUADRON, ROYAL ARMOURED CORPS, BURMA, 1945

Aurora was one of four Scorpions, accompanied by a Valentine Porcupine mine-roller pilot tank, that moved from India to the fighting front in Burma in November 1944. Some sources suggest that in Burma a pale blue was used, instead of white, for any symbols painted on vehicles in order to reduce visibility in regions where fighting ranges were short. This cannot be confirmed, but a hint of blue has been used here on the Allied star and the tank's name and number. The Scorpions were attached to 254th Indian Tank Brigade, whose insignia is shown, but they never seem to have found any minefields to clear, and in any case, the close jungle environment was not always conducive to their use; *Aurora* seems to have been particularly accident prone. Notice that in this theatre the Grant Scorpions were fitted with T49 steel tracks with bar tread instead of the more common rubber block type. (Art by Tony Bryan, © Osprey Publishing)

Back in Egypt by mid-1943 the workshops had now come up with a twin-engine version of the Scorpion powerful enough to spin more chains. An experimental prototype was mounted on a Grant II. Petrol for the flail engines was stored in a tank that can just be seen on the rear deck. The Grant II had a diesel engine.

The Grant Scorpion IV does not look that different from the Scorpion III at first glance, although from this side the more robust rotor support arm is obvious. The photo was taken in Tripoli, during practice for the forthcoming Sicilian landings.

Another Grant Scorpion IV, now with the flail rotor uncovered and a Browning machine gun mounted on the turret, lands from an LCT (4). This is How Beach, near Avola, on 10 July 1943.

Matilda, but more important was that it was available, as it was replaced in combat regiments by the Sherman. In order to fit the flail apparatus, which was essentially the Scorpion II arrangement from the Matilda, it was necessary to remove the Grant's greatest asset, its hull-mounted 75mm gun. However, the vacated space turned out to be an ideal location for the flail operator.

Less sensible was the removal of the tank's turret, with its 37mm gun and co-axial Browning. Presumably this was done in line with the previous practice of disarming the Scorpion II, although in this case it was not necessary. Indeed it tended to be more dangerous for, when the first of these tanks were issued to the newly recreated C Squadron, there was quite a large hole in the top where the turret had been, and crews did not like this. This new equipment was designated Scorpion III.

C Squadron received 11 Grant Scorpions on 17 March 1943, eight of which were earmarked for action at Wadi Akarit on 6 April 1943. Temporary measures were taken to provide at least some protection to the top, but in the event the Grants were not used. Some 12 days later, six 37mm turrets turned up and were duly fitted. No doubt much to the dismay of C Squadron, four of these were then handed over to A

Squadron to supplement their dwindling stock of Matildas, and they used them at Takroum on 21/22 April in support of the 2nd New Zealand Division. It was not an auspicious start. Mechanically, the Grant Scorpions did all that was required of them and the crews liked the turret and the taller hull, which gave them a better view. Where they came unstuck was due to the effect of detonating mines and rough ground, which caused the flail driveshafts to buckle and rotors to split. This malfunction was put down to the fact that the arms supporting the rotor did not have enough give in them and reacted badly to violent shocks. The Takroum action was the only occasion that records show the Scorpion III being used in combat, so it seems that production was probably curtailed.

Even if the first Grant Scorpion had worked properly, its useful days would have been numbered since, at 13ft 8in. (4.2m) wide, it was just too wide to pass through the bow doors of existing landing craft. Apart from a bit of clearing up there was not a great deal to do in North Africa any more. Yet flails would still be required, so it was decided to improve the design and it emerged, in May 1943, as the Scorpion IV. Outwardly the most obvious change, which serves to identify the new model, is a redesign of the gantry arms. Instead of an arrangement of two sets of girders, spaced slightly apart, the Scorpion IV had a single set made from much stronger members. Indeed, although it is not so obvious a number of components were strengthened, including the rotor itself. This effectively reduced the width; it would still be a tight fit, but if the tank was lined up correctly on the landing craft and driven with care it was possible to pass through the gap with about 5in. (12.7cm) to spare on each side.

Production appears to have moved closer to the scene of action, since C Squadron recorded receiving 12 of them from No.3 Army Base Workshops in Tripoli in June. Thirty more were made available for the other two squadrons at about the same time, but no source is given. Most of these would have been Scorpion IIIs modified in production, plus a few new machines and ultimately the original group handed in for conversion. With Operation *Husky*, the landings in Sicily, no more than a month away, trials were also conducted at Tripoli with landing craft.

At around this time it was decided to expand flail operations in the Mediterranean theatre with the creation of two more units, which ultimately became 400th and 401st Independent Scorpion Squadrons, equipped with a dozen Scorpion Mark IVs along with two Valentine pilot tanks each. The 401st was shipped out to the Far East in October 1943, while the 400th was stripped of its tanks and the personnel shipped back to the UK where, according to legend, they joined 30th Armoured Brigade, which was to operate flails in 79th Armoured Division.

Operation *Husky*, the Allied assault landing in Sicily, began on 10 July 1943 and B Squadron, which at the time had a full complement of 15 Scorpions, came ashore with 50th Division, mostly in the Acid North sector on the east coast. The geology of the island did not really lend itself to the creation of large minefields; the rocky terrain was sufficiently difficult to deal with, so the squadron was employed mainly behind the lines, clearing secondary routes. They were joined by C Squadron about a month later.

Experience on Sicily emphasized something that was already suspected and threw up another problem. The new difficulty concerned the RE's latest and most marvellous tool, the Bailey Bridge. It was not quite wide enough to cope with a Scorpion IV. However, those concerned with flail development had already concluded that the existing Scorpion system was not strong enough to deal with a new generation of German mines.

SHERMAN SCORPION V* (TWIN) FLAIL, B SQUADRON 'A' ASSAULT REGIMENT, AQUINO AIRFIELD, ITALY, JUNE 1944

'A' Assault Regiment was formed in May 1944 from the 1st Scorpion Regiment plus a detachment of Royal Engineers. It was to comprise A Squadron, with Churchill-based assault equipment operated by the RAC and the RE, plus B and C Squadrons with the new Sherman Scorpions, although it seems that the latter was never completed. Aquino airfield, west of Cassino, was the only location at which these flails were called upon to do any work. B Squadron supplied two troops with five Scorpions to assist an airfield construction unit, but it was soon found that the flail chains were not up to the work and when improved chains also failed, the crews resorted to clearing mines by hand. They spent ten days on this work, which included towing away wrecked German aircraft. After that there was nothing more for Scorpions to do in Italy. The insignia is that of 25th Armoured Engineer Brigade, but there is no evidence to show that it was ever actually painted on the tanks. (Art by Tony Bryan, © Osprey Publishing)

SHERMAN V CRAB I, 22ND DRAGOONS, 30TH ARMOURED BRIGADE, NORMANDY, 6 JUNE 1944

The 22nd Dragoons put two squadrons ashore on D-Day. In Sword sector A Squadron landed with the British 3rd Infantry Division, while next door, on Juno, B Squadron was with 3rd Canadian Division. On occasions, where Sherman DD tanks were not available, the Crabs used their guns to silence the opposition. Otherwise it was a matter of clearing lanes across the beaches and through the dunes and then tackling the lateral roads. Formal operations were impossible under the circumstances; it was a time for quick and innovative thinking. A report, issued about a week after D-Day, singled out the Crabs for high praise. Not only did they manage to clear more than 50 per cent of the required exit lanes from beaches, they also used their guns to considerable effect. It is worth saying that some senior officers were very doubtful about the value of flails on sandy beaches. They imagined that large craters would appear every time a mine was detonated, and would prove to be as big an obstacle as the mine itself; however, this does not seem to have been a serious problem. Our tank is shown storming ashore with the flail thrashing, but still sporting the special Deep Wading Gear designed to help it through deeper water; but this would be jettisoned at the first opportunity. (Art by Tony Bryan, © Osprey Publishing)

An early production Crab I with the arms raised. The flails are made from ordinary chain with no weights at the bottom. An armoured box covers the place where the drive emerges from inside the hull. This is said to be the first photograph of a flail tank released for publication.

OPPOSITE The same twin-drive arrangement as the experimental Grant II Scorpion was mounted on a Sherman V (M4A4) and four or five were built. One was sent to Britain for comparison with a Crab, while the remainder saw limited use in Italy.

During their time in Egypt the two independent squadrons had assisted in a number of trials. Most of these trials had to do with the design of the flail itself, and was largely empirical, trial-and-error work, but the most important development was a matter of common sense. It became clear that in order to make a better job of clearing a given area of mines it would help if more flails could be added to each tank's rotor, but there was not sufficient power in the existing engine to achieve this. The solution was to use two engines to drive each flail; this configuration would not only handle more flails, but probably also hit the mines harder.

Under the existing system two engines meant greater width, so the designers came up with a new idea, first tested upon a turreted Grant. The original experiments appear to have involved Ford V8 power units, but ultimately Dodge engines were employed. To reduce width, these were located more or less above and behind the tank's turret, which effectively reduced its ability to traverse, and then drove forwards by means of long, universally jointed shafts, to each end of the rotor. Despite the fact that there seems to have been a shortage of new German mines to test it against, the new twin arrangement was clearly approved and authority given for No.7 Base Ordnance Workshops to convert 24 Sherman tanks to this role. These were designated Sherman Scorpion Mark V (Twin) and later Scorpion Mark V* when the latest type of flails were fitted.

Wire had started to become a menace during the latter stages of the campaign in North Africa, but no attempt seems to have been made to fit cutters, as had occurred in the United Kingdom. Instead, crews had started to use an explosive charge contained within a metal tube, carried on the tank, which were detonated in the wire to break it up before the tank attacked it. Later developments enabled the crew to launch and detonate these tubes without leaving the tank and with the Scorpion V this equipment became a standard fitting. Another refinement, albeit not one to be used when action was imminent, was that the entire gantry assembly could be dismantled and stowed on the tank for transport purposes.

Generally speaking, it has to be said that away from the wide expanse of the desert the Scorpion system failed to work as well as might be hoped. It clearly did not suit European conditions, but there was also a serious failure in the quality of materials used to make the actual flails. Even so, one example of the Sherman Scorpion V equipment was shipped to Britain where it was compared with a Sherman Crab and judged by the experts to be almost as good.

THE CRABS MOVE IN

By August 1943 a prototype Crab was ready for examination at Southall, based on a Sherman V (M4A4) and subjected to initial trials the following month. Compared with the fully developed model it was very basic. The arms that supported the rotor looked particularly flimsy, and did not include hydraulic equipment. There were no wire cutters at the ends of the rotor drum. The mechanical arrangements were extremely simple compared with what had gone before and were very much on display.

Inside the tank a sprocket was driven from the propeller shaft between the engine and transmission. From here drive passed via another sprocket and two loops of roller chain, to a third sprocket outside the armour on the right side. This meant that a hole had to be cut in the tank's side armour, but in order to protect the crew, this chain drive was enclosed in a light metal casing. Outside the hull the final sprocket was fitted to the end of a Cardan shaft, which carried the drive forward along the right arm to a spiral bevel gear, which in turn rotated the flail drum.

Probably unique, a Crab I based upon the radial-engined M4 (Sherman I) which, by any calculation, should be seriously underpowered for this work. There are at least three surviving views of this machine, but no explanation as to why it was developed.

For the first time (except in the case of the Pram Scorpion) no separate engine was required to drive the flail. In action the driver would engage the flail with the tank in first gear only and then move forward. What Rackham had recognized, but everyone else seems to have ignored, was that since tanks only flailed at very low speeds a lot of potential power from the tank's own engine was going to waste. Under normal circumstances the Chrysler-powered M4A4 in first gear, at 2,000rpm with the flail engaged, moved forward at 1.62mph (2.6km/h) while the rotor turned and flailed at 180rpm. Since this did not change when the tank started flailing uphill, it was clear that there was power to spare.

However, the real key to the success of the Crab was the way that the flail chains were attached to the rotor drum. Hitherto the trend had been to attach rows of chains to the drum, and these chains struck the ground in succession. In Rackham's design, if one looks at it closely, it can be seen that the attachment points are arranged as a series of parallel spirals so that the chains thrash the ground much more evenly than before.

A production prototype Crab was tested a month later in October 1943 and there is some evidence to suggest that it was on an M4 (Sherman I) tank. The original plan was to produce a number of Crab and Marquis flails for competitive trials, but the superiority of the Crab was recognized at once so this scheme was dropped. The production prototype not only featured stronger support arms for the rotor, these in turn were now controlled by the same hydraulic system that had been developed for the Marquis. During the trials a number of recommendations were made which would be incorporated into the production machines. Externally these included the provision of armoured covers to protect the flail drive mechanism and, inside, a selection of navigational aids, including gyro and projector binnacle compasses and a distance indicator calibrated in yards.

SHERMAN V CRAB I, WESTMINSTER DRAGOONS, 30TH ARMOURED BRIGADE, 79TH ARMOURED DIVISION, 1944

This cutaway has been arranged in particular to show how the drive from the tank's engine is conveyed to the rotor drum. A system of chains and sprockets takes the drive from the tank's main propeller shaft and through a narrow opening in the side of the hull. Within the tank, for safety reasons, this is all encased within a mild steel cover. Outside, the link to a jointed Cardan shaft is protected by an armoured cover and from there drive is taken forward to a gearbox at the end of the flail rotor drum. Inside the tank things are otherwise similar to a conventional Sherman except that there are alterations to the ammunition stowage on the right side. The other changes are two independent compass systems and a device for measuring distance travelled in yards. The most obvious compass is the binnacle compass that pokes through a hole in the top of the tank's turret and is elevated to its full height when required in order to get it as far away from the mass of metal as possible. This compass can be read via a repeater inside the turret and gives the normal magnetic bearing. The other is a gyro compass, which has to be preset in order to give the driver a precise course to follow across a minefield. The yard counter enables the driver to keep an accurate check on the distance covered. (Art by Tony Bryan, © Osprey Publishing)

Key

1 Air inlet
2 Tarpaulin cover
3 Spare chain holder
4 Left fuel tank filler
5 Radiator filler
6 Turret stowage box
7 Binnacle compass projector retracted
8 Binnacle compass projector extended
9 'B' aerial base
10 M2 Browning .50-cal. machine-gun
11 'A' aerial base
12 Commander's hatch
13 Vane sight
14 M3 75mm gun
15 Side rotary wire cutter
16 Ventilator
17 Flail jib cross-member and shield
18 Flail rotor drum
19 Flail chain attachment point
20 Flail drive bevel gearbox
21 Flail chain
22 Wire deflector
23 Flail drive shaft
24 Flail drive shaft cover
25 Right side flail boom
26 Jib elevating piston
27 Drive sprocket
28 Right side flail boom support bracket
29 Armoured cover for rear flail drive gearbox
30 Rear flail drive gearbox
31 Flail chain drive upper case
32 Co-driver's seat
33 Flail chain drive lower case
34 Flail drive power take-off
35 75mm gun cover locker
36 Driver's seat
37 Flail activating lever
38 Suspension unit
39 Main drive shaft
40 Machine-gun ammunition stowage
41 Loader's seat
42 Turret basket
43 Track idler wheel
44 Tail light
45 Steel chevron track
46 Engine deck hatch
47 Engine access doors
48 Towing lug
49 Idler wheel mounting bracket
50 Lifting ring

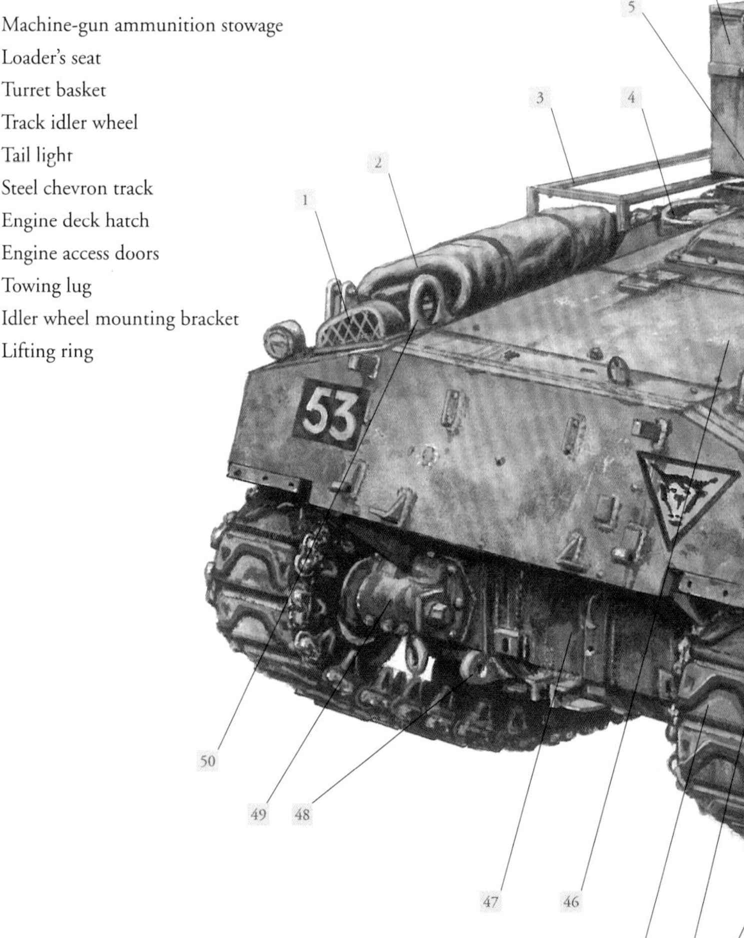

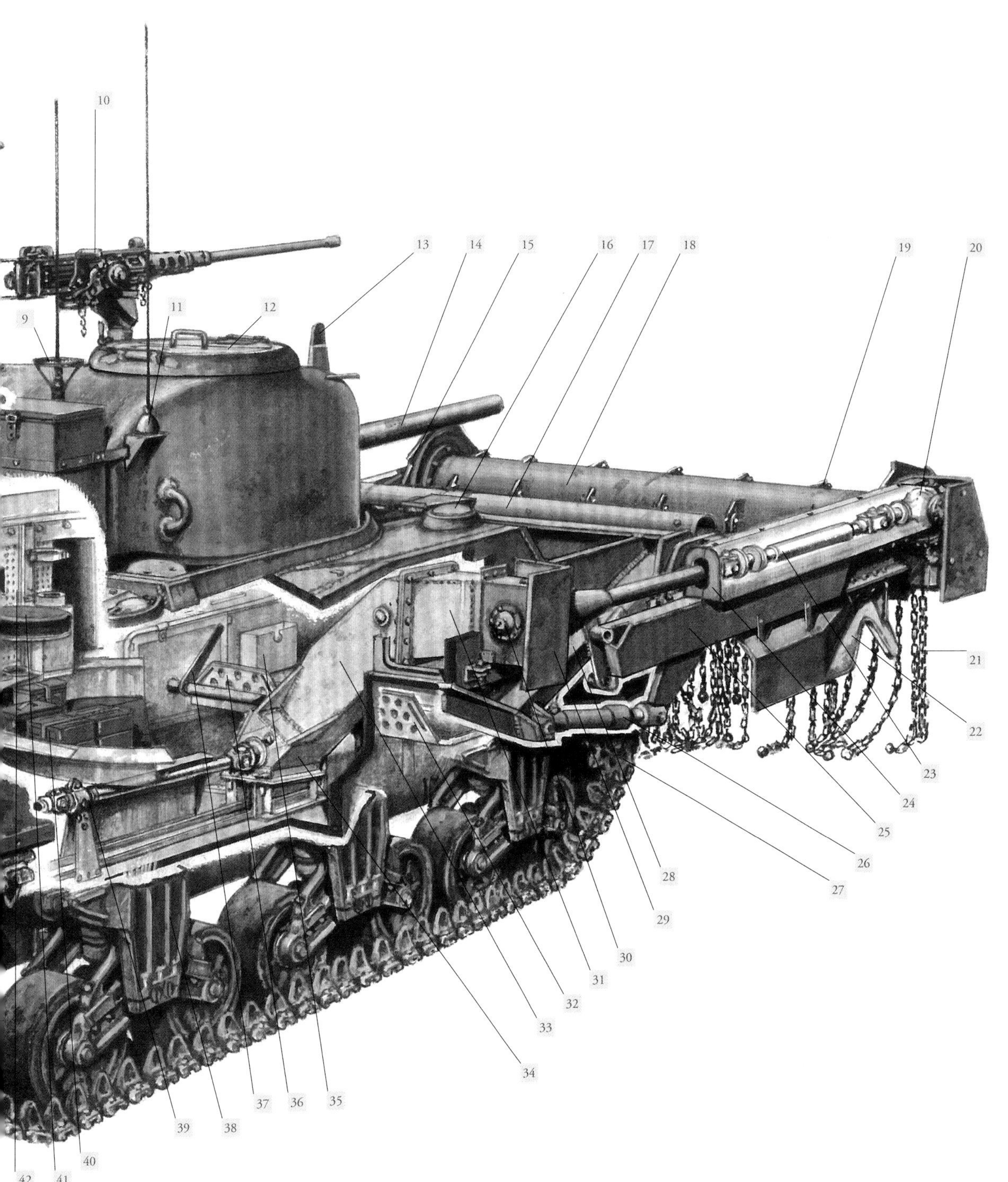
9
10
11
12
13
14
15
16
17
18
19
20
21
22
23
24
25
26
27
28
29
30
31
32
33
34
35
36
37
38
39
40
41
42

Training for the assault, a Crab with its chains securely wrapped in canvas tackles a breach in a training wall. At this point the driver is unable to see anything worthwhile and relies on the commander to guide him.

As soon as these trials were completed, an initial order for 330 Crabs was placed, to be ready by March 1944. The work was to be shared by Curran Brothers in Cardiff, Milner's Safe Company in Manchester, T. C. Jones & Co. in London and J. Hibberts Ltd of Darwin in Lancashire. So, in terms of design, all of the eggs were in one basket and as if on cue, a serious fault suddenly put in an unwelcome appearance. Further comparative trials revealed that the Crabs involved were not scoring very high figures in terms of mines destroyed in a typical flailing run. It even reached the point where

A Crab I of 739th Tank Battalion, US Army, passing through Vicht, Germany, on 21 February 1945. The flail chains are an early type and the bracket on the turret for smoke-bomb dischargers is a typical British fitting.

A snapshot, said to have been taken in Villers-Bretonneux, shows a Crab with camouflage netting around the turret, and the flail chains wound around the rotor, passing an ambulance convoy in a narrow street.

a much-despised Baron put up a better show. Fortunately, before everyone went back to the drawing board, someone decided to check the quality of flail chains being supplied and discovered that many were nowhere near up to standard. As a result, those companies that could not reach the required standard were dropped and immediately the detonation rate began to rise again.

It is also worth noting that in February 1944 a Staffordshire firm, T. B. Welling & Co., submitted a flail of riveted construction, quite unlike any traditional chain, which twisted rather than broke with the blast and was regarded as promising for future development.

Contemporary official records should be the raw material from which all works such as this are created, but they are of variable value, not always to be dipped into lightly. For example, the RAC six-monthly report issued at the end of 1943 not only gives some very optimistic production figures (which reveal, among other things, that 576 Shermans earmarked for production as Marquis would now be Crabs), but also includes the extraordinary statement that Shermans fitted with Chrysler and Ford engines would not be suitable for conversion to Crabs because at least 460bhp (343kW) was required in order to drive the flail equipment. In practice, that ruled out all versions of the Sherman although, of them all, the Ford-engined M4A3 (Sherman IV) came closest at 450bhp (335kW); the Chrysler was 375bhp (279kW) as was the twin GM diesel pack, while the Continental radial was only 350bhp (261kW).

Given that the chances of the British acquiring suitable quantities of Ford-powered Shermans were slim at best, that part of the statement could be interpreted as sour grapes, yet a mere six months later the report on the Crab starts with the line; 'The Crab is based on the Sherman V…' which is, of course, the Chrysler-powered model. The report includes certain other interesting snippets. To begin with it states that, by that

These vehicles are believed to be of the 22nd Dragoons, carrying infantry of the 51st (Highland) Division towards Blerick, on the Dutch–German border in December 1944. The name *City of Gloucester* painted on the rotor arm of the nearest Crab is probably an acknowledgement of sponsorship rather than a regimental name.

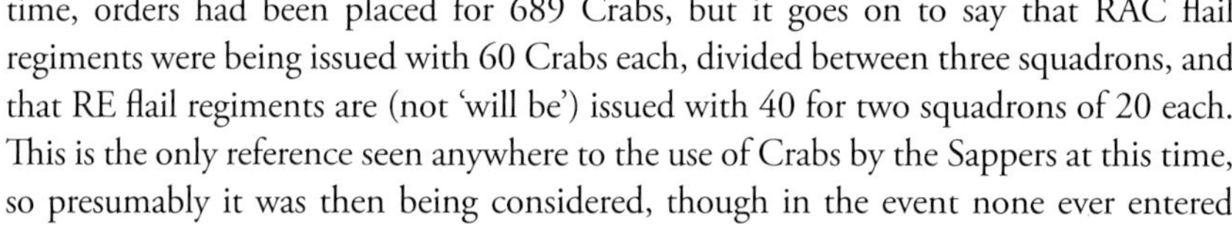

time, orders had been placed for 689 Crabs, but it goes on to say that RAC flail regiments were being issued with 60 Crabs each, divided between three squadrons, and that RE flail regiments are (not 'will be') issued with 40 for two squadrons of 20 each. This is the only reference seen anywhere to the use of Crabs by the Sappers at this time, so presumably it was then being considered, though in the event none ever entered service. Going back to the RAC regiments, although a very simple sum will show that they would also have 20 Crabs per squadron under this arrangement, a further line indicating that these would be organized on the scale of four troops (per squadron) each of five Crabs has been crossed out in the original document.

This Crab of the 1st Lothian & Border Horse carries the most common type of station-keeping device, involving discs on posts. Subsequently the Lothians themselves developed a more effective system that used chevrons instead of discs.

What this tells us, of course, is that things were constantly changing and that one should be extremely cautious in interpreting an isolated entry, even in an official document. Even so, two other comments in this particular report are worth noting. The first states that all Crabs would be fitted with a hook to tow the Centipede roller device to detonate S-mines not set off by the flail. There is one poor-quality photograph showing this, presumably on trial, but no evidence that it was used in practice. The second reference is to another Sherman modification optimistically named as the Canadian Indestructible Roller Device (CIRD) which, we are told, would be issued to RAC flail regiments on the scale of one troop per squadron, to act as pilot vehicles to locate the edge of a minefield. Once again, there is no evidence that this was ever done, or indeed that CIRD saw any active service at all.

This is a stationkeeping device developed by the Department of Tank Design but being tested here by F Wing, 79th Armoured Division, at Gheel in Belgium. Projecting from the side of the tank, this device uses a wire, attached to the tank in front, to activate dials that give the driver a precise indication of his position relative to the leading tank.

Thus far, one might say, engineering had been the driving force behind flail development, but not science. However, it seems that the Humber Company in Coventry, otherwise not known to be involved in flail development, worked out that if the rotor arms could be balanced correctly, the flail could be made to follow the contours of the ground unassisted. Trials on the Marquis prototype and an early production Crab showed the possibilities and subsequent refinements by AEC evolved into an effective system.

Following trials by 79th Armoured Division at the end of April, the design was authorized for production in May 1944 as the Contouring Crab, or Crab II. The type is best identified from the left, or near side in British terminology, for here one can

A Crab II in India beating across hard, dry ground. The strips of metal welded to the ends of the rotor were intended to make it easier to remove wire when it became wrapped around the drum.

Rackham's prototype Crab, viewed from the right, shows how the flail drive emerges from the side of the hull and links to the geared drive at the end of the rotor by two jointed shafts. The rotor arms are fixed and no wire cutters are fitted to the ends of the rotor.

see that the hydraulic cylinder has been removed, the rotor arm extended beyond its pivot point and a cast counterweight of about 112lb (51kg) bolted on instead. This system, aided by the centrifugal force generated by the rotor, and the weight of the rotor when the chains are in contact with the ground, kept the arm at around 4ft 3in. (1.3m) high. A stop could be engaged to keep the rotor arms level for wire cutting and the hydraulic arm on the right side, in addition to raising the arms in the normal way, acted as a form of shock absorber during flailing.

The Crab IIs, as they became available, were gradually issued to regiments in the months after D-Day. They were first used operationally at Le Havre, then at Walcheren and were the standard type by the time of the Rhine crossing.

THE CRAB IN ACTION

Major-General Nigel Duncan, who commanded 30th Armoured Brigade when it operated flails, provided a very realistic picture of a typical, albeit rather formal, mine-clearing operation, written in 1947. A flail troop consisted of five tanks, on the basis that in order to clear a path 24ft (7.3m) wide through a minefield three flails would be required, plus two more waiting on the sidelines to replace casualties and provide fire support in the meantime.

As the troop approached the edge of the minefield the three tanks earmarked for flailing formed up, one behind another, about 75ft (23m) apart, while the other two stopped and prepared to engage the opposition. At the edge of the minefield the leading tank halted, engaged the flail drive and at a steady 1.5mph (2.4km/h) began to crawl forwards. The second flail then followed, still maintaining that 75ft (23m) gap but echeloned itself so that there was a 1ft (0.3m) overlap between its path and that of the leading tank. The third tank followed in the same way, and the direction of the echelon, left or right of the leader, depended on the wind direction to avoid blowing dust. The flail drum on a Sherman Crab was 9ft (2.7m) wide so, allowing for the overlap, the three could clear a lane 24ft (7.3m) wide across the minefield, this being the agreed width to suit not just conventional tanks but also other assault engineer equipment required for the operation; at all times the Crabs had to consider themselves as part of an assault team.

OPPOSITE A superb view of a pair of Crabs of 22nd Dragoons, fully stowed for active service. Features to note on the nearest tank are the frame for a Whyman lane marker near the back, a frame to hold spare flail chains beneath the turret and two spare road wheels near the front.

Within each tank all was concentration. A very high standard of driving was required to ensure that tanks did not wander off course, but the cloud of dust or mud kicked up by the flailing chains was almost impenetrable up to turret height, so that the driver had to rely on the elevated station-keeping devices on the tank in front. Visibility was not that good inside either. Such light as there was came filtered through a constant cloud of dust that penetrated despite the various seals applied to keep it out. The detonation of a Teller anti-tank mine was not as exciting as one might expect. Inside it sounded as a dull thud, accompanied by a slight shock running through the vehicle. More telling was a sudden increase in engine noise when the

blast from the mine caused the flail jib to jump upwards so that the flail drum revved a bit faster before falling back into place.

Naturally, there were many different combat considerations. Ian Hammerton, a troop commander in B Squadron, 22nd Dragoons (see Bibliography), tells how during the assault on Groesbeek in the Reichswald, his troop, echeloned to the right, had been warned of the presence of a German self-propelled gun in the neighbourhood and, feeling very exposed on a broad, treeless plateau, flailed the course with turrets trained to the right and gunners ready, just in case. On an earlier occasion, during operations to clear the Scheldt estuary, Hammerton's troop assisted the Canadians by flailing along the top of a dyke, high above the surrounding countryside, for all to see and working in the muddiest conditions imaginable. It was the kind of operation that no previous training could really have prepared them for.

FAR LEFT The Whyman lane-marking device was originally developed to mark out where mats had been laid over beaches, but was later taken up by the flails. Three of the long marker poles remain, which could be fired into the ground as the tank proceeded, marking the edge of the swept lane.

CENTRE TOP One of the first station-keeping devices for flails involved four very tall posts with coloured lights on top which the following driver was trained to keep station on. The system was abandoned, however, because it prevented the turret from traversing very far.

ABOVE These extensions to the driver's and co-driver's periscopes not only helped to protect them from mud and dust, they were also marked to relate to the station-keeping equipment. This picture also gives a clear view of the special mantlet cover fitted to flail tanks to seal it from dust.

SHERMAN CRABS BREACHING A MINEFIELD

This somewhat idealized and simplified diagram shows a troop of flail tanks clearing a lane through an enemy minefield. Three of the five tanks are flailing steadily across the danger zone in a dead straight line at 1.5 mph (2.4km/h). The wind is blowing from the west and the tanks are echeloned to the right so that they are not blowing dust over the tanks behind them. They are keeping station, 75ft (23m) apart and each slightly overlapping the path of the tank in front to create a reasonably safe lane 24ft (7.3m) wide for other elements of the breaching team to follow. The other two tanks remain in reserve, using their guns to cover for those that are flailing but ready at a moment's notice to replace any flailing tank that might become a casualty. Minefields in Normandy appear to have been clearly marked to prevent German troops and local civilians from straying into them. (Art by Tony Bryan, © Osprey Publishing)

ERMAN V CRAB I, 1ST LOTHIAN & BORDER HORSE, 30TH ARMOURED BRIGADE, WINTER 1944–45

:r was never a good time for flail tanks. Either the terrain quid mud that got plastered all over the tank and its crew, s making the task of detonating mines more difficult; or it be bitterly cold, freezing the crews even inside the tank naking the ground rock hard, which made flailing sible. And then, of course, there was snow. This tank a mine, and then settled in the mud that later froze. Once ea had been cleared it would be recovered and repaired. othian & Border Horse was a yeomanry regiment, like the Westminster Dragoons. Both had been armoured car companies of the Royal Tank Corps between the wars, which became fully fledged tank regiments on the outbreak of war, although for a while the Westminster Dragoons was an officer cadet training unit. Within the 30th Armoured Brigade the three flail regiments were organized in the order 22nd Dragoons, 1st Lothian & Border Horse, Westminster Dragoons. (Art by Tony Bryan, © Osprey Publishing

Hammerton also remarks that, in the final months of the war, when the mine problem was nothing like as great as it had been, their eager new commanding officer volunteered the regiment for virtually any job going, to the point that plans were made to remove the flail equipment and have the Crabs operate as conventional gun tanks; a suggestion that was not greeted with very much enthusiasm by the specialist crews.

The Crabs also appeared in Italy in the final months of the war, forming B Squadron, 51st RTR, in the 25th Armoured Engineer Brigade; while A and C Squadrons had Crocodile flamethrowers. The Crabs saw some action during the advance to the Reno and Senio rivers, but not enough to suffer any casualties at all, and they spent the last weeks clearing routes through minefields well behind the lines.

THE AMERICAN ANGLE

On a number of occasions during the development of the Scorpion flail, the authorities in Washington DC asked London to supply information. Indeed, at one time they even asked for a sample vehicle. The response was not encouraging. Each time the request was rejected, on the grounds of security, which seems an odd way for Allies to behave. True, the Americans were working on their own designs, and had some flails operating in Tunisia by 1943, but clearly the British were regarded as the pioneers.

The pusher contraption, borrowed from the Americans and fitted to a Crab II, so that another tank could bank it up steep hills. The Crab also displays station-keeping equipment and an angled marker box on each side that dispensed illuminated pegs along its route.

In February 1944 a committee of engineers from the US First Army examined a number of British devices on behalf of General Eisenhower, including both the Scorpion and the Crab (which they described as an American version of the British Scorpion) and one gets the impression that the Scorpion, in American eyes, killed the Crab. Two US Armored Division commanders turned the Crab down as an organic part of their divisions, largely on the grounds that it appeared to be too slow, while the First Army team had three objections: lack of mobility, meaning that it was too slow, mechanical unreliability and sensitivity to terrain, all of which suggest that it was the Scorpion that was being judged. However, they had three alternatives to suggest: the Snake explosive device, the bulldozer tank and the traditional methods of lifting mines by hand, all of which they deemed more effective.

Even so, experience soon altered views and on a number of occasions British flail regiments, and particularly 2nd Lothian & Border Horse, were called upon to assist General Simpson's US Ninth Army when mines were expected, on one occasion with tragic results. On the night of 26 February 1945, two troops of A Squadron moved out to assist two tank companies of the 743rd Tank Battalion in an attack on the

Flailing over frozen ground was never a very rewarding experience and it is difficult to tell whether these crews, believed to be from the Westminster Dragoons, are searching for mines the hard way or just making a fire to keep warm. The route appears to have been taped already, while the men, as usual, are wearing every variation of uniform.

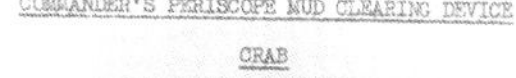

villages of Kich and Troisdorf. The Crabs led the way in the dark until the leading American company peeled off to the right to take up fire positions off the road. At this point the leading Crabs were reversing back down the road when they were spotted by tanks of the second company which, unable to recognize them in the dark, opened fire and knocked out three Crabs. Ultimately, a handful of Crabs were handed over to the Americans, where they were operated by the 739th Tank Battalion.

ABOVE Flailing in thick mud was a messy business. This thoroughly plastered Crab was being used in post-war trials to test special devices to clean periscopes using water sprays. Cleaning the tank afterwards must have been a difficult chore.

ABOVE LEFT The Westminster Dragoons provided crews for four Crabs to take part in the British Victory Parade in 1946. They are shown here, in a highly polished state, formed up near the Tower of London and ready to move off, followed by a pair of Churchill bridgelayers.

POST-WAR DEVELOPMENTS

The Crabs and their crews emerged from the war with everyone's praise ringing in their ears. They had performed a dangerous and thankless task with great competence and skill. Statistics are always difficult to play with because they never reveal the full story but, for what they are worth, the following refer to flail operations during the first four months of operations in north-west Europe. Each squadron destroyed, on average, 440 mines in an overall average flailing time of eight hours, and over the same period only 15 tanks were destroyed beyond repair through mine damage. The future was looking good.

Snow trials were held at Petawawa in Canada over the winter of 1948–49. This is a Crab II with the flail attachment on full elevation. The trials seemed to show that flailing in deep snow was ineffective.

A SHERMAN V CRAB II WITH STATION-KEEPING EQUIPMENT, BRITAIN, 1945

The problems of station-keeping for flail tanks in action exercised many minds and resulted in various solutions. However, nothing teaches so well as experience, and the chevron device shown here seems to have originated with an idea by the Lothian & Border Horse. The theory was that the driver of a following tank had to line up two chevrons so that he could see an X through his periscope. A similar structure on top of the turret could be observed from the tank in front, from a periscope in the commander's hatch. In order to indicate the safe path to following vehicles, lane markers were fired at regular intervals from special dischargers on the side of the hull. The binnacle compass can also be seen on top of the turret. Experiments continued into the immediate post-war years and the agency involved was a truncated team from 79th Armoured Division, using the same insignia, and now known as SADE, the Specialised Armour Development Establishment. (Art by Tony Bryan, © Osprey Publishing)

As part of the experiments to develop a post-war flail, a remote control Crab was tested against much more powerful mines. This was the result. Clearly in the future something a lot more robust would be required.

A CHURCHILL TOAD FLAIL, ROYAL ENGINEERS, SALISBURY PLAIN, 1958

There is no evidence available to show whether Churchill flail tanks were ever issued for operational use, but it seems unlikely. In the main they would have been kept in store. For the purpose of this illustration we are imagining a demonstration on the British Army training area of Salisbury Plain in Wiltshire. For this reason no markings are shown on the tank itself. The end of the lane-marking dispenser is shown raised so that the mechanism can be seen and an individual marker is shown inset. Compared with wartime flails, the Toad was immensely powerful; indeed the driver was instructed to get the vehicle moving before the flail was activated, otherwise it was found that the flail chains excavated a hole which the tank, as soon as it moved, fell into. By the late 1950s virtually all specialized armour was operated by the RE, whose post-1953 cap badge is shown. (Art by Tony Bryan, © Osprey Publishing)

Long term, it was intended to include a flail (FV204) as part of the Universal Tank Programme, until this collapsed in a mixture of financial melt-down and technical nightmares. In the meantime the Crab II became the focus of numerous experiments, some of the more interesting of which are shown in the photographs. One might be mentioned here since it had implications for the future. Towards the end of the war the Germans had started to counter the success of the Crab by linking conventional mines to more substantial explosive devices – aerial bombs, depth charges or large artillery shells for example. The Crab detonated the mine, the mine detonated the bomb and the bomb destroyed the Crab. This was clearly a short-term solution that might not be used after the war, but more powerful mines were very likely. To explore this possibility a Crab II was tested by the FVPE in 1947 against a 40lb (18kg) anti-tank mine, and the results were impressive. The FVPE staff were unwilling to risk a human crew at this stage, so the trial tank was 'manned' by a crew of rabbits, each in its own cage, and FVPE fitted a remote-control clutch so that the tank could be started from outside. The result was certainly spectacular since the mine blew off the rotor and created a large crater, but the rabbits appear to have been unharmed – at least until each one was subjected to an autopsy.

The partially armoured AEC Matador flail dynamometer, with what appears to be the armoured cab of a Deacon. Projecting from the back is the sub-frame that carries a Ford engine at the front end, driving the multiple discs to which different types of flail chain could be attached.

A final production Churchill flail or Toad, shown with the rotor drum and arms folded backwards in the travelling position; it made a particularly tall load for a tank transporter. It enables us, however, to see the shelf across the front that reduced mud splash and, higher up, the array of smoke bomb dischargers.

For the future, however, there was a problem to be resolved. The Sherman Crab could not go on for ever and in any case it was an American tank, technically on loan. FV204 was a non-starter and no plans had ever been made to develop a flail version of Centurion, although this might have been the better solution even now. Instead, by about 1953 (and one feels in some desperation) plans were drawn up to create a flail version of the Churchill for the RE under the designation FV3902. There were still plenty of Churchills around, many in nearly new condition, and it was a type familiar to the Sappers, but as a basic design it was very long in the tooth and not, at first glance, ideally suited to such a conversion.

In total 42 Churchill Flails – or Toads as they were nicknamed – were built between 1954 and 1956 by a consortium that included the Distington Engineering Company of Cumberland (preparation of drawings and design parents), Robinson & Kershaw of Dunkinfield (hull conversion and new superstructure) and British Railways workshops at Horwich (flail mechanism and final assembly). There were three successive variants of the Toad, but the basic layout was the same and can be described first. The hull was that of a late production A22F Churchill, stripped of its turret and fitted instead with a large superstructure that covered the entire front half of the tank. At the very front, raised well above his original position, sat the driver, with the commander (the only other crew member) on his left; behind them the rest of the superstructure was occupied by the fuel-injected M120 version of the Rolls-Royce Meteor V12 (the Conqueror tank engine) aligned fore and aft but facing back to front. There was also room here for air cleaners plus fuel and lubricating oil tanks for both engines. Already it was a step backwards by introducing a separate engine to drive the flail.

To be fair, the designers were anticipating a new generation of mines that the poor old Crab would not have had the stamina to deal with (Toad was a much more

A Crab 2 with a post-1948 registration. Viewed from the left side one can see the counterweight that replaced the hydraulic gear on that side and enabled the rotor arm to follow the contours of the ground. With the vehicle on a hard surface it is evident how the added weight of the flail gear bears down on the front of the suspension.

powerful machine by any standards), to which end they needed a bigger rotor drum with more flails attached and, by definition, much stronger support arms. This was the most novel feature of the new design, in that the arms were pivoted against the sides of the hull in such a way that for travelling the entire flail arrangement could be folded back to rest on top of the superstructure when not required. Drive to the flail rotor ran through the left, or nearside arm.

The first two Toads, the prototypes, featured a counterbalance system for the rotor (to permit contouring) located in cylinders each side, operated by a hydraulic system that also activated the flail to and from its stowed position and retracted an ingenious lane marking device at the back. In 1955 six interim design flails appeared in which, among other things, all the hydraulic gear had been deleted. Counterbalancing was now achieved by concentric springs inside much larger cylinders, the lane-marking device became a permanent fixture and if the flail boom had to be retracted for stowing, a rope and pulley system was employed.

As always, everything goes around in circles, and the final design that appeared at the start of 1956 was a re-incarnation of the Pram Scorpion. The entire counterbalance system was done away with and replaced by a pair of curved skids, fitted under each end of the rotor drum, and incorporating a castoring roller. It was as if Abraham du Toit had got his way after all.

Flailing along the beach at COXE (Combined Operations Experimental Establishment) in North Devon, with Appledore just across the water, this Toad has been fitted with deep-wading gear. The engineers observing this trial may not have known it, but this was the twilight of the wartime flail tank.

CHAPTER 7

OTHER AMERICAN-BUILT TANKS

T14 ASSAULT TANK

The difference between what the Americans called an 'assault tank' and the British preference for the term 'infantry tank' is always difficult to assess. In America the term normally applied to tanks with thicker armour (which inevitably made them slower), much like a British infantry tank. However, American assault tanks such as the M4A3E2 (22mph) or T14 (24mph) were still a good deal faster than the archetypal British infantry tank, the Churchill, which had a top speed of 15mph. However, the British equivalent to the American T14, the mid-war A33 prototype, was also rated at 24mph top speed; classed as a heavy assault tank to make it more comparable with its American equivalent, it was also considered in Britain as an infantry tank to replace the Churchill.

The two designs stemmed from a meeting, held on 30 March 1942, between the Chief of Ordnance at Aberdeen Proving Ground and members of the British Tank Mission, at which it was decided that two prototypes would be produced in each country for a common type of assault tank that both could use. The American T14 was based on the new Sherman while the British A33 used some components of the Mark VIII Cruiser, the Cromwell – notably the Meteor engine, Merritt-Brown transmission, and 75mm gun, but not the suspension.

The American Locomotive Company (ALCO) contracted to build two pilot models which were subsequently sent to Aberdeen Proving Ground for evaluation. The second pilot was ultimately shipped to Britain where it still survives as an exhibit at the Tank Museum. T14 was powered by the 520hp Ford V8 Model GAZ petrol engine which drove through a regular Sherman gearbox and final drive, albeit with changed ratios to allow for the extra weight (47 tons instead of about 33 tons for a typical Sherman). The suspension, derived from the heavy tank M6, used horizontal volute sprung bogies, but with three per side rather than the four on the M6; the new tank featured double-width track of the M6 pattern as well. However trials revealed

One of the two T14s in America with its side skirts removed to show the suspension.

a regular tendency to shed tracks, a fault that was never entirely cured, while fitters constantly complained about the difficulty of raising sections of skirting plates, half an inch thick, simply to adjust track tension – never mind other, more serious repairs and replacements.

The hull was of welded construction, sloped at the sides and front. Armour plate was between 2 and 2.5in thick on the sides and a maximum of 4in on the front, with 2in-thick sloped plate above. The main armament was the regular 75mm weapon in an M34A1 mount and the co-axial machine gun could be either a .50-calibre weapon or a .30-calibre, although the front hull machine gun was intended to be a .50-calibre Browning with its own telescopic sight; perhaps this was a concession to the British, although an adaptor was provided for a .30-calibre weapon to be fitted instead. The turret otherwise fitted the same diameter turret ring as the Sherman but was larger, with 3in thick sloping plate at the front and 4in on all vertical surfaces at the sides and back, with two hatches on the roof and a 2in smoke bomb discharger.

In America the Armored Force never liked the tank, or indeed any heavy tank.

T14 shown from the rear with the heavy side skirts in place.

T1E2 with the cast hull was the pilot for the original M6. Weighing around 50 imperial tons it was deemed too heavy, and in any case the Americans thought it made more sense to ship more, lighter tanks across the Atlantic.

The British contender failed even before it left Britain and the British decided that the Churchill would now fill the role. But when the US Army decided to abandon the tank in 1944 that was the end of the programme. Even so the British, having originally put in a request for 850, seem to have increased that number to 1,000 on an unnumbered contract card and even allotted the WD numbers T236775 to T237774 – although they only ever received one tank.

THE HEAVY TANK PROJECT

Even before America entered World War II, and drawing heavily on British experience of tank fighting, the Americans decided that they needed a heavy tank capable of lending fire support to their M3 Medium Tank design. Although at first conceived as a multi-turreted design, it later resolved itself into a single-turret tank mounting a modified 3in M7 anti-aircraft gun in a combination mount with a 37mm M6 gun and the usual profusion of machine guns. Incidentally, the turret had a 69in diameter turret ring, giving the lie to any suggestion that the Americans were unable to produce such a turret at that stage.

In fact the biggest problem at the outset was to settle upon a suitably powerful engine. This was decided in favour of the Wright G-200 Model 781C9GC1, a nine-cylinder air-cooled radial rated at 960hp at 2,300rpm, which was as close as they could get to the 1,000hp required. The only trouble was finding a suitable transmission to go with it. Ultimately this resolved itself into a sophisticated petrol-electric transmission in the T1E1, which was regarded as the American version. The export version had a Timken mechanical system linked to a Twin Disc torque converter (Model 16001), driving through a Hycon two-speed-and-reverse hydraulic gear change and controlled differential steering. This drivetrain gave a top speed of 22mph for the T1E2 and T1E3, which were standardized as the M6 and M6A1 heavy tanks respectively, the only difference being that the M6 had a cast hull and the M6A1 a welded one. Eight of the former and 12 of the latter were completed at the Baldwin Locomotive Works, all for service with the British Army, although none were ever

The M6A1 was a big tank. This version was of welded construction, but apart from this there was very little difference between the M6 and M6A1. Sixty-five of these tanks were scheduled to go to Britain.

delivered. Apparently there was no requirement for heavy tanks in north-west Europe, and in any case the Americans felt that it was better to ship over two 35-ton tanks instead of one weighing nearly twice as much. In addition, the heavy tank was a rather antiquated design by then and the crew locations were not up to the latest standards.

An effort has been made to liken the M6-series tanks to the German Tiger 1, both being examples of the early type of heavy tank. The German tank seems to have the edge in most respects, being somewhat heavier and faster and mounting a better gun, but there is not a lot in it. The maximum armour thickness is quite similar and the American suspension seems to be a little less likely to get blocked up with mud or snow. However, the two tanks never got close to confronting one another in action, so it remains an improbable 'might have been'.

THE M22 LIGHT TANK LOCUST

The M22 was designed and built by the Marmon-Herrington Company of Indianapolis. It was originally designed as the T9 airborne tank, which was to be flown into the battle zone by a Douglas C-54 Skymaster, a four-engined transport which after the war evolved into the DC-4 airliner. The plan was to carry the hull of the tank slung beneath the fuselage of the aircraft, while the quickly detachable turret, and the three-man crew of course, travelled inside the aircraft. One disadvantage was that the tank could only be flown to the nearest airfield to the battlefield, reassembled and then moved, either on its own tracks or by transporter, into battle.

A development of the T9, the T9E1 showed some quite striking changes to the T9, including such fundamental things as the shape of the hull and the layout of the driver's position. In an effort to save weight the fixed, forward-firing hull machine

An M22 Locust in front of a Hamilcar glider. The serial number 41, on top of a green-above-blue square (the arm-of-service marking of a Royal Armoured Corps Reconnaissance Regiment) indicates 6th Airborne Reconnaissance Regiment.

guns were eliminated, as was the power traverse for the turret and the stabilization gear for the gun. Additions included four substantial brackets on the hull sides to attach the lifting gear to when the hull was slung beneath its C-54 transport, and two hatches in the turret roof instead of one. Most unusual was a bar, linking the suspension units on each side. The T9E1 was standardized as the M22.

The M22 was an incredibly small tank, just 13ft long, 7ft wide and only 6ft high. It weighed just over 7 tons and was powered by a Lycoming 0-345T air-cooled engine (six cylinders, horizontally opposed) rated at 192bhp driving through a four-speed gearbox into a controlled differential final drive to front-mounted sprockets, giving a respectable top road speed of 35mph. The suspension was vertical volute, two bogies each side, with a substantial idler at the rear. The little tank had a crew of three, a driver and two men in the turret. It was armed with a 37mm gun M6 with a co-axial .30-calibre Browning machine gun in a fully rotating turret.

A surviving Locust in RAF service in the Middle East after the war. The senior officers look a bit too exalted to constitute the normal crew.

The tank was never used in action by American forces but there is a contract card (s/m/1280) for 500 of the little tanks, for which the British numbers T158877–T159376 were allotted, and dated 29 March 1943. But according to the late Richard P. Hunnicutt only 260 of these tanks were allocated to Britain under the Lend-Lease programme.

British use of the M22 Locust required the addition of a pair of external smoke grenade dischargers mounted on either side of the turret, and in some cases a version of the Littlejohn squeeze bore adaptor was fitted to the 37mm gun. This device, attached to the muzzle of the gun, allowed the firing of a Super Velocity tungsten round that gave an enhanced armour-piercing performance, but while it was attached no other type of ammunition could be fired, and the American 37mm gun's barrel had to be shortened to accept it. All told 12 tanks, of Sixth Airborne Reconnaissance Regiment, were used in the airborne role for Operation *Plunder*, the Rhine crossing in March 1945, and all arrived safely on the German side

apart from one tank that broke through the floor of its glider over the river. Of those that landed, five or six were knocked out while the others performed some useful work in support of the airborne forces. Each tank was carried in a General Aircraft Hamilcar glider, towed by a four-engined aircraft. The Hamilcar had the advantage that it flew right to the battleground and disgorged its tank complete and in fighting trim. The C-54 had much greater range, but carried the tank in two pieces and could only land on a proper airfield.

The Locust was also used as a commanding officer's charger attached to a mechanized Royal Artillery regiment, but to what extent is not known. At least one served with the Royal Air Force Police at an airfield in the Middle East but how this came about is not clear either.

M24 CHAFFEE

Although in terms of armour thickness the new M24 Light Tank was the same as its predecessors, the M3- and M5-series light tanks, it was far better arranged with hardly a vertical surface visible. However, the main reason for developing a new light tank was to arm it with a better gun; a new version of the 75mm M3 gun was developed and entered service as the lighter M6 version, with a concentric recoil system that worked in the new turret. In fact the gun had been developed from a lightweight 75mm installed in the nose of the North American B-25 Mitchell bomber. Secondary armament came in the form of two .30-calibre Browning machine guns, one in the front of the hull and the other co-axial with the main armament in the turret, to the right of the 75mm gun. A larger .50-calibre Browning was mounted on top of the turret, on a hefty tripod and within reach of the commander's cupola.

Laughing Boy, an M24 Chaffee in British service, photographed at a victory parade in Germany at the end of the war, passing the saluting base and Field Marshal Montgomery. The tank carries the curious double sign seen only on vehicles of 7th Armoured Division; the stag's head symbol of 22nd Armoured Brigade above the numbered arm-of-service marking, in this case 52 which suggests 1st Royal Tank Regiment.

A sample M24 in Italy, posed alongside an M5A1 Stuart VI.

The new tank, which first appeared in prototype form in 1943, had a similar drivetrain to the M5/M5A1 Light Tanks, consisting of a pair of Cadillac V8 engines, each coupled to its own automatic Hydramatic transmission, but a new, manually operated transfer box was now fitted in place of the automatic one developed for the earlier tank. This not only gave the driver the option of using speeds in low or high ratio, it also enabled the tank to move at relatively high speed in reverse, which was useful in certain tactical situations. Final drive (including the inevitable controlled differential steering system) was in the nose of the tank, covered by a bolt-on plate. Drive sprockets were at the front of the tank and for the first time in an American tank issued for service, a form of torsion bar suspension with five wheel stations was employed (although it had already appeared in the M18 tank destroyer). Weight was a little over 18 tons and the top speed reckoned to be a respectable 35mph.

The new tank carried a five-man crew although sometimes, in American service, this was reduced to four men, so that the assistant driver was expected to slip out of his seat and slide back into the turret to act as loader when required. In British service a full five-man crew was carried, the loader being trained to also serve as the wireless operator when required. The driving controls were standard for an automatic tank, and duplicated so that the assistant driver was also able to operate the tank. On some earlier tanks, and the M18 tank destroyer, the steering levers were pivoted at the top, effectively above the driver's head, but on the M24 they were pivoted at the bottom and worked in the usual way. The tank was of all-welded construction, both hull and turret, with an elongated back to the turret to contain the wireless set, a cupola for the commander on the right side, and an ordinary hatch on the left.

The M24 entered production in the summer of 1944 and the first arrivals in Britain were not until later in the year. They then had to undergo various modifications to make them suitable for British service, so it was 1945 before any were ready, and some seem to have entered regimental service just in time to participate in various parades marking final victory in the war in Europe. Although 400 M24 tanks were requested on the original contract card and WD numbers allotted for 600 tanks, Britain only received 298, and most of them too late to make any real difference.

M26 PERSHING MEDIUM TANK

The tank which evolved into the M26 actually began life as an idea in May 1942, and a prototype, designated T20 No. 1, was rolled out from the Fisher Body Plant in Detroit, a division of General Motors, almost precisely one year later. As might be expected, it owed a lot to contemporary in-service tanks, notably the latest version of the M4 Medium. This included a long-barrelled 76mm gun, Ford V8 (Model GAN) engine and an early form of horizontal volute suspension. But the transmission now relied on a Torqmatic system and was shifted to the rear, and for the first time in an American tank since the days of Walter Christie, it had a rear-mounted drive sprocket.

Further prototypes appeared over the next 18 months with a gradual move towards a torsion bar suspension system, a longer and harder-hitting 90mm gun with a co-axial Browning machine gun and a similar .30-calibre weapon in the front of the hull, and a slightly more powerful 500hp Ford V8 (Model GAF) engine linked to a fully automatic Torqmatic three-speed transmission. The resulting T26E3 was standardized as the M26 and named Pershing, and production began at the Fisher Tank Arsenal in November 1944 and at the Detroit Tank Arsenal from March 1945. This was despite a disagreement between the Ordnance Board and the Armored Force Board in America. Although both were in favour of the new, more powerful weapon, the Ordnance Board was quite happy with the idea of mounting it in a new tank, while the Armored Force Board preferred it to be installed in an existing tank. They saw no need for a new tank at all.

The M26, one of at least three sent to Britain, taking part in a display at Gallows Hill near Bovington.

The M26 Pershing photographed at Lulworth, home of the Royal Armoured Corps Gunnery School.

Armour thickness was to a maximum of 102mm – much thicker than the Panther, marginally thicker than the Tiger, but well short of the Tiger II. Weight by British calculation stood at 46 tons and the top speed is given as 24mph. The tank had a crew of five, with two men at the front and three in the turret. The commander was provided with a cupola with all-round vision. The tank had six medium-sized road wheels at each side and five return rollers. A larger .50-calibre air-cooled Browning machine gun could also be mounted on top of the turret. By this time the M26 had been reclassified as a heavy tank.

In Britain, General Richardson, who had recently returned from an exhaustive tour of tank-producing facilities in the United States, advised the Director of the Royal Armoured Corps to place an order for some M26s, although he himself had not even seen so much as a wooden mock-up. The order was ultimately placed to the tune of 500 tanks; this was despite the fact that, firing Armour-Piercing Capped Ballistic Cap ammunition, the 90mm gun was only marginally superior to the British 17-pounder except at longer range, although the M26 did offer much better armour protection than the Sherman Firefly.

Since they were in rather short supply to begin with Britain only received a few of the new tanks as samples (one of which remains in the Tank Museum collection), and with the ending of the war in Europe the main order for 500 was never fulfilled. Thus the M26 never saw action in British service, despite wearing a British War Department number. A handful were used experimentally by the US Army on the final thrust into Germany at the end of the war, but although it was judged superior to the original Tiger (a 1942 design), it was still considered inferior to the Tiger II in terms of firepower and armour protection, and as an all-round tank design to the Panther (which was about the same weight). Although it was not invulnerable, the M26 normally proved more than a match for the Soviet-built T-34/85 tank in Korea a few years later.

An M10 of 73rd Anti-Tank Regiment, Royal Artillery, in the XXX Corps area at the eastern end of Gold Beach in Normandy.

M10 TANK DESTROYER

Although the M10 was not a tank, but a tank destroyer, it looked like a tank from most angles and had a fully traversing turret, so it is included here for that reason. The M10 used the automotive components of the M4A2 tank – a pair of General Motors diesel engines – on Sherman running gear, and was the only diesel-powered armoured vehicle the US Army used. As a matter of policy the Americans had decided to standardize on petrol-fuelled vehicles except for training. So the M10 was an exception.

A regular M4A2 Sherman (or Sherman III to the British) weighed around 31 tons in fighting trim, whereas an M10 in similar condition weighed 29 tons. This was the essence of the tank destroyer concept – it was supposed to be lighter and faster than contemporary tanks, despite its powerful anti-tank gun, and the weight reduction was achieved by reducing the armour thickness. Thus an M10 carried 1.5in of armour on its upper hull front, and a maximum of .75in elsewhere on the hull, although its hull armour was sloped all around and therefore effectively a bit thicker against a horizontal shot. The turret was slightly thicker than the hull, 2.25in at the front around the mantlet and just 1in at the sides and rear. It was open at the top. On the early M10 Mark 1 the turret rear was V-shaped; later models had counterweights fitted, and this so-called 'duck bill' signifies a Mark II. Both types saw service with the British Army. The total number of M10 tank destroyers sent to Britain was 1,654.

An M10 could manage a steady 25mph on the road but was capable of short bursts up to 30mph – which was exactly the same as an M4A2 tank. However in terms of firepower it had the edge; the 3in M7 gun fitted to the M10, firing M62 Armour Piercing Capped shot, had a maximum range of 16,100 yards, more than

An M10 Mark IIC armed with the British 17-pounder gun and with more than its regulation turret crew of three, advancing near Nijmegen in Holland. Notice the machine gun at the back of the turret and the typical British stowage arrangements.

2,000 yards greater than similar M61 shot fired from a 75mm gun. It also gave a proportionate increase in armour-piercing performance, for instance 3.5in at 1,000 yards against 2.4in over the same distance. However none of the tank destroyers mounted a co-axial machine-gun, instead they carried a .50-calibre weapon on a flexible mount at the rear of the turret. Some crews unofficially mounted extra machine guns firing over the top of the armour at the front.

This seems as good a spot as any to mention the M4A3/M10A1. Despite what one reads elsewhere there never was an M10A1 in British service. It was planned to develop an M10-style hull and turret on the Ford-engined M4A3 chassis, but the majority were completed as M36 tank destroyers with the 90mm gun, a type that never entered British service anyway. Many of the others were completed as M35 turretless gun tractors, a few of which were shipped to Britain, while the remainder were finished as genuine M10A1 tank destroyers but only used for training in the United States. So none served abroad with the US Army and certainly not with the British.

When M10 production began a new style of gun mounting and mantlet was introduced with fixed trunnions in the turret. This was so that the original 3in gun and mounting could be removed and changed for a 105mm Close Support weapon or even a British 17-pounder. Although this never actually happened, the British did rearm some of their M10s with the 17-pounder. The Mark V version of the gun was selected and fitted to the original 3in gun mounting, adapted to suit. Since the barrel of the British gun was slimmer than that of the American weapon, albeit considerably longer, a metal sleeve was introduced where it passed through the original opening. This acted as a counterweight and another weight, attached like a collar, was mounted at the front end, just behind the muzzle brake. Although it had a somewhat slower rate of fire than the American weapon the British gun was a lot more lethal, with a vastly improved armour-piercing capability, even better than the 90mm gun of the M36. The conversion was done at the Royal Ordnance Factory in Leeds. Of the total of 1,654 M10s that were sent to Britain, 1,017 were rearmed with a 17-pounder.

In British service the M10 was issued to the Royal Artillery, who marshalled them into self-propelled anti-tank batteries. A Royal Artillery Anti-Tank Regiment of 1944 comprised four batteries, two batteries of towed guns and two of self-propelled guns. Each battery had two or three troops; there were four guns to a troop. On certain occasions, notably in the advance to the Rhine crossing, some units, the Guards Armoured and 11th Armoured Divisions in this case, used their M10 (17-pounder) self-propelled guns to stiffen the firepower of their tanks, converting the crews of their towed artillery into infantry men to escort these improvised tanks. However earlier attempts to use these vehicles as extra tanks had not always been successful.

The M10, both the 3in and the 17-pounder versions, saw service with the British Army in north-west Europe from the D-Day beaches right through to the end of the war in Europe; it also fought to a lesser degree in the Italian campaign with British and Commonwealth forces. After the war the 17-pounder version continued in service with the British Army, but latterly with the Royal Armoured Corps rather than the Royal Artillery.

Although the name Achilles was selected for the vehicle, in keeping with other anti-tank vehicles in British service (for instance Archer and Avenger), it only appeared in official documentation and was not adopted by soldiers in the field. The name was applied to all variations of the M10 – the Achilles I and Achilles II were applied to M10 Marks I and II with the 3in gun, and for the version with the British 17-pounder a suffix C was added. Thus there were officially Achilles IC and IIC although the former is rarely seen.

CHAPTER 8

STAGHOUND ARMOURED CAR

The Staghound medium armoured car was a rarity among World War II US armoured vehicles. It was one of the only American designs that was manufactured exclusively for other armies and never used by the US Army. The Chevrolet T17E1 was originally based on a joint US Armored Force and British requirement. By the time the T17E1 was ready for production, the US Army had ruthlessly restricted its armoured car acquisition to a single type, the M8 light armoured car. As a result, the Chevrolet M6 medium car never entered US service. However, British forces still saw a need for an armoured car in this class and so encouraged serial production of the design, which they called the Staghound. The entire production run except for a handful of pilot models was supplied to Britain.

By the time the Staghound arrived in service in early 1944, battlefield conditions had changed. The vehicle was designed for long-range desert reconnaissance missions, but British and Commonwealth armoured-car regiments were now knee-deep in the

mud of the Italian winter. Although a dependable and robust vehicle, the Staghound was also large and cumbersome on Italy's poor mountain roads. The Staghound fared better once the Italian campaign turned mobile in the summer of 1944. The vehicle was also widely used in north-west Europe starting in the summer of 1944, seeing service primarily in the headquarters of armoured-car regiments. Its most extensive use was by Canadian regiments. The Staghound was durable and dependable enough that it remained in service after World War II. Many were cascaded down to NATO allies such as the Netherlands, Italy and Denmark, while others were exported to the countries in the Middle East. They saw combat use in several Middle Eastern wars, and remained in Lebanese service well into the 1980s. The Staghound continued to pop up in unexpected places around the globe, including Cuba during the revolution of the 1950s, and in Nicaragua during the civil war of the 1980s.

DEVELOPMENT

ORIGINS

At the time that the US Army formed the Armored Force in the summer of 1940 in response to the shocking defeat of France, one of the technical lessons from the campaign was the German use of wheeled armoured cars for reconnaissance. At the time, the US Army was in the process of acquiring the M3A1 scout car for its mechanized cavalry force. The M3A1 was essentially a lightly armoured truck with no overhead armoured protection. There was some debate regarding the ideal reconnaissance vehicle, with options mooted including light armoured cars, medium armoured cars and light tanks. The pre-war cavalry had used both armoured cars and light tanks, the latter called 'combat cars'. The advantages of armoured cars over tanks were that the former were faster on roads and quieter, which was helpful when scouting. Armoured cars also tended to be more reliable and require less maintenance than tracked vehicles. On the negative side, armoured cars had restricted mobility in cross-country travel, especially in adverse environmental conditions such as in deep mud or snow. This was an inevitable consequence of having wheeled suspension, since the footprint of their tires was inevitably much heavier than the wider and longer footprint of a tracked vehicle. Light tanks were attractive due to their better mobility in all conditions and the fact that their chassis permitted the use of better armoured protection and heavier firepower. On the other hand, tracked vehicles were noisy, consumed more fuel, and required more daily maintenance attention than armoured cars. To some extent, the choice was linked to tactics. If the reconnaissance doctrine stressed the need to fight for intelligence, a more robust vehicle such as a light tank was better suited to the role. If the tactics placed more stress on stealth and speed, armoured cars were a better choice. In 1940–41, the Armored Force had not made up its mind about tactics or technology – indeed, the debate has continued up to the present day. As a result, the US Army in 1941 was willing to sponsor the development of both armoured cars and light tanks until such time as these tactical issues were settled.

Besides the Armored Force, two other combat arms had some interest in future armoured reconnaissance vehicles. The Tank Destroyer Center had a standing requirement for a fast scout vehicle, since a central element of the new tank-destroyer tactics was to put out a screen of reconnaissance troops in front of the tank-destroyer companies to locate any approaching enemy force. There was some debate whether

OPPOSITE The last significant armoured car developed by the US Army prior to World War II was the archaic T11 developed by the Four Wheel Drive Auto Company in 1934–36. Six of the original T11s and six of the T11E1s were manufactured in 1934–35. Only this single pilot of the final T11E2 was completed, which incorporated a new turret. No serial production was authorized due to weak suspension and poor engine cooling. (NARA)

The Trackless Tank is seen here during its demonstration for the Armored Force Board on March 19, 1941. The performance of this medium armoured car was promising enough to initiate the development of medium armoured cars for the US Army. (Patton Museum)

such troops should use a light unarmoured vehicle such as a Jeep, or a light armoured car. The rump of the cavalry force was also in the process of organizing mechanized cavalry squadrons which would serve both as organic divisional scout troops as well as corps- and army-level scout formations. Light tanks and armoured cars were being examined as options for these formations as well. As a result of these related tactical requirements, the Ordnance Department began development work on three categories of armoured car in 1941: light, medium, and heavy. These differed primarily in the amount of armour protection rather than the level of firepower, as all initially used the 37mm tank gun as their principal weapon.

To further complicate matters, British military representatives in the United States were active in encouraging the development of armoured vehicles by the US Ordnance Department that would suit British army requirements. The North African desert campaign was in full swing, and the British purchasing agents were especially interested in armoured cars. The inventory of armoured cars available to the British Eighth Army in early 1941 was motley and far from ideal. Many of these vehicles consisted of commercial automobile or light truck chassis with light armoured bodies. They were not especially durable, their armament was not impressive, and they offered only minimal armoured protection. While newer types were in the process of being delivered, there was still a desperate need for modern armoured cars. The desert fighting put a premium on armoured cars not only for traditional scouting missions, but also for a wide range of mechanized-cavalry missions including flank security and raiding. Under these demanding conditions, range and durability were major requirements.

TRACKLESS TANK

The first effort in medium armoured-car design was not initiated by the US Army, but was a private venture offered by industry. The Trackless Tank Corporation of New York had developed an elaborate wheeled armoured vehicle with eight wheels, all with independent suspension and shock absorbers. This suspension arrangement offered significantly better cross-country performance than conventional truck-type arrangements that used conventional full-width axles and leaf-spring suspension. The Trackless Tank, as the company's name implied, was envisioned as a wheeled alternative to tracked light tanks such as the existing M2A4. However, the US Army showed little interest in this concept since wheeled vehicles invariably had poorer mobility in adverse soil conditions than full-tracked vehicles. Ordnance was also sceptical of the company, as it was new and small, so had no track record and limited resources. However, even though Ordnance rejected the project, the Armored Force was intrigued enough by the idea as a potential reconnaissance vehicle to ask for a demonstration at Aberdeen Proving Ground, Maryland, in March 1941. These initial trials were promising enough for the US Army to fund the manufacture of two pilot examples for further tests; this was soon followed by an Adjutant-General order for 17 more vehicles, now designated Medium Armored Car T13.

After the United States was dragged into World War II in December 1941, a furious effort was made to ramp up military production. In several cases, armoured vehicles that were still in development and unproven were hastily ordered into production; among these was the Trackless Tank, now fitted with a Rock Island Arsenal turret and designated the T13E1. The Armored Force wanted approval of the production of 1,000 of these as reconnaissance vehicles for the new armoured divisions. Later in the year more sober judgments were made, as it became clear that the Trackless Tank Corporation was in no position to manufacture a satisfactory pilot vehicle, never mind mass-produce the design. The army began to pressure the corporation into teaming up with an experienced automotive manufacturer, or simply selling the design patents to the government. Eventually, the large truck manufacturer, Reo Motor Company, was dragged into the programme. The T13E1 effort proved a total disappointment due the technical immaturity of the design and Reo's inability to redeem the inherent flaws in the design. The vehicle's powertrain proved a repeated source of problems, and in June 1942 the Armored Force Board was forced to send back both pilots to the Trackless Tank Corporation for substantial redesign. In July 1942 development was suspended, and the programme ended in acrimony and a Congressional investigation.

The Ford T17 Deerhound was the competitor to the Chevrolet T17E1 Staghound for the medium armoured car requirement. The types used a common Rock Island Arsenal turret, but were otherwise completely separate designs. The Ford design had more protracted automotive problems than the Chevrolet design, and the 250 that were built as the M5 medium armoured car were used without armament in the United States by military police units. (NARA)

However, in the summer of 1941 British army representatives in the United States had raised the issue of medium and heavy armoured-car designs suitable for reconnaissance work, based to some extent on field experience against German heavy armoured cars such as the SdKfz 232. The British army's staff dithered over the specific requirements sought, but at that time the US Armored Force was also considering the adoption of such a vehicle for the new armoured divisions. Ordnance's suspicions about the technical limitations of the Trackless Tank Corporation encouraged senior officials to push for a parallel medium-armoured-car programme that could be competitively bid to industry. In July 1941, Ordnance solicited industry offers for the T17 medium armoured car and the T18 heavy armoured car.

The March 1942 table of organization and equipment for the new US Army armoured division envisioned the allotment of 49 armoured reconnaissance cars to the divisional reconnaissance battalion, but a decision was yet to be made whether this would be a light, medium, or heavy armoured car pending their development.

THE CHEVROLET T17E1

Designs for the T17 requirement were offered by two firms, so each design received a separate medium-armoured-car designation. The Ford Motor Company design was designated the T17 while the design from the Chevrolet Division of General Motors Corporation received the T17E1 designation. Despite sharing a common designation, the only physical component the designs shared was the turret, developed by the Army's Rock Island Arsenal. The cast turret closely resembled other Ordnance turrets of the time, such as that developed for the M3 medium tank in 1940. However, British input into the requirement as well as changing US tactical doctrine led to several important changes in turret configuration. To begin with, the British insisted on having a minimum of two crewmen in the turret, side-by-side on either side of the

The Ford M5 Deerhound medium armoured car had a number of structural differences from the Chevrolet T17E1, including the use of a large hull casting for the bow section instead of plate armour. Here, one of the production vehicles is seen during trials at the Armored Forces Board at Fort Knox. (Patton Museum)

This is one of the first two T17E1 pilots built by Chevrolet. At this stage, the design lacked the production stowage such as the stowage bin and auxiliary fuel tanks eventually fitted to the hull side. (NARA)

gun. In addition, British practice was to situate the vehicle radio close to the commander, so a bustle was added at the turret rear to accommodate this equipment.

The two T17 designs offered similar levels of armour protection, less than 1in on the hull front and 1in on the turret face, to their unloaded weights were similar. The Ford T17 used a 6x6 configuration and was the heavier design at 28,600lb unloaded, while the Chevrolet T17E1 used a 4x4 configuration and weighed 27,200lb unloaded. The original Ford design was powered by two Ford 90hp engines, but to improve standardization the Army requested substitution of the Hercules JXD 110hp engine. The latter was already in use in the M3A1 scout car and in 2½-ton trucks, so was preferred over the commercial Ford engines.

While Ford was working on the T17, Chevrolet began work on its T17E1. The T17E1 programme was headed by Earl S. MacPherson, a British-born engineer working for Chevrolet who later became famous for the MacPherson strut so widely used in post-war automotive designs. The T17E1 was powered by two General Motors 97hp truck engines. British liaison officers were able to influence MacPherson regarding the features they sought in the design and in the end, the T17E1 began to emerge along lines more in tune with British requirements in the desert campaign. Brig G. MacLeod Ross, a British liaison officer in the United States, later recalled in his memoirs: 'We had managed to influence MacPherson sufficiently to obtain all the features we had built into the ill-fated [British army] armoured car in 1935'.

These medium-armoured-car programmes became caught up in the same production frenzy as the T13E1 programme. In January 1942, Ford was authorized to manufacture 2,260 T17 armoured cars even before the first pilot had been completed. This production was assigned to the St Paul plant, and in June 1942 a contract option was exercised, increasing production by 1,500 vehicles to 3,760 armoured cars. The first pilot was manufactured in March 1942. Likewise, the army authorized the production of 2,000 Chevrolet T17E1s in January 1942. The British Purchasing Commission, especially pleased with the Chevrolet T17E1 design, formally requested the manufacture of 300 T17E1s in December 1941 and this order was formally confirmed in March 1942 after the first pilot was completed.

The Chevrolet T17E1 was one of the most sophisticated armoured cars of its day. The driver's tasks were eased by the pioneering use of automatic transmission and power-assisted steering, which made it an easy vehicle to drive even in demanding conditions. (MHI)

The design programme for the Chevrolet T17E1 proceeded faster than that for the Ford T17, and an initial pilot was delivered to Aberdeen Proving Ground in March 1942, followed by a second pilot to the General Motors automotive test track. The initial series of tests encountered numerous flaws, but all seemed correctable. The design was quite sophisticated, including automatic transmission and a stabilized gun in a power-operated turret. The results were satisfactory enough that a further 1,500 T17E1 armoured cars were added to the Chevrolet production contract in April 1942. The main issues uncovered by the tests were associated with the gearbox, differential, and universal joints, and arose due to Chevrolet's decision not to use available commercial components but to develop new and more robust parts. In the short term, until the components matured, this caused problems, but in the long term it considerably boosted the design's durability. While these powertrain issues were being settled, a wooden mock-up was constructed with stowage features heavily influenced by British desert-warfare requirements. Long range was an especially useful feature in operations in the desert, so the design incorporated a pair of auxiliary fuel-tanks on special racks on the hull side that could be dropped before entering combat to avoid any fire hazard.

The Armored Force became concerned about the performance of these medium armoured cars in cross-country travel, as their conventional truck axles offered poor ride. As a result, yet another medium armoured car effort, the T19, was authorized

In contrast to most previous armoured cars, which were built on conventional automobile chassis, the Chevrolet T17E1 used unibody construction with the armour hull serving as the chassis frame. The suspension was conventional, essentially based on reinforced truck axles and leaf springs rather than the independent spring suspension promoted by the Trackless Tank and the later Chevrolet T19 design. (MHI)

This T17E1 on trials at Aberdeen Proving Ground shows the initial production turret which had pistol ports on either side, and lacked the eventual 2in smoke mortar on the forward right corner of the turret roof. (NARA)

on January 29, 1942. This was another Chevrolet design, but unlike the T17E1 and like the T13 Trackless Tank it used six independently sprung wheels. In its original form it bore a strong resemblance to the T17E1, except for its 6x6 configuration.

By the summer of 1942, the US Army had a growing number of armoured-car programmes under way, including not only the T17 medium armoured car effort, but a Ford and Studebaker light armoured car, a Yellow Truck and General Motors heavy armoured car, and a host of other experimental designs. The frenetic demand for equipment at the beginning of 1942 had led to a confusing excess of development efforts by the Armored Force, the Cavalry, and Tank Destroyer Command. The headquarters of Army Ground Forces was insistent that some standardization be imposed, so in the early autumn a Special Armored Vehicle Board – better known as the Palmer Board – was formed, under BrigGen W. B. Palmer of the Armored Force. The board's officers first met on October 14, 1942, and proceeded to Aberdeen Proving Ground to examine the numerous types of armoured cars under development.

The board had no sympathy at all for the wide variety of types under development, and had a strong bias in favour of a small, cheap, light vehicle, on the presumption that the tactical requirement was for reconnaissance and not close combat. The Palmer Board was from the outset opposed to any armoured car heavier than 20,000lb, which immediately ruled out the medium and heavy armoured cars. Consequently, when the board released its findings in December 1942 it recommended that all the programmes be terminated in favour of the Ford T22 37mm gun motor carriage, a vehicle originally designed as a light tank destroyer. This eventually emerged as the M8 light armoured car (see Osprey New Vanguard 53: *M8 Greyhound*

1
2
3
4
5
6
7
8
9
10
19
20
21
22

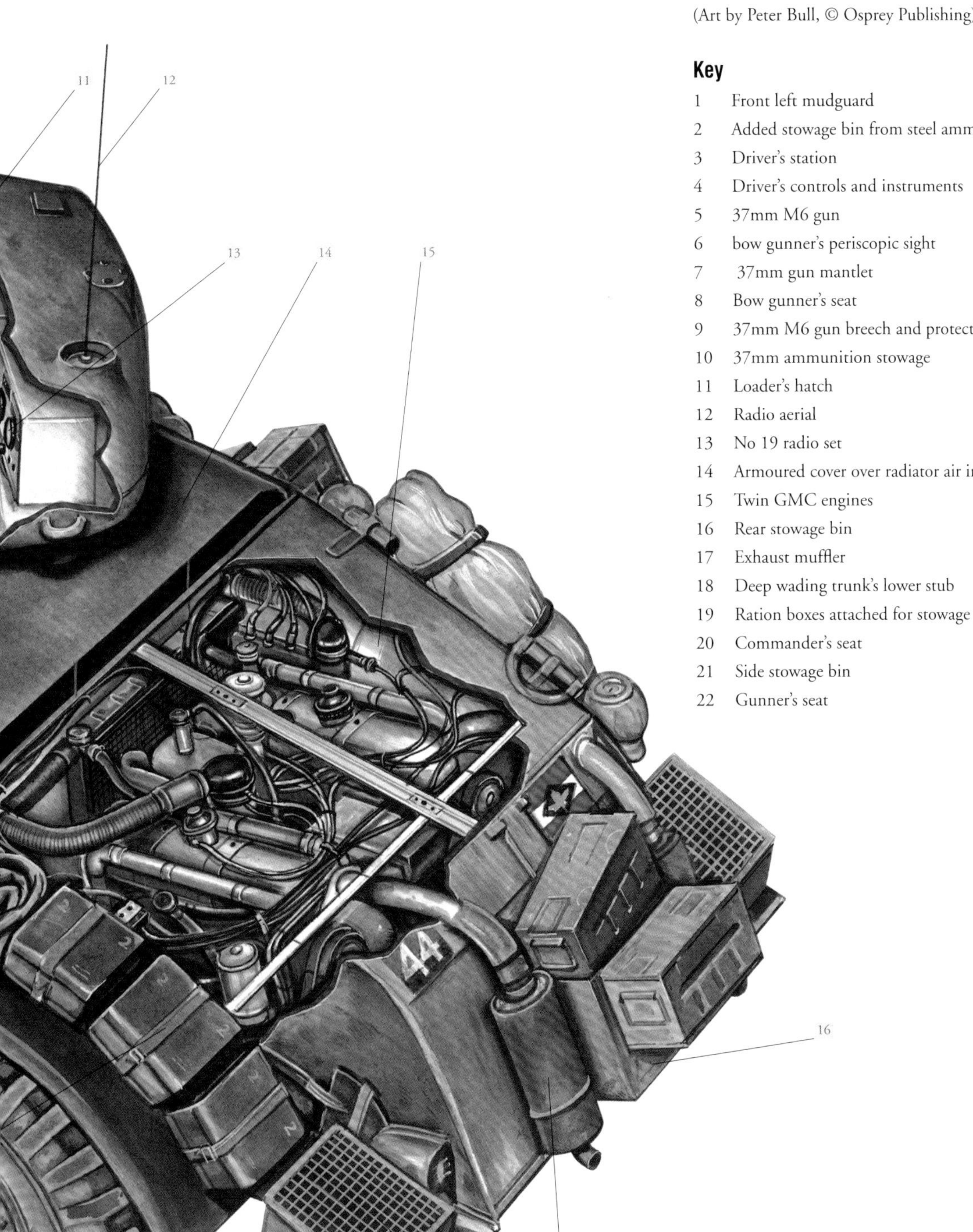

STAGHOUND MK I

(Art by Peter Bull, © Osprey Publishing)

Key

1 Front left mudguard
2 Added stowage bin from steel ammunition box
3 Driver's station
4 Driver's controls and instruments
5 37mm M6 gun
6 bow gunner's periscopic sight
7 37mm gun mantlet
8 Bow gunner's seat
9 37mm M6 gun breech and protective shield
10 37mm ammunition stowage
11 Loader's hatch
12 Radio aerial
13 No 19 radio set
14 Armoured cover over radiator air intake
15 Twin GMC engines
16 Rear stowage bin
17 Exhaust muffler
18 Deep wading trunk's lower stub
19 Ration boxes attached for stowage
20 Commander's seat
21 Side stowage bin
22 Gunner's seat

The late-production batch of T17E1s introduced a new turret casting that omitted the two pistol ports on either side and added a 2in smoke mortar on the right front corner of the turret, at the request of the British army. (NARA)

Light Armored Car). Although there was general acquiescence within the army over this decision, the Armored Force continued to press for a larger and more capable armoured car, with the Chevrolet T19 medium armoured car being favoured. However, the Armored Force was overruled, and the M8 light armoured car was standardized. However, the 1943 mechanized cavalry squadrons used a mixed organization based on M8 light armoured cars and M5A1 light tanks, not exclusively armoured cars as in British practice.

The heavy counterpart of the T17 medium armoured car was the General Motors T18E2 Boarhound heavy armoured car. It was substantially larger and more thickly armoured than the medium armoured cars and armed with a 57mm (6-pdr) gun. All of the 30 built were supplied to Britain, but none saw combat use. (NARA)

The Armored Force was interested in a further evolution of the Chevrolet T17E1, but with independently sprung suspension instead of conventional truck axles with leaf springs. The original T19 pilot, seen here, is strikingly similar to the T17E1. (NARA)

Regardless of the Palmer Board's belated recommendations, the industrial process started in early 1942 had built up considerable momentum. The Chevrolet T17E1 programme had proceeded much more smoothly than the Ford T17 one, even though there were some unexpected delays in preparing the production plant for serial manufacture in the autumn of 1942 due to the shortage of machine tools. T17E1 manufacture started at a slow pace in October 1942 and only 157 examples were finished by the end of the year. Meanwhile, Ford T17 production was further delayed by lingering problems with the powertrain and only 32 examples were completed in 1942.

The British Army did not share the US Army's fixation on standardization and continued to show interest in the medium armoured cars. The US Army Desert Warfare Board was asked to conduct automotive trials on both the T17 and T17E1 medium armoured cars, and these were completed in February 1943. The Chevrolet

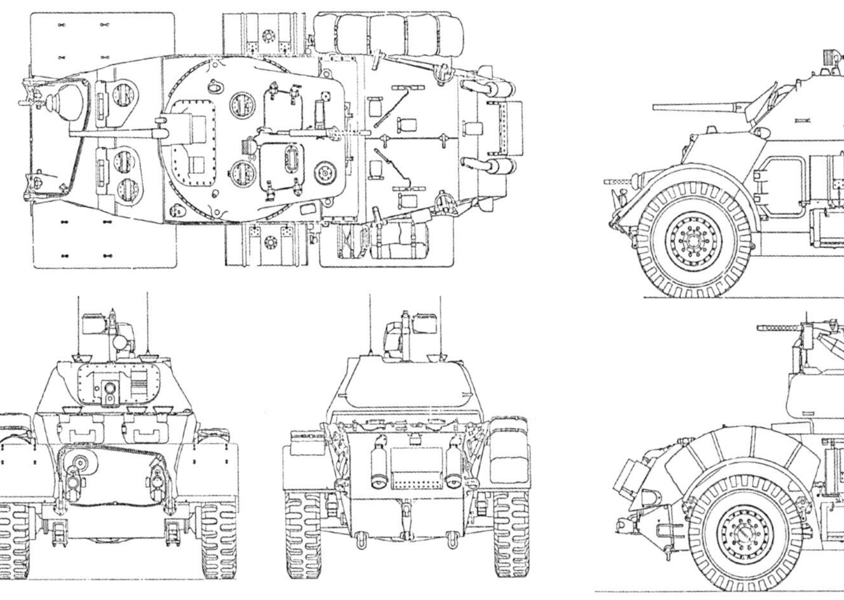

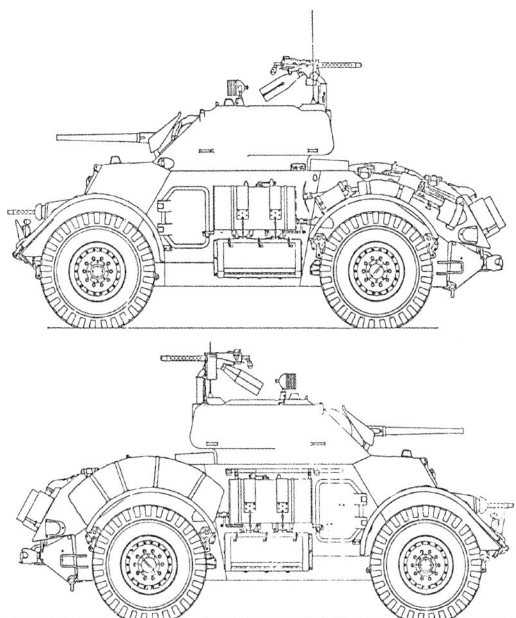

Scale plan of exterior. (US Army)

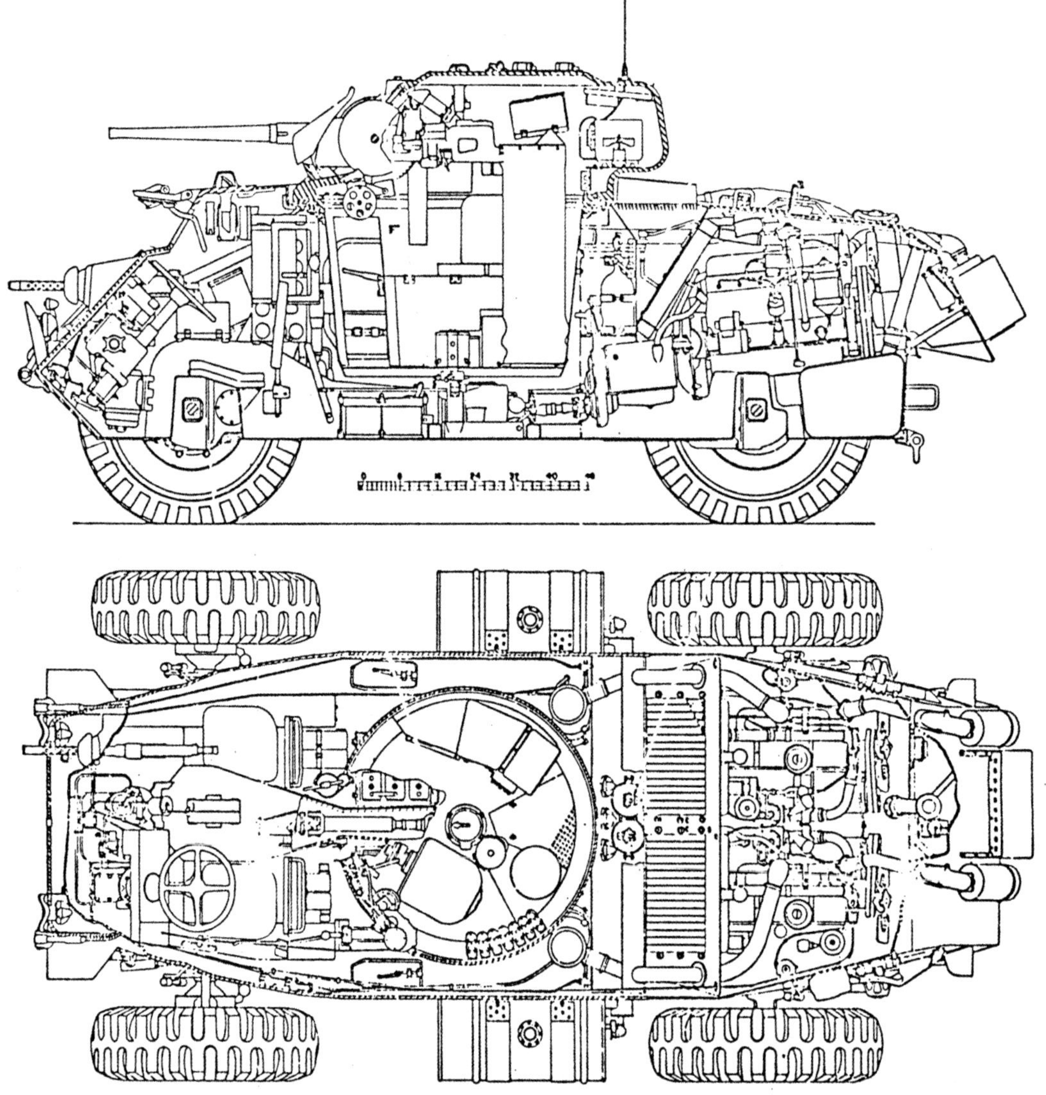

Scale plan of interior. (US Army)

T17E1 emerged as the clear winner, with substantially better automotive reliability than the Ford T17. As a result, the British army requested continued manufacture of the type for its procurement through the Lend-Lease programme. The average unit cost of the T17E1 was $31,433; by way of comparison, the M8 light armoured car cost $22,587.

Although Britain's selection of the Chevrolet T17E1 led to a termination of Ford's T17 production contract, the US Army authorized Ford to complete 250 vehicles to serve as a stopgap until plants were ready to manufacture the preferred M8 light armoured car. These T17 armoured cars were initially allotted to International Aid, with the intention to ship them to Britain; there, they were nicknamed the 'Deerhound'. However, after the Desert Warfare Board tests, the British army lost interest in the Ford armoured car. As a result, the US Army was stuck with the 250 vehicles that were completed by the end of May 1943. They were not fitted with their intended 37mm main-gun armament and the US Army assigned them to military police units in the continental United States for patrol duty. The type was sometimes referred to as the M5 medium armoured car even though this type was not formally standardized. Likewise, the T17E1 was sometimes referred to by its intended US designation of M6 medium armoured car, and this designation can be found on production plates and contract documents. The T18 heavy armoured car also reached serial production, starting in December 1942, but only two were manufactured that year. The Palmer Board decision meant the contract was terminated, with a total of 30 having been completed by May 1943.

In contrast to the Ford T17, Britain proved willing to accept the T18 under the Lend-Lease programme, with the type being designated 'Boarhound'. However, these T18s were used only for trials and were never put into troop service. They were substantially more expensive than the T17E1, costing $60,820 each.

The United States began to ship Staghound armoured cars to Britain in 1943, with a total of 2,620 delivered in 1943 and the final batch of 216 in 1944. In keeping with the '-hound' tradition for naming US-supplied armoured cars, the T17E1 was called the 'Staghound'. By June 1943, a total of 398 Staghounds were in British hands, with 204 in the UK, 120 in the Middle East outside Iraq, 38 in Iraq, 24 in North Africa, 11 in Australia and one in Canada.

A number of production changes occurred during the course of Staghound manufacture. The most noticeable change was in the turret design. The initial production configuration used the E5221 turret casting which had small pistol ports on either side of the turret front. However, this compromised the turret's protective quality without offering much advantage, so the ports were deleted on the improved E5229 turret casting. This turret variant also incorporated a 2in smoke mortar sought by the Royal Armoured Corps (RAC). Other small improvements included a D78272 .30-calibre machine-gun pintle on the turret and a stowage bin on the hull rear between the mufflers. As Staghounds began to arrive in Britain, the Director of the RAC set up a committee to discuss possible improvements. Some of these, such as additional stowage features, could be implemented locally. Other features were sought for safety reasons, such as a counterbalance or spring to prevent turret hatches slamming on fingers. While some of these improvements were undertaken during manufacture, other suggestions arrived too late to be incorporated into the production plan or were simply not approved. Examples of the latter originally requested by RAC but never adopted included a modified turret seat to make it easier for the commander to sit with his head out of the hatch while traveling, and a cupola with 360-degree view. The Logansport traverse system was not as popular as the Oilgear design used in other US Lend-Lease vehicles, but this was not changed, and there were discussions about improving the gyrostabilizer but no such change took place.

VARIANTS

STAGHOUND ANTI-AIRCRAFT (T17E2)

In February 1943, while Staghound production was still under way, British officials raised the issue of an anti-aircraft variant. British armoured-car units in the Western Desert had come under frequent Luftwaffe attack and now mobile air-defence capability was sought. The obvious solution was to use the British-designed Frazier-Nash twin .50-calibre machine-gun turret, which was already being manufactured in the United States by the Norge Division of the Borg-Warner Corporation, as the

ABOVE The T17E2 represented an effort to develop an anti-aircraft version of the Staghound armoured car with a twin .50cal heavy machine-gun turret. Although 1,000 were built, they were the least successful version of the type as there was little need for air defence against the Luftwaffe in the final year of the war. (NARA)

RIGHT The T17E2 Staghound AA substituted an armoured Norge N80 twin .50cal heavy machine gun turret for the usual 37mm gun turret. In this overhead view, the guns are at full elevation but pointed towards the rear of the vehicle. (NARA)

N80 turret for British motor torpedo-boats. This had to be adapted to an armoured-vehicle configuration including a turret race, turret basket, and armoured turret. The turret was too small to accommodate the vehicle radio, so this was stowed in the hull in place of the bow machine-gun. The T17E2 pilot was shipped to Aberdeen Proving Ground for firing tests in March 1943 and returned to Chevrolet for modification and final development work. Improvements included a General Electric power-booster ammunition feed and an improved gunsight. The turret was redesigned, using welded construction and curved plates for a more efficient layout. The crew of the vehicle was reduced from five to three due to the limited space in the turret. A total of 2,610 rounds of ammunition were stowed. British representatives were happy enough with the design that the existing production contracts were modified so that instead of the 3,800 T17E1 armoured cars planned under the schedule of September 1, 1942, a total of 1,000 units would be diverted to the T17E2. The first production vehicle was completed in September 1943 and in December sent to Fort Knox for troop tests and to the Antiaircraft Artillery Board at Camp Davis, North Carolina, for firing trials. Some modest modifications were made during the production run based on these tests. Production was completed in April 1944. In the end, however, this proved to be the least successful version of the Staghound as by the time it arrived in Italy and north-west Europe in the summer of 1944, the Luftwaffe threat had largely evaporated.

HOWITZER STAGHOUND (T17E3)

In the autumn of 1943, British army officers in Washington forwarded a request to Ordnance for the design of a fire-support version of the Staghound for dealing with roadblocks and other tactical obstructions too formidable for the Staghound's small 37mm gun. Since the requirement was for only 100 vehicles, the project did not warrant the development or expense of a new turret. Ordnance had already developed a 75mm howitzer turret for the M5 light tank that had been accepted for service as the M8 75mm howitzer motor carriage in May 1942 and was already in production. This was readily adaptable to the Staghound hull, and Chevrolet quickly constructed the T17E3 pilot in October 1943; this was sent to the Erie Proving Ground in December 1943. However, British interest in the requirement waned and the project ended by late December 1943, even though it was not officially cancelled until late 1944.

Even though the T17E3 project never proceeded beyond the pilot, the requirement still existed. As detailed below, the New Zealand Divisional Cavalry Regiment in Italy had developed a field modification by substituting 3in Mk I howitzers for the usual 37mm gun. These conversions, undertaken in Italy and variously referred to as the 'Staghound 3in' or 'Staghound II'.

A more elaborate fire-support variant was proposed in Britain in the autumn of 1943 using surplus Crusader Mk III tank turrets. A new turret ring was adapted to the Staghound and the Staghound turret basket was modified to fit the Crusader turret, which was re-armed with a more powerful Mk V 75mm gun and a co-axial Besa machine-gun. A Staghound III pilot was put together in December 1943 and eventually sent for trials at the Fighting Vehicle Proving Establishment at Farnborough. However, the trial results were not entirely satisfactory. To begin with, the Crusader turret accommodated only two crew instead of the three in the normal Staghound turret, so the commander had to double as the loader. This created a tactical disadvantage since the commander, distracted by these duties, could not observe the fall of shot when the gun fired to provide any necessary corrections. The tests dragged on until January 19, 1945, and the requirement was trimmed from the original 100 vehicles down to 50. In the end, only 32 vehicles were converted by war's end and the first three were sent to the Canadian XII Manitoba Dragoons in Germany. The Canadians concluded that the Staghound III was 'probably the best all-round 75mm armoured car available' but the type's significance proved to be negligible due to its late arrival.

US MEDIUM AND HEAVY ARMORED CAR PRODUCTION				
	M5 (T17)	**M6 (T17E1)**	**M6 (T17E2)**	**M7 (T18E2)**
1942				
Oct		28		
Nov	8	54		
Dec	24	75		2
1943				
Jan	66	100		1
Feb		68		
Mar	124	312		9
Apr	26	275		7
May	2	256		11
Jun		322		
Jul		279		
Aug		335		
Scp		228		
Oct		198	12	
Nov		147	71	
Dec		167	128	
1944				
Jan			220	
Feb			200	
Mar			225	
Apr			144	
Total	250	2,844	1,000	30

SPECIALIZED STAGHOUNDS

A variety of requirements were established for specialist Staghound variants, primarily oriented towards command issues. A command version that was mooted would have had the gun removed and map and filing desks added inside the turret. Although two of these were nominally authorized under war establishment for each armoured-car regiment, few if any of these conversions were formally undertaken. Instead, many commanders used normal Staghounds fitted with a second radio in the hull. However, some senior commanders preferred more spacious alternatives. One conversion in north-west Europe was the Staghound Charger, sometimes carried out using surplus Staghound AA cars. These had the turrets removed and a plastic windshield fitted at

STAGHOUND MK I, 1 TROOP, A SQUADRON, CAVALRY REGIMENT, 2ND NEW ZEALAND DIVISION, ITALY, SPRING 1944

Typical of most British and Commonwealth armour in Italy, this Staghound is finished in an overall camouflage pattern of Light Mud with rolling bands of SCC 14 Blue-Black. This Staghound is named 'Pukeko', after the New Zealand bird. The squadron marking is a black triangle. The unit marking, usually carried on the left hull front or on the ammunition box on the left-hand bumper, consists of the divisional insignia on top and the arm-of-service marking (white '77' over green/blue square) below. (Art by Peter Bull, © Osprey Publishing)

the front of the opening. This gave the regimental commander more room and better visibility. A second authorized command type was designated 'Staghound control', with four assigned to each armoured-car regiment. These headquarters vehicles had a second No 19 radio set added along with a stowage box on the outside of the turret; the main gun was retained. The Canadians built their own equivalent, the 'Staghound Rear-Link'. On this version the 37mm gun was deleted but a long-range CR-299 radio and associated antennae were added. As the designation implies, this vehicle

The T17E3 combined the turret from the M8 75mm howitzer motor carriage with the T17E1 hull to provide a fire support version. However, it never entered production beyond this pilot. (NARA)

One of the more awkward contraptions fitted to the Staghound was the Bantu mine-detection system, which used a set of magnetic detectors contained in wooden drums. (IWM MH 14033)

served as a communications link between the armoured-car regiment and corps or other headquarters to the rear.

There was also some interest in fielding an engineer version of the Staghound to counter the threat of German anti-tank mines. A prototype was constructed in the spring of 1944 using the Bantu mine detector. This elaborate contraption contained detector coils within wooden drums that were pushed in front of the Staghound. A corresponding device, the AMRCR (anti-mine reconnaissance caster roller), was a mine-rolling system designed to detonate anti-tank mines sufficiently far in front of the Staghound to prevent damage from the blast. However, both systems proved too cumbersome for actual field conditions and in neither case did development proceed beyond trials.

STAGHOUNDS IN SERVICE

THE STAGHOUND ENTERS COMBAT

Between the time the Staghound was first ordered in March 1942 and the time it became ready for shipment into combat in the autumn of 1943, the British army's tactical requirements underwent a substantial change. To begin with, by 1943 the army had finally received an acceptable armoured car for its requirements, the Daimler Mk 1 armoured car. This was smaller and lighter than the Staghound, but armed with a comparable 2-pounder gun. This vehicle was already deployed with the three corps-level armoured-car regiments in the Italian theatre, the 1st Household Cavalry (V Corps), the 1st King's Dragoons (XIII Corps), and the 12th Lancers (X Corps). The Staghounds were first delivered to Egypt in the summer of 1943 for re-equipping a variety of units slated for the Italian theatre; the majority of these were Commonwealth or Polish units.

The most influential Staghound unit in the theatre was the Divisional Cavalry Regiment of the New Zealand 2nd Division, which was refitting in Italy in August–September 1943 following its participation in the Western Desert campaign, in which it had been equipped with Stuart light tanks. Aside from being one of the first combat units equipped with the Staghound, the New Zealand unit had a penchant for innovation and vehicle modification that percolated through the other Staghound units in the Mediterranean. The regiment was concerned that the flat trajectory and small high-explosive charge of the Staghound's 37mm gun were not ideal to counter the threat posed by German anti-tank guns. Two of the regiment's lieutenants promoted the idea of substituting a 3in Mk I howitzer for the 37mm gun. The Staghound turret was sufficiently large and robust to accommodate the howitzer, and after some careful work the design was demonstrated to the divisional commander. With his approval, the upgrade was demonstrated to General Headquarters, Mediterranean Expeditionary Force, which approved it for general use. As a result, a programme was initiated in Egypt to re-equip each troop with one 3in Staghound, a type which was later called the 'Staghound Mk II'.

Another issue was the performance of the Staghound in muddy and wintry conditions. The obvious solution to these traction problems was tyre chains, but to facilitate their use chains had to be located, issued and properly stowed on the Staghounds. An alternative solution hit upon was to cut a rectangular opening in the front fenders and weld steel 25-pounder ammunition bins there for stowage of the chains until needed. This feature was adopted throughout the Mediterranean theatre, but was later extended to some units in north-west Europe as well.

The first British Staghound armoured-car regiment to deploy to Italy was the 27th Lancers, which replaced the 1st Household Cavalry as V Corps' reconnaissance regiment starting in October 1943. The third Staghound regiment into Italy in the autumn of 1943 was the Polish Carpathian Lancers (*Pułk ułanów karpackich*, or PUK) which was initially the armoured-car regiment of the Polish II Corps. Besides the units based upon the Staghound, other armoured-car regiments equipped with the smaller Daimler or other armoured cars were often allotted Staghounds for their headquarters since the latter vehicles' more spacious interior was more satisfactory for staff and in terms of extra radios.

Unfortunately, the Staghound's debut in Italy was not opportune due to weather and geography. The type had been designed with the lessons of the desert campaign in mind – here, endurance, durability and speed being paramount. On the Italian mountain roads and in Italy's muddy winter fields, the Staghound was too large and cumbersome. The problem was not confined to the Staghound, but more broadly affected the role of the armoured-car regiments and other light armoured reconnaissance formations. During the Western Desert campaign the armoured cars had played a vital role in probing enemy defences. They could freely operate on a broad front using their speed and mobility to best effect, since virtually all the terrain was navigable. Along the Sangro front in Italy in the winter of 1943–44, they were confined to mountain roads and predictable approach routes which limited their tactical manoeuvrability and virtually negated their value in conducting deep reconnaissance for corps and divisions. Reconnaissance had to be conducted using dismounted troops or aircraft. The armoured-car regiments' other major tactical role – exploiting successful attacks with rapid penetrations deep into enemy territory – became irrelevant once the front line bogged down around Monte Cassino, since there were no penetrations to exploit. Nor did the vehicles have the firepower or armoured protection to conduct the type of close infantry support undertaken by Sherman tanks. In February 1944, the Staghound crews of the New Zealand Divisional Cavalry were temporarily converted into infantry during the fighting along the Rapido river near Monte Cassino – a state of affairs they dubbed 'infantcavalry'. This would not become permanent until December 1944, but reflected changing tactics in the Italian theatre and the reduced value of armoured cars in such weather and terrain conditions.

The number of Staghounds in Italy continued to increase with the arrival of additional Canadian and Polish Staghound units. The Royal Canadian Dragoons

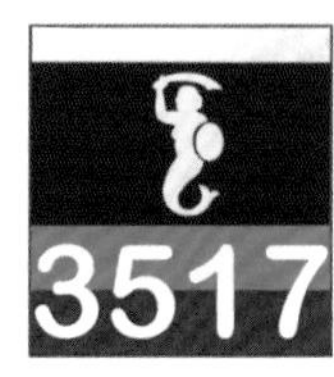

STAGHOUND AA, HQ SQUADRON, POLISH CARPATHIAN LANCERS REGIMENT, ITALY, 1944

The Carpathian Lancers Regiment (Pułk ułanów karpackich) was the reconnaissance unit of the Polish 2nd Corps in Italy and one of the biggest users of the Staghound in that theatre. As a result, the unit insignia seen on the left front of the hull consisted of the corps emblem, a white Warsaw mermaid on red square, over the cavalry arm-of-service insignia, a white 3517 on a green/blue rectangle. In this particular case the insignia has been painted as a shield instead of the usual square format. This particular vehicle is named after the town of Obertyn. (Art by Peter Bull, © Osprey Publishing)

had been equipped with Daimler armoured cars in December 1943 but had begun to receive some Staghounds in February 1944. The British tended to favour the smaller Daimler, but the Canadians were not at all pleased with it, preferring the Staghound due to its better reliability and automotive durability. The Daimler required one to three hours' maintenance per day, but with the Staghound it only took a few minutes to check fuel and lubricant levels. Dissatisfaction with the Daimler became so pronounced that the regimental commander recommended it be entirely replaced with the Staghound. This was duly approved in March 1944, although the much-prized 3in Staghound did not become available to the Canadians until December 1944.

In the Polish case, the arrival of more II Corps units from training camps in Egypt and Palestine led to the increase in the number of Staghound regiments from one to three, with the addition of two divisional armoured-car regiments: the 12th Podolski Lancers (12. Pułk ułanów podolskich) with the 3rd Carpathian Infantry Division, and the 15th Poznan Lancers (15. Pułk ułanów poznan´skich), with the 5th Kresowa Infantry Division. However, the increasing numbers of Staghounds did not imply increased armoured-car activity. In the Polish case, in May 1944 all three cavalry regiments were committed to fighting at Monte Cassino in a dismounted role. Following the capture of Monte Cassino, the Polish Staghound units underwent a substantial reorganization, with the Carpathian Lancers switching to Sherman tanks, the 12th Podolski Lancers taking their place as the corps reconnaissance regiment, and the newly arrived 7th Lublin Lancers (7. Pułk ułanów lubelskich) and 25th Wielkopolski Lancers (25. Pułk ułanów wielkopolskich) taking over divisional reconnaissance slots. By the summer of 1944 the Polish II Corps had ended up with the most Staghounds of any of the various contingents in Italy.

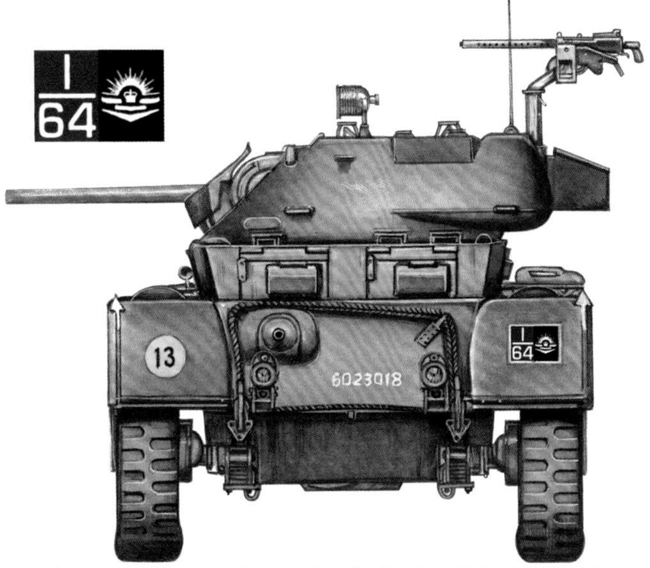

STAGHOUND MK I, 1ST AUSTRALIAN ARMOURED CAR SQUADRON, BRITISH COMMONWEALTH OCCUPATION FORCE, JAPAN, 1946

The Australian contingent of the BCOF included an armoured-car squadron raised at Punkapunyal in 1946, which included 18 Staghounds. These were in the usual finish of dark khaki green and one of the few local adaptations was the addition of a stowage bin at the rear of the turret based on the Sentinel tank type. Markings were quite simple consisting of an arm-of-service square adjacent to the marking of the Australian BCOF which was based on the insignia of the 34th Infantry Brigade, which formed the core of the force; the BCOF insignia mainly consisted of a sunburst patterned on the Australian Commonwealth Forces cap-badge over a boomerang. The Australian army retained the US registration number, though repainted locally on the glacis, and there is a yellow/black bridging circle on the right bumper. (Art by Peter Bull, © Osprey Publishing)

STAGHOUND MK II, POLISH CARPATHIAN LANCERS REGIMENT, ITALY 1944

British workshops in the Italian theatre frequently modified the front bumpers of Staghound armoured cars by cutting out a rectangular portion and welding an ammunition box into the cavity so as to create more stowage. In the case of this Mk II of 2nd-Lt Półchłopek, the regimental insignia is painted on the left bumper ammunition bin. This unit often painted the vehicle name on the glacis plate, but in this case no name is present. (Art by Peter Bull, © Osprey Publishing)

Hercules, the command Staghound of LtCol H. A. Smith of the 2nd Household Cavalry, triumphantly moves through Brussels in September 1944, following the liberation of the city. This was the armoured-car regiment of VIII Corps and operated Daimler 2-pdr armoured cars as well as a small number of Staghounds in command functions. A second command radio has been fitted in the hull and the antenna can be seen fitted to the periscope mount above the bow machine-gunner's station. (IWM BU 482A)

The Staghound regiments finally had their moment in the sun when the Italian campaign regained its momentum in the summer of 1944, during the advance on Rome. The battlefield became fluid enough for armoured-car regiments to play a role in pursuing retreating German forces. By September 1944, Staghound strength in Italy had reached more than 600 armoured cars. However, by the autumn of 1944 Italy had become a backwater and was starved of resources which were directed to north-west Europe instead. Some units which had been reorganized with Staghounds were sent elsewhere. The Italian front became bogged down again in the winter of 1944–45, with predictable results for armoured-car operations. For example, in late November 1944 the New Zealand Divisional Cavalry was once again dismounted and used as infantry to reinforce the rest of the division. The Staghound squadrons saw another flurry of activity in the spring of 1945 when the front became mobile again and Allied formations headed north towards the Alps.

A significant number of Staghounds were deployed to the Middle East in 1943–45, including training units in Egypt. A number of units were deployed on garrison duty in Palestine, and the Indian 31st Armoured Division in Iran employed Staghounds in the 13th Lancers and later the 3rd Hussars.

THE STAGHOUND IN NORTH-WEST EUROPE

In 1944, the war establishment for a British armoured-car regiment nominally included 45 Daimler cars in four squadrons, a headquarters squadron with 14 Staghounds including two command and four control cars, and up to five Staghound AA cars. However, not all of these specialized types were available on D-Day, and in the summer of 1944 actual Staghound strength in the regiments was often less. The Staghound was popular for its rugged durability, but acclaim was far from universal. According to the 11th Hussars' regimental history, troops 'found it unwieldy and it never earned their affection'.

The main exception to the organization scheme detailed above was the Canadian army, which continued to show a preference for the Staghound over the Daimler. During 1943, the Canadian army's Armoured Car Subcommittee had studied the various British and American armoured cars that were likely to be available including the Staghound, the Daimler and the M8 Greyhound. On September 25, 1943, a formal decision was made in favour of the Staghound for the armoured-car regiments, but for the lighter Daimler for the reconnaissance regiments within infantry divisions, since there was an established policy limiting divisional bridging to Class 9 (nine tons), which excluded the heavier Staghound.

The II Canadian Corps' armoured-car regiment was the XII Manitoba Dragoons (18th Armoured Car Regiment), which had been re-equipped with the Staghound starting in the summer of 1943. The Staghound was very popular with the unit due to its automotive reliability. As with the New Zealand units in Italy, the Manitoba

The command Staghound of MajGen G. L. Verny, commander of the 7th Armoured Division, enters Ghent, Belgium, during the liberation of the city in September 1944. Like many command Staghounds, this vehicle has additional radios with two added mounts fitted to the two front hull periscope openings. (IWM BU 769)

STAGHOUND AA, 1ST BELGIAN INDEPENDENT ARMOURED BRIGADE GROUP, BELGIUM, SEPTEMBER 1944

The Belgians served with Montgomery's 21st Army Group, so markings practices followed the British pattern. The vehicle is finished in overall olive drab. The unit insignia is on the left bumper while the arm-of-service square is on the right. The yellow/black bridging circle is on the centre of the glacis plate, with the census number below in white. A white Allied star is carried on either side of the turret while the standard Allied air-identification star is painted on the engine deck. (Art by Peter Bull, © Osprey Publishing)

Dragoons liked to tinker with their vehicles. One innovation adopted in Normandy was adding fittings on the hull side for carrying a pair of 12ft sections of No 9 track bridge to assist in handling craters, small waterways, damaged bridges, trenches, and other obstacles. These were usually deployed at the ratio of one set per squadron HQ.

The initial fighting in Normandy through early August was very frustrating for the regiment as there was little freedom of action in the constricted bridgehead until the breakout started on August 8, 1944. As a result, the unit was frequently employed in a dismounted role. It was during the August breakout beyond Falaise that the XII Manitoba Dragoons was finally able to operate in a classic cavalry role – exploiting the Allied breakthrough, conducting deep reconnaissance and raids, disrupting the German retreat and providing flank security to the corps. The regiment served in a flank security role on the easternmost flank of the 21st Army Group advance during Operation *Tractable* – the advance on Falaise on August 14–16.

During the fighting for the Falaise Gap the regiment was sent to make contact with the Polish 1st Armoured Division, in an isolated spearhead near Trun. Reports of German traffic fleeing out of the pocket near St-Lambert-sur-Dives led the regimental commander, LtCol James A. Roberts, to send two Staghound squadrons to block the exit on August 20. Lt Woodward McKeough's troop was the first to

STAGHOUND MK III, 11 TROOP, C SQUADRON, 12TH MANITOBA DRAGOONS, II CANADIAN CORPS, GERMANY, 1945

The rebuilt Staghound Mk III was refinished in SCC 15 Olive Drab, a colour adopted by the British army in April 1944 to avoid the need to repaint the many US vehicles received via Lend-Lease. The British colour was essentially similar to US olive drab. As the corps reconnaissance unit, the arm-of-service insignia is the usual green/blue square with a white band above. The corps insignia is seen on the left side. The squadron insignia is a white circle on black background on the glacis plate and rear turret side; inside is the troop number and vehicle number. A movement marking is chalked on the right bumper. The vehicle census number F116572 is painted on the glacis plate under the squadron marking. (Art by Peter Bull, © Osprey Publishing)

arrive and described the ensuing firefight as 'shooting fish in a barrel'. The troops destroyed three half-tracks, two tanks, and several trucks and damaged two more tanks. The troop expended all its 37mm ammunition, before the remainder of B and C Squadrons arrived and joined in the one-sided attack. The unit's war diary remarked: 'This particular incident is a job that armoured car troops sometimes get. They put their heart and soul into it as it is a reward for the long and cautious patrols they may be called on to do when firing their guns is only permissible for their protection.' The next day, the same troop had its first encounter with a German 8x8 armoured car, probably a SdKfz 234. The latter was quickly knocked out by Sgt D. L. Yonge's Staghound. The unit war diary recorded: 'This is another dream for the armoured car troops, to meet their equal and show who is better. The natural outcome was that Sergeant Yonge reported knocking out and brewing one 8-wheeled armoured car.' Sgt Yonge received the Croix-de-Guerre for his role in reconnoitring the Falaise Gap the day before, knocking out several German armoured vehicles in the process.

The most famous incident involving the Canadian Staghounds in France occurred on August 30, 1944, during the race beyond the Seine. The Staghound of Sgt Ross J. Bell from C Squadron was on patrol when troop commander Lt W. Laird's vehicle up ahead was knocked out by a Panzerfaust anti-tank rocket. Sgt Bell's Staghound was

A column of heavily stowed British Staghounds passes a column of German prisoners in Gudow, Germany, on May 2, 1945. (IWM BU 5035)

trapped in close country and could not turn around, so Sgt Bell ordered his driver to proceed at full speed down the sunken country road. Careering down the road at 60mph, the Staghound overran a German infantry unit of some 60 soldiers with three anti-tank guns. On the approaches to the village of Bierville, a German tank blocked the Staghound's way. The unit war diary remarked: 'They politely made room for each other to pass. No fire was exchanged.' Beyond the village, the Staghound encountered a German artillery battery on the move on the Rouen–Neufchatel road, and shot up the column, killing or wounding 70–80 horses and 200–300 troops. The Staghound crew was now deep behind German lines and out of ammunition, and it took a day to work its way back to Allied lines with the help of local French Resistance units. Sgt Bell received the Military Medal for his exploits.

If the August fighting demonstrated the potential of armoured cars during mobile operations, it also highlighted the costs. The XII Manitoba Dragoons suffered a third of its entire wartime casualties during a few weeks of fighting. The main cause of vehicle casualties was entrenched German anti-tank guns. The Staghound's thin armour could not withstand such weapons, but at least the vehicle's construction did serve to reduce crew losses. The guns frequently hit the running gear which made up a large fraction of the hull exterior, and these hits tended to blow off wheels and suspension rather than penetrate the hull itself. During the advance beyond the Seine, the Staghounds spearheaded the race up along the coast, probing the Dunkirk defences and later leading the Canadian columns into Ostend. By the first week of September the regiment had advanced some 400 miles. The remaining months of 1944 saw the regiment engaged in static warfare, holding the Bruges–Zeebrugge canal for most of October and then shifting into the Netherlands along the Maas and Waal rivers from November to February.

During this period, the regiment began a series of experiments to improve the firepower of its Staghounds. The most critical need was for more high-explosive firepower, given the puny high-explosive round of the 37mm gun and the delay in receiving enough 3in or 75mm Staghounds. The regiment attempted to acquire some surplus M7 105mm HMC self-propelled howitzers, but these were not part of war establishment and the request was turned down. The regiment was also aware of attempts to mount aircraft rockets on Sherman tank turrets, nicknamed 'Tulips', and decided to try the same approach on the Staghound. Some launch rails and rockets were obtained from an RCAF Typhoon squadron and mounted on a Staghound turret with two launchers on either side. Test firings were conducted on November 26, followed by a demonstration to senior officers on December 2. The rockets were not especially accurate at long range, and at short range the fuze often failed to detonate the warhead. First Canadian Army recommended further study, but cancelled a February 1945 plan to convert enough to issue to serving units. Instead, Canadian Military Headquarters sponsored an effort in Britain by No 1 Canadian Base Workshop to adapt the Land Mattress artillery rockets to the Staghound turret. This placed four rockets in box launchers on either side of the turret. The main problem with this arrangement was that the backblast from the rockets was so severe that it damaged the rear mudguards. Another Canadian experiment was to mount four 20mm automatic anti-aircraft cannon in an improvised open turret in place of the usual turret. This was demonstrated to senior officers in the Netherlands on December 2, 1944, but the scheme was turned down as by now there was little need for an air-defence vehicle in view of Allied air superiority, and the open turret reduced the value of the vehicle in reconnaissance missions.

After frustrating months of static warfare, in late February 1945 the XII Manitoba Dragoons was again assigned as corps reconnaissance for the advance of II Canadian Corps in its operations into Germany across the Rhine. The regiment had a hard slog in the mud of the forested Hochwald, which severely restricted mobility. In early April, I Canadian Corps shifted from Italy to north-west Europe, bringing with it the Staghounds of the Royal Canadian Dragoons and expanding the Canadian contingent in Montgomery's 21st Army Group to a full army with two corps – the First Canadian Army. By war's end the XII Manitoba Dragoons had about half its Staghounds lost or damaged, with 21 written off and eight damaged but put back into action. As mentioned earlier, three of the Staghound IIIs with 75mm guns belatedly arrived in April 1945, in time for the final fighting in Germany.

By the end of the campaign in Europe the two Canadian regiments constituted almost half of the Staghound combat strength in 21st Army Group; the remaining Staghounds were scattered among British armoured-car regiments and sundry command and headquarters troops. Staghounds also served in small numbers in the Polish 1st Armoured Division and the Belgian Brigade Piron. The Staghound was the second most common armoured car with Montgomery's forces, with around 250 in service at war's end compared to about 350 Daimler 2-pounder armoured cars. One of the more obscure Staghound operators was the Royal Navy's 30 Assault Unit – a multi-service unit promoted by the creator of 'James Bond', Ian Fleming, who served in naval intelligence during the war. This unit deployed field teams with specially equipped Jeeps, tasked with conducting deep-reconnaissance missions to collect technical intelligence. To reinforce these teams and provide fire support, a small number of Staghound and Humber armoured cars were used.

The Canadians' employment of the Staghound in north-west Europe highlighted the tactical limitations of armoured car regiments against a determined opponent in constricted terrain. While such regiments could prove enormously useful in a cavalry role, exploiting a breakout as occurred in the Falaise fighting in August 1944, in the more typical close-combat conditions the limited armoured protection provided by armoured cars significantly restricted their utility compared to better-armoured tanks. This shortcoming was not peculiar to the Staghound regiments, but was suffered by other armoured-car regiments in Europe as well. Although designed with desert warfare in mind, the Staghound saw nearly all its employment in continental Europe, where battlefield circumstances did not permit the type of mobility envisioned for such a vehicle.

APPENDIX: US TRANSFERS OF ARMORED VEHICLES TO THE UK: MAY 1941–JULY 1945

	1941–42	1943	1944	1945	TOTAL
M3A1 Light Tank	1,355	907	0	0	2,262
M3A3 Light Tank	0	1,539	506	0	2,045
M5A1 Light Tank	0	3	1,128	290	1,421
T9, T9E1 Light Tank	0	107	153	0	260
M24 Light Tank	0	0	203	99	302
M3 Medium Tank	2,643	212	0	0	2,855
M4, M4A1 (75mm) Medium Tank	268	752	2,018	90	3,128
M4A1 (76mm) Medium Tank	0	0	1,330	0	1,330
M4A2 (75mm) Medium Tank	456	4,083	501	8	5,048
M4A2 (76mm) Medium Tank	0	0	0	20	20
M4A4 (75mm) Medium Tank	147	5,385	1,631	5	7,168
M4 (105mm) Assault Gun	0	0	488	105	593
M26 Heavy Tank	0	0	1	6	7
TANKS SUB-TOTAL					**26,439**
M14 MGMC	0	1,525	0	0	1,525
M16 MGMC	0	2	0	0	2
T48 57mm GMC	0	30	0	0	30
M18 76mm GMC	0	2	0	0	2
M10, M10A1 3-in GMC	0	1,128	520	0	1,648
M7 105mm HMC	143	655	30	0	828
T64E1 155mm HMC	0	0	0	1	1
M35 Prime Mover	0	0	12	0	12
M8 Armored Car	0	2	454	40	496
T17E1 Armored Car	0	2,620	216	0	2,836
T17E2 Armored Car	0	34	965	0	999
T18E2 Armored Car	0	30	0	0	30
M3A1 Scout Car	1,757	4,295	558	0	6,610
Canadian Scout Car	286	849	0	0	1,135
M2, M2A1 Halftrack	0	10	0	0	10
M9, M9A1 Halftrack	0	404	649	0	1053
M3, M3A1 Halftrack	2	0	0	0	2
M5, M5A1 Halftrack	0	188	0	0	188
LVT-1	0	200	0	0	200
LVT-2	0	0	100	0	100
LVT-4	0	0	203	50	253
T16 Carrier	2,522	2,205	9,358	1,704	15,789

Source: Monthly Progress Reports, US Army Service Forces: International Aid, Section 2G, 1942-1945.

SELECT BIBLIOGRAPHY

Anon., *79th Armoured Division Final Report*, official publication, Germany: 1945

Anon., *Final Report of the Specialised Armour Establishment RAC*, War Office: 1951

Anon., *The Story of 79th Armoured Division*, Berlin: 1945

Birt, Raymond, *XXII Dragoons 1760–1945 The Story of a Regiment*, Gale & Polden Ltd (1950)

Chase, Daniel, *Design, Development, Engineering and Production of Armored Cars 1940–1944* (Ordnance Department, 1944)

Dingwall, Don, *Canadian Armour in the Italian Campaign 1943–45* (Canadian Tracks, 1999)

Ellis, Major L. F., *History of the Second World War, Victory in the West Vol. 1: The Battle for Normandy*, HMSO: 1962

Fletcher, David, *Matilda Infantry Tank 1938–1945* (1994)

Futter, Geoffrey W., *The Funnies*, Model & Allied Publications: 1974

Hammerton, Ian C., *Achtung Minen! The Making of a Flail Tank Troop Commander*, The Book Guild (1991)

Harrison, Gordon A., United States Army in World War II, Cross Channel Attack, Washington: 1951

Hills, Stuart, *By Tank to Normandy*, Cassell & Co.: 2002

Hopkinson, Major General G. C. et al, *A History of the 44th Royal Tank Regiment in the War of 1939–45*, Ditchling Press (undated)

Hughes, David, et al., *The British Armies in World War Two: An Organizational History. Vol. 4* (Nafziger Collection, 2002)

Hunnicutt, Richard, *Armored Car: A History of American Wheeled Combat Vehicles* (Presidio, 2002)

Hunnicutt, R. P., *Sherman*, Taurus Enterprises: 1978

Koch, Tomasz, et al., *Samochód pancerny T17E1 Staghound* (Rossagraph, 2007)

Kemp, Lieutenant Commander P. K., *The Staffordshire Yeomanry*, Gale & Polden: 1950

Kořán, F., et al., *Staghound T17E: In Detail Special No. 9* (Wings & Wheels

Publications, 2008)
Jarvis, Robert B., *Chariots of the Lake*, Heritage Workshop Centre: 2003
Lane, John, *Trackless Tank* (Ordnance Department, 1945)
Lawson, C. C. P., and Private N. Huw-Williams, *A History of the Westminster Dragoons 1901 to 1967* (1968)
Lindsay, T. M., Sherwood Rangers, Burrup Mathieson & Co: 1952
Littell, Edmund, *Armored Car T17E1* (Chevrolet, 1945)
Loughnan, R. J. M., *Divisional Cavalry* (New Zealand War History Branch, 1963)
Lucy, Roger, *The Staghound in Canadian Service* (Service Publications, 2007)
Magnuski, Janusz, *Wozy bojowe polskich sił zbrojnych 1940–1946* (Lampart, 1998)
Miller, Major General Charles H., *History of the 13th/18th Royal Hussars 1922–1947*, Chisman Bradshaw Ltd: 1949
Plowman, Jeffrey and Thomas, M., *2nd New Zealand Divisional Cavalry Regiment in the Mediterranean* (Kiwi Armour, 2002)
Stacey, Colonel C. P., *Official History of the Canadian Army in the Second World War Vol. III: The Victory Campaign*, Ottawa: 1960
Stirling, Major J. D. P., *The First and the Last, The Story of the 4th/7th Royal Dragoon Guards 1939–1945*, Art & Educational Publishers: 1946
Tascona, Bruce, *XII Manitoba Dragoons: A Tribute* (Manitoba Dragoons, 1991)
Woolward, Private W. A., *A Short Account of the 1st Lothians and Border Yeomanry* (1946)

INDEX